ENVIRONMENTAL
ETHICS

ENVIRONMENTAL ETHICS

An Introduction to Environmental Philosophy

JOSEPH R. DESJARDINS

College of Saint Benedict

Wadsworth Publishing Company
Belmont, California
A Division of Wadsworth, Inc.

Philosophy Editor: Kenneth King
Editorial Assistant: Gay Meixel
Production: The Book Company
Print Buyer: Karen Hunt
Copy Editor: Linda Purrington
Cover: Winslow Homer, *October Day*. Sterling and Francine Clark Art
Institute, Williamstown, Massachusetts
Printer: Malloy Lithographing, Inc.

*This book is printed on
acid-free recycled paper.*

1 2 3 4 5 6 7 8 9 10—97 96 95 94 93

Library of Congress Cataloging-in-Publication Data

DesJardins, Joseph R.
Environmental ethics : an introduction to environmental philosophy
Joseph R. DesJardins.
p. cm.
Includes bibliographical references and index.
ISBN 0–534–20046–X
1. Human ecology—Moral and ethical aspects. I. Title.
GF80.D49 1992
179'.1—dc20
92-32464
CIP

*To Michael
and
Matthew*

PREFACE

One winter evening several years ago I re-read Aldo Leopold's *A Sand County Almanac*. This occurred a few months after moving to rural Minnesota from suburban Philadelphia. I came upon Leopold's entry for February:

> There are two spiritual dangers in not owning a farm. One is the danger of supposing that breakfast comes from the grocery, and the other that heat comes from the furnace. To avoid the first danger, one should plant a garden, preferably where there is no grocer to confuse the issue. To avoid the second, he should lay a split of good oak on the andirons, preferably where there is no furnace.

This passage struck me in a way that it never could have had I still been living in a metropolitan area. The fact that it was 27 degrees below zero outside and I was sitting in front of a roaring oak fire might have had something to do with this. I recognized that there are more than just two spiritual dangers in not owning a farm; one other concerns divorcing one's life from one's work. I realized that evening that teaching courses on environmental and ecological issues would mean more to me now, personally and professionally, than they could have in the city. This book has grown out of that commitment to redirect personal and professional attention to environmental and ecological concerns.

The primary aim of this text is simple: to provide a reasonably clear, systematic and comprehensive introduction to the philosophical issues underlying environmental and ecological controversies. These controversies, concerning such diverse issues as energy use, population growth, wilderness and species preservation, air and water pollution, resource conservation, and toxic waste disposal will determine the quality of life for both present and future generations. Indeed, human activity even threatens our planet's atmosphere and climate, the very conditions required for the survival of all life on Earth.

The tendency in our culture is to treat such issues as simply scientific, technological, or political problems. But they are much more than this. These environmental and ecological controversies raise fundamental questions about what we as human beings value, about the kind of beings we are, about the kinds of lives we should live, about our place in nature, and about the kind of world in which we might flourish. In short, environmental problems raise fundamental questions of ethics and philosophy. This text seeks to provide students with a systematic introduction to these philosophical issues.

OVERVIEW

A significant amount of philosophically interesting and important research on environmental and ecological issues has taken place during the past decade or two. The structure of this text implicitly tells the story of how the fields of environmental ethics and environmental philosophy have been developing during that period.

Two initial chapters introduce students to the relevance of philosophy for environmental concerns and to some traditional ethical theories and principles. The following two chapters survey topics that essentially fit the "applied ethics" model. Traditional philosophical theories and methodologies are applied to environmental issues with the aim of clarification and evaluation. The applied ethics model, it seems to me, accounts for much of the early work in environmental ethics.

Philosophers soon recognized that traditional theories and principles were proving inadequate to deal with new environmental challenges. In response to these challenges, philosophers began to extend traditional concepts and principles so that they might become environmentally relevant. The next several chapters examine attempts to extend moral standing to such things as individual animals, future generations, trees, and other natural objects. Within much of this thinking, traditional theories and principles remained essentially intact, but their scope and range are extended to cover topics not previously explored by philosophers.

In recent years, many philosophers working in this field have come to believe that mere extensionism is an inadequate philosophical response to environmental issues and controversies. To many of these thinkers, traditional ethical theories and principles were part of a worldview that has been responsible for much environmental and ecological destruction. What is needed, in their eyes, is a more radical philosophical approach, an approach that includes rethinking metaphysical, epistemological, and political, as well as only ethical, concepts. At this point, the field previously identified as environmental ethics is better conceived of as environmental philosophy. The final five chapters examine several of these more radical environmental and ecological philosophies. These views include: biocentrism (the view that all living things deserve moral standing); ecocentrism (the view that shifts away from traditional environmental concerns to a more holistic and ecological focus), deep ecology, social ecology, and ecofeminism.

TO STUDENTS AND TEACHERS

There are two intellectual dangers in writing a textbook like this. One is the danger of supposing that students are as motivated by and interested in abstract philosophical issues as their teachers. The other is that in pointing to the immense practical relevance of environmental ethics, one ignores or understates the importance of careful and rigorous conceptual analysis. I have tried to address these dangers in a number of ways.

Each chapter begins with one or two descriptive cases that can be used as an entry into the philosophical discussion that follows. These cases describe issues that are at the forefront of the contemporary environmental scene and implicitly raise fundamental ethical and philosophical questions. My hope is that after some directed reflection and discussion, students will see the need to address philosophical questions in their own pursuit of environmental and ecological answers. Each chapter also ends with a series of study questions that can be used either as the basis of a chapter review or as the basis of further study.

To avoid the second danger, I have tried to follow the philosophical debates far enough to provide an accurate example of how philosophers reason and how reasoning can make progress. There can be no substitute for a careful study and reading of the many primary sources that I have used in this text. But the nature of textbooks require that these debates not be so developed that students get lost in, or bored by, the detail.

I have not always been successful in my own teaching at balancing a relevant introduction to the issues with an in-depth analysis. Without a clear context to motivate the need to know, students often get lost in philosophical analysis. On the other hand, without depth students can become convinced too easily that they now know all the answers. Class time spent providing context, of course, takes away from time spent developing analysis; time spent following through on the debates prevents the forest from being seen for all the trees.

This text was written to address that tension. I suspect that fo many teachers, the text will provide a context and introduction allowing class time to be used for fuller development of selected issues. This might be accomplished in a number of ways: by reading classic or contemporary primary sources; by studying more empirical resources like the Worldwatch publications; by using some of the many excellent videos on environmental topics that are now available; by addressing the claims of more activist groups ranging from the Sierra Club to Earth First!. However individual instructors choose to develop their own courses, I hope that this text can provide a context to ensure that students remain as connected to the important philosophical issues as they so often are to the practical environmental ones.

ACKNOWLEDGMENTS

Like all textbook writers, I owe my greatest debts to those thinkers who are doing the original research in this field. I have tried to acknowledge their work at every turn, but if I have missed someone I hope this general acknowledgment will suffice.

The reviewers who read this text for Wadsworth provided thorough, insightful, and tremendously helpful advice. I must especially acknowledge Claudia Card of the University of Wisconsin at Madison, Arthur Millman of the University of Massachusetts at Boston, and Ellen R. Klein of the University of North Florida. While their advice improved this text immeasurably, the usual disclaimers of responsibility apply. My thanks also to: Ned Hettinger, College of Charleston; Dale Jamieson, University of Colorado, Boulder; Donald C. Lee, University of New Mexico; Joan L. McGregor, Arizona State University; and Charles Taliaferro, Saint Olaf College.

My students at The College of St. Benedict and St. John's University worked through early versions of this text. We were all students in those classes, and their comments helped substantively as well as pedagogically. The College of St. Benedict, through the office of the Dean, Dolores Super, provided financial support for research during the writing of this book. Heidi Heintz, my student research assistant, also contributed in many ways. Finally, everyone associated with Wadsworth Publishing proved once again why they are simply the best textbook publishers around. Thanks especially to Ken King for his enthusiasm for this project.

One morning this summer, while driving through the countryside, my four-year-old son asked, "Daddy, what are trees good for?" Sensing a precious moment of parenthood, I began gently to explain that as living things they don't need to be good *for* anything, but that trees do provide homes to many living things, that they make and clean the air that we breathe, that they can be majestic and beautiful. "But daddy, I'm a scientist and I know more than you because you forgot the most important thing. Trees are good for climbing."

I hope that I have not missed too many other such obvious truths in writing this text, which I dedicate to Michael and Matthew.

CONTENTS

PART III   Theories of Environmental Ethics   139

BASIC CONCEPTS

1

Ethics, Science, and the Environment

CASE ONE

Technological Solutions

Just after midnight on March 24, 1989, the oil tanker *Exxon Valdez* ran aground in Prince William Sound near Valdez, Alaska. Over the next few days, about 11 million gallons of oil poured out of its tanks, creating the worst oil spill ever in U.S. coastal waters. The oil killed tens of thousands of birds, hundreds of sea otters, and uncountable fish and other sea life. Hundreds of miles of shoreline were covered with oil, threatening the health and livelihood of local residents.

As part of the attempt to clean up this spill, workers used pressurized hot water to remove some of the tarlike oil covering the shoreline. The hot water softened oil that had been thickened by the cold Alaskan temperatures, making its removal from the rocks and sand easier. Pressurized hot water cleaners appeared to be a helpful solution to one small aspect of the cleanup. Unfortunately, few people considered the effects that hot water might have on microscopic and other life-forms that live among the rocks and sand of the shoreline. Few recognized at first that these life-forms, which contribute both to the biological decomposition of the oil and to the re-emergence of plant and animal life, would be killed when sprayed by hot water.[1]

On the opposite side of the earth, the agricultural lands bordering Egypt's Nile River had been subjected to annual flooding for as long as humans have lived in this area. Although these floods brought needed water for the crops, the extent, timing, and length of the flood could neither be predicted nor controlled. Erratic and unpredictable flooding was something that farmers had lived with for millennia. All this ended in the 1960s with the construction of the Aswan Dam.

The dam was built to supply hydroelectric power, and to provide irrigation and flood control. In many ways, these goals have been met. For example, many crops survived severe droughts in the early 1970s because of the water available from the dam. However, the dam has also created a multitude of environmental problems never envisioned by its original designers.

Although flooding was a major problem, it also fertilized these lands by depositing a layer of silt, washed away salts that built up in the soil, and helped remove snails that spread the parasitic disease schistosomiasis. As a result of the dam, this agricultural land now must be treated with costly chemical fertilizers. Salinization is slowly destroying the productivity of much of the land, and the incidence of schistosomiasis infections has risen steadily. Furthermore, the silt that was once spread across the land by floods now is building up in the waters of Lake Nasser behind the dam. The lake is slowly filling up with mud rather than water. Downriver, the Nile has so eroded its riverbed that smaller dams, bridges, and shorelines are being undermined. The increased erosion is due to the lack of sediment now in the Nile's waters. The lack of sediment also means that the Nile delta is eroding as well, allowing sea water to advance inland and destroy the productivity of other agricultural land. Since the river no longer deposits this nutrient-rich silt into the Mediterranean Sea, marine life around the Nile delta has been so depleted that Egypt's sardine, mackerel, shrimp, and lobster industries have been devastated. Finally, when a rare earthquake struck the Aswan area in 1981, some geologists suggested that the very weight of Lake Nasser itself was responsible.

1.1 INTRODUCTION

As we approach the twenty-first century, it is fair to say that human beings face environmental challenges unprecedented in the history of this planet. Largely through human activity, life on earth faces the greatest mass extinctions since the end of the dinosaur age 65 million years ago. Some estimates suggest over a hundred species each day are becoming extinct and that this rate could double or triple within the next few decades.[2] The natural resources that sustain life on this planet—air, water, and soil—are being polluted or depleted at alarming rates. Human population growth is increasing exponentially. The 1990 world population of 5.5 billion people will increase by a billion people (nearly a 20 percent increase) within ten years. The prospects for continued degradation and depletion of natural resources multiply with this population growth. Toxic wastes that will plague future generations continue to accumulate around the world. The world's wilderness areas, its forests, wetlands, mountains, and grasslands are being developed, paved, drained, burned, and overgrazed out of existence. With the destruction of the ozone layer and the potential for a "greenhouse" effect, human activity threatens the very atmosphere and climate of the planet itself.

Although the pessimists among us might despair at this reality, many others look to science and technology for solutions. If only we could engineer more efficient solar panels, or harness the energy potential of geothermal, wind, or tidal power. If only we could develop alternatives to the internal combustion engine. If only we could master cold fusion. If only we could develop more productive and sustainable agricultural technologies. If only we could arrange economic incentives to discourage pollution.

For many people in our culture, and especially for many in policy-making positions, science and technology offer the only hope for solving environmental problems. Because environmental problems often involve highly technical matters, it is only reasonable to turn to experts in these technical areas for answers. Furthermore, since science offers objective and factual answers in an area where emotions run high and controversies abound, science seems an obvious candidate from which to seek help with environmental concerns.

Unfortunately, turning to science with the optimistic hope for a quick fix is not very different from the pessimistic attitude. Each involves individual citizens relinquishing the authority to make decisions about their world. Although it is tempting to turn to science and technology in the hope for a quick fix, environmental challenges are neither exclusively nor even primarily problems of science and technology. Environmental issues raise fundamental questions about what we as human beings value, about the kind of beings we are, about the kinds of lives we should live, about our place in nature, and about the kind of world in which we might flourish. In short, environmental problems raise fundamental questions of ethics and philosophy. Reliance on science or technology (or even economics or the law) without also considering the ethical and philosophical issues can raise as many problems as it solves. Leaving environmental decisions to the "experts" in science and technology does not mean that these decisions will be objective and value-neutral; it only means that the values that do decide the issue will be the values these experts themselves hold.

This text provides an introduction to the many ways in which philosophical ethics can contribute to the creation of a sane and judicious environmental policy. Environmental issues raise fundamental questions about how we should live. Such questions are philosophical and ethical questions, and need to be addressed in a philosophically sophisticated way. Another assumption is that environmental policy ought to be decided in the political arena and not in scientific laboratories, corporate boardrooms, or government bureaucracies. A further goal of this text is to empower citizens to become full participants in these crucial public policy debates. Familiarity with the philosophical issues involved in these debates is a necessary first step in this direction.

1.2 SCIENCE WITHOUT ETHICS

As the cases that begin this chapter suggest, people take risks when they treat environmental problems merely as technical problems awaiting solution from some specialized discipline. In part this is because the dimensions of environmental issues are seldom limited to the specific boundaries of any one particular discipline. It is impossible to find an important environmental issue that does not cross boundaries between the sciences, economics, public policy, law, medicine, engineering, and so forth. Building the Aswan Dam and confronting the resulting problems, for example, has involved engineering, geology, agriculture, marine biology, medicine, chemistry, economics, politics, anthropology, and law. But it is equally impossible to find an environmental issue that does not raise basic questions of value. Approaching any serious environmental issue with the hope of discovering a technical "quick fix" guarantees only a narrow and parochial understanding of what is at stake. History testifies to the dangers inherent in this approach. Too often past technological or scientific "solutions" have resulted in as many new problems as they have solved.

But the danger in overreliance on science and technology extends beyond this simple point of technological complexity. Science is not as value-neutral as many assume. A very deep belief in our culture, so deep and unexamined that it takes on the dimensions of a cultural myth, views science as the ultimate authority on questions of knowledge and truth. This "myth of scientific objectivity" says that unless our beliefs are validated by science, they remain in the realm of mere opinion: personal, subjective, arbitrary, biased. Although it is important not to overstate this point—science does have tremendous potential for helping us to understand and solve environmental problems—science is not the purely objective and value-neutral resource that so many people assume it to be.

This is not the place for a full discussion of the issue of scientific objectivity. However, I can mention several points that should give us pause when we are tempted to turn solely to science and technology for solutions to environmental problems. To help sort through these issues, it may be helpful to distinguish several common understandings of science. In common understanding, science is understood to be a *method for attaining knowledge, a body of information or "facts"* gained through that method, and a tool for controlling and changing the world.

In some ways the scientific method is nothing other than a careful, detailed, precise, and documented approach to knowledge. The practice of science demands that its practitioners minimize assumptions, seek to eliminate bias, verify results, and limit conclusions to what can be supported by the evidence. In this sense there is a very real "ethic" of the scientific method, which aims to ensure impartial, accurate, and rational results. To the degree that scientific practice measures up to this ethic, we can have confidence in the rationality of its result.

Nevertheless, hidden assumptions in this method may influence scientific practice. For example, in later chapters I discuss some observers who claim that modern science is dominated by models imported from physics. In that view, we best understand something (such as a physical object) when we reduce that object to its most simple elements (such as atoms or electrons) and investigate the forces that work on those elements (such as gravity and electromagnetism). But according to these critics, that approach is inappropriate when exported to other fields. Social sciences such as economics, sociology, and political science, for example, may well distort reality when "society" is reduced to a mere collection of individuals mechanically driven by the forces of self-interest.[3] More relevant to this book, some biologists believe that the physics model is particularly misleading in the study of ecosystems. The reductionist tendency can ignore or distort the complex relations that exist within an ecosystem. Reductionism literally fails to see the forests for the trees.

Likewise, a commitment to mechanistic explanations can also distort our understanding of ecological relationships. For example, debates concerning our understanding of animal behavior are sometimes framed in mechanistic terms: *either* animals' behavior is caused by environmental conditioning, *or* it is controlled by genetic programing. Either way, the explanation can be stated in invariable, deterministic, mechanistic "laws of nature." Again, for many biologists this represents a distorted and oversimplified account of animal behavior. Even the simplest organism is capable of changing its environment as much as it (and its progeny) is changed by the environment. Biological and environmental changes seem to occur as much through random chance as according to deterministic laws.[4] Accordingly, a policy of wildlife management, for example, that was based on a mechanistic model of animal behavior would have very different consequences and recommendations from a policy assuming that change rather than constancy is the norm.

Thus despite the fact that the practice of science is committed to the values of impartiality and objectivity, the scientific method is not always the unbiased procedure it is taken to be.

Science is also sometimes understood not as a method or procedure but as a body of information or facts. Surely facts are objective, and if science discovers the facts, scientific knowledge must be objective; or so the myth of scientific objectivity would have us believe.

How comfortable should we be when we rely solely on scientific information to resolve environmental challenges? Even assuming that the facts are established through a careful, methodical, and verified procedure, we need to recognize that the "facts" seldom tell the whole story. Reliance on even well-established scientific information can be risky if that information fails to give us a complete explanation. Perhaps the biggest obstacle to getting the whole story is not science's inability to get answers, but science's limits in asking questions. Before relying on scientific answers to resolve environmental problems, we need to know what questions the scientists were asking.

Amory Lovins, an internationally recognized energy scientist, makes a similar point by reminding us that "the answers you get depend on the questions you ask."[5] Lovins uses an example from energy policy to make this point. If we define the energy problem as a supply problem, it is easy to conclude that people are running out of energy and are in need of new energy sources. Science and technology can help supply many answers to these problems. Science can document the facts of resource depletion; calculate the known reserves of coal, oil, and uranium; compare the technological advantages of various energy sources; predict the costs and efficiencies of generating plants powered by coal, oil, and nuclear energy; and so on. We might thus imagine collecting a significant amount of relevant scientific data on the various alternatives of energy production. We may also imagine, given these facts, that one alternative (for example, nuclear fission breeder reactors) emerges as the most reasonable option. This decision, we may well imagine, is based on the objective, neutral "facts" of science.

But if we define our energy problem as a question of demand, we will come up with very different answers. Defined this way, we begin to ask questions about energy use, about matching energy source with energy use, about energy efficiencies, about appropriate technologies, and so on. A scientist who asks these questions is more likely to focus on such issues as home heating, insulation, efficiency of electric motors, lighting, appliances, fuel-efficient cars, or, better yet, mass transportation, solar power, and so forth. We can understand that the information emerging from these questions, as factual and as objective as the information coming from supply questions, will suggest very different energy policies. These "facts" might well prove that heating homes with electricity is quite unreasonable, even if the source of that electricity is safe and efficient when compared to alternative sources.

We have thus imagined a situation in which we have two sets of facts, each equally valid and objective from a scientific point of view, but each leading to quite different policy recommendations. One set of facts supports building new power plants, the other set supports a greater emphasis on appropriate technologies. In such a scenario, the scientific facts alone tell us nothing about which alternative we ought to choose. In later chapters, I examine the more general difficulties involved with reasoning from "facts" to "values." Philosophers have long recognized that descriptions of how the world is do not, in themselves, commit us to any particular value conclusions about how the world should be. Simply acknowledging the gap between statements of fact and statements of value is enough, at this point, to caution us against overreliance on science and technology.

But more to the point, we need to be especially careful in determining which questions are being asked by environmental scientists. If the questions are limited, so too will the answers be, and so too will be the policy recommendations that society adopts based on those answers.

So where do scientists get their questions? The answer—not as cynical as it might sound—is that scientific questions are formed to a large degree by the people who pay for scientific research. Contemporary, state-of-the-art scientific research is very expensive.

Typically it is funded by government and private industry. The projects that get funded are the projects that answer questions being asked by government and industry. Science conducted under these conditions certainly does not always supply the answers that government and industry wants, but the likelihood of such science supplying radically different answers is seriously restricted.

For example, most of what is known about nuclear energy is the result of research supported by the U.S. government. Specifically, the Department of Defense has spent billions of dollars developing nuclear weapons. In fact, the standard design for a nuclear power plant is a modified version of the nuclear reactor that powers submarines. Thus, our knowledge about nuclear energy is directly traceable to political decisions made in a very different context.

This is not to suggest that such knowledge is somehow less reasonable or valid than it might be. However, we need to acknowledge that the environmental decisions we make depend on the available information and technology and that these depend on the types of questions being asked by scientists. You need only imagine the knowledge and technology that we would have about solar power, for example, if the money spent on nuclear weapons and nuclear research over the past fifty years had been spent instead on solar energy research.

Finally, another common understanding of science views it not only as a method for knowing or a body of information, but as a powerful tool for shaping the world. Here science is identified with technology and engineering and is seen as a major factor in humankind's progress and development. Science is seen as a major tool for controlling disease and early death, for conquering hunger and for helping humans to better survive in the world.

Science—understood generally to include engineering, technology, and the social sciences—does of course have much to contribute in resolving environmental problems. Its track record for explaining and controlling both human behavior and the natural environment is impressive. We should turn to science for help with environmental problems because it is a powerful tool for understanding and controlling the world. But like all tools, its use depends on the user's values and purposes. The time to examine these values and purposes is *before* we begin to use the tools.

If nothing else, intellectual honesty demands that we not overgeneralize the expertise of scientists. We should not deceive ourselves into thinking that because science demands objectivity and neutrality in its practice, all its uses are objective and value-neutral. Even if the scientific enterprise is committed to impartial and objective methods and even if its findings are reasonable and true, the practical *uses* we make of scientific information may not be. We should also not deceive ourselves into thinking that simply because many environmental problems involve technical issues they do not raise ethical questions as well. The myth of objectivity that sometimes surrounds science can obscure these points. As we'll see, one role of environmental philosophy is to make explicit the hidden value assumptions of alternative environmental policies. And sometimes this requires us to examine the value assumptions implicit in science and technology.

1.3 ETHICS WITHOUT SCIENCE

Nevertheless, it would be a mistake to think that some abstract ethical theory can resolve environmental controversies. Ethical and philosophical analysis done in the abstract, ignorant of science, technology, and other relevant disciplines, has little to contribute toward resolving environmental problems. The alternative to looking to science for some quick fix is not looking instead to philosophical ethics.

How we understand the world, and therefore how and what we value, is significantly shaped by what science tells us about that world. The only serious alternative is to recognize that both science and ethics are essential if we hope to make meaningful progress in meeting the environmental challenges that confront us. We can capture this perspective by adapting an old philosophical adage: "Science without ethics is blind; ethics without science is empty." This book surveys the variety of ways in which philosophers seek to provide such a vision for environmental science and for environmental policy.

Most of this text focuses on the first half of this adage: without an ethical vision to guide environmental policy, science and technology at best can only provide haphazard success. Given that emphasis, perhaps it will be useful at this point to review briefly some reasons why it would be equally risky to rely exclusively on ethics and philosophy for guidance.

This text assumes that philosophical ethics can make significant contributions to environmental studies. It also assumes that the best of these contributions must be informed by environmental science. However, many philosophers would deny the relevance of science to issues of philosophical ethics. In their view, the primary role of the philosopher is to articulate and defend some abstract theory or principle. Only in a secondary sense might the philosopher then apply this theory to some practical issue such as the environment.

Because this book rejects such an abstract view of ethics, a helpful first step in understanding the relevance of ethics to environmental issues is to consider how empirical disciplines contribute to ethics.

First, much of ethics is concerned with offering and defending normative judgments; for example, "Deforestation of tropical forests is wrong," "Continued depletion of natural resources is irresponsible," "Sustainable agriculture is praiseworthy." But surely it is irresponsible, if not irrational, to make such judgments without a firm grasp of the facts. If you lack a clear understanding of the ecological effects of deforestation, or the extent of resource depletion, or the biology of pesticide-free farming, you are in no position to take a stand for or against such practices. To avoid offering irrelevant and irresponsible advice, environmental ethics must be grounded in the facts of environmental science.

Second, even the ability to recognize and understand an ethical issue *as* an ethical issue depends on information provided by empirical sciences. The more we learn about such issues as global warming, ecosystem ecology, and toxic waste disposal, the more likely we are to discover ethical issues and ethical complexity. Naive and simplistic ethical judgments, including the judgment that no ethical controversy exists, can often be traced to naive and simplistic understandings of the facts.

Third, ethical analysis as practiced by philosophers is a fairly abstract enterprise. Philosophers deal with such general concepts as "rights," "justice," "goodness," and "respect." But these abstract concepts provide little practical guidance unless they are given specific interpretations, interpretations that can only be "filled out" in specific contexts. The meaning and implications of "individual freedom" applied to people living in isolation in the wilderness are quite different from their meaning when applied to people living in New York City. The "right" of private property will have a meaning to a hunter-gatherer society different from its meaning to an industrialized, capitalistic society. Translating ethical concepts from the abstract to the more practical level requires knowledge of particular social and scientific facts.

Finally, there is a standard formula to which philosophers refer when discussing this issue: "Ought implies can." This formula suggests that it makes little sense to discuss what we ought to do if we don't understand what can be done. We cannot reasonably hold people responsible for doing what is impossible, and we surely can't blame them for failing to do what they cannot do. To know what can and cannot be done, in turn, requires that we know a good deal about what human beings are like. In more general terms, it requires us to know a good deal about human nature.

For some philosophers, studying human nature is a purely conceptual matter. They say philosophy should abstract from particular human characteristics a common "essence" shared by all humans. This essence, which admittedly not all people manifest (it remains a human "potential" in other people), serves as the standard for ethical evaluation and prescription. More often, philosophical claims about human nature are grounded in a careful, and scientific, study of what humans actually are like. Aristotle, for example, thought the study of biology and psychology was essential for thinking about ethics. This required, at a minimum, knowledge of basic human needs, common capabilities and potentials, human motivation, and so on. In short, there is an important role for the sciences, both social and biological, to play in supplementing the philosophical account of what human beings are like.

Of course, this does not mean that philosophical appeals to human nature, even those firmly grounded in science, are without problems. Sometimes, what is taken to be an essential truth about human nature turns out to be more a result of cultural bias and limitation. It is difficult to read Aristotle's discussions of the "nature" of women and "natural slaves," for example, without concluding that his ethical views were extremely limited by his own cultural assumptions about women and non-Greeks. It is equally difficult to read a philosopher such as Thomas Hobbes without recognizing how some modern views about human nature are also shaped by the political and economic forces of his time.

Three themes emerge from this point that are worth mentioning early in this book. First, we should be careful in discussing "nature" and "human nature." At best, these terms are very ambiguous and can be responsible for much unclear thinking. At worst, they can hide powerful and controversial claims under the disguise of uncontestable and simple observations. Given the central role that the concept of "nature" plays in many environmental discussions, the significance of this point cannot be underestimated. Philosophical appeals to "nature" that are not firmly grounded in scientific observations of the natural world, should be treated with suspicion. We should be equally suspicious of scientific or technological appeals to what is "natural." They, too, can contain hidden value assumptions that must be explicitly examined. Very often, it is assumed that because something is natural it must be good.

Second, we should be alert to the biases and limitations of our own common ways of thinking. As we shall see, some writers claim that certain environmental problems result from biases and hidden assumptions in some traditional philosophical and ethical theories. This is especially important to keep in mind when we begin to survey some of the recently emerging theories of environmental ethics. We also need to be equally alert to hidden value assumptions and prejudices in our own patterns of thinking.

These considerations do not deny the value of "pure" philosophical reasoning. Conceptual analysis and philosophical theorizing are two important contributions that philosophy can offer. Indeed, they are essential for any adequate resolution of environmental controversies. However, we cannot lose sight of the fact that ethics is essentially *practical*. It is concerned with how we should live, how we should act, and what kind of people we should become. Because ethics is essentially practical, it should not be used without paying close attention to empirical information about the world.

I began this section with the claim that the role of ethics is to provide a "vision" for environmentalism. I then reviewed some reasons why it would be misleading to think that this vision can come from a purely abstract ethical theory. At this point, let's look in more detail at the ways in which ethics can contribute to meeting environmental challenges.

1.4 WHAT IS ENVIRONMENTAL ETHICS?

In general, *environmental ethics presents and defends a systematic and comprehensive account of the moral relations between human beings and their natural environment.* Environmental ethics assumes that human behavior toward the natural world can be and is governed by moral norms. A theory of environmental ethics then must go on to (1) explain what these norms are, (2) explain to whom or to what humans have responsibilities, and (3) show how these responsibilities are justified.

A variety of environmental ethics emerge with differing answers to these questions. Some philosophers argue that our responsibilities to the natural environment are only indirect—that the responsibility to preserve resources, for example, is best understood in terms of the responsibilities that we owe to other humans. Other philosophers argue that we have direct responsibilities not only to plants and animals but also to ecosystems and species, and that these responsibilities are based on the moral standing of these natural objects. Later chapters examine these answers in detail. First, however, we should think in more general terms about ethics itself.

1.5 DESCRIPTIVE ETHICS

Talk of "ethics" can sometimes be a bit confusing or intimidating. Ethical issues often involve our most fundamental commitments and values, and it is difficult to question these. Many people are also unwilling to do the careful and hard thinking that is necessary in ethics. Simply, philosophical ethics is something many people prefer to avoid, despite the fact that these same people regularly make ethical judgments. To help overcome this hesitance, it is useful to distinguish between different types of ethical judgment and ethical reasoning.

Sometimes when we speak of "ethics," we are simply describing the particular values and principles that someone holds. In this *descriptive* sense, "environmental ethics" refers to those values, whatever they turn out to be, associated with the environmental movement. As the name suggests, *descriptive ethics* involves describing, classifying, listing, and summarizing ethical beliefs.

It might seem that there is little of philosophical interest in descriptive ethics. Describing ethical beliefs might appear to be more the domain of social scientists and pollsters than of philosophers. However, one of the first and most serious challenges in any study of ethics involves identifying an issue *as* an ethical issue. We all need to be taught to recognize—and to practice recognizing—ethical issues. For example, some authors speak of different levels of "environmental consciousness"[6] which suggests that people will understand the world in different ways depending on their ethical and environmental sensitivity. One constant challenge for environmental ethics is to help people notice environmental problems that they might otherwise miss. Philosophy can help train us to recognize otherwise hidden issues.

For example, in the classic environmental essay "The Land Ethic,"[7] Aldo Leopold retells the story of Odysseus' return from the Trojan War. Odysseus hanged a dozen women slaves whom he suspected of misbehavior. Since slaves were seen as property, the Greeks apparently saw nothing ethically wrong with this action. Leopold uses this example to call for an "extension of ethics" to include human relations to the land. Just as Odysseus was ethically insensitive to the evil of killing innocent slaves, we fail to notice the wanton destruction of the land. Leopold's point is that to be capable of noticing an ethical issue, sometimes we need to work intellectually. At times we can be limited by our own perspectives on the world.

Uncovering the limitations of our own ethical and environmental consciousness is a regular theme in the following chapters. Such limitations may also turn out to be the cause of some of the frustration that characterizes ethical discussions and that therefore prevents us from following through on the careful thinking required in ethics. Many environmental controversies rest, at bottom, on very different perspectives for understanding the world. Few things are as frustrating as having our fundamental perspectives challenged. But we all need to be open to the possibility that, like Odysseus, we ourselves may suffer from ethical ignorance. A primary goal of *descriptive* ethics is to constantly stretch our understandings, shift our perspective and consciousness, and help us escape the limitations implicit in common ways of thinking.

1.6 NORMATIVE AND PHILOSOPHICAL ETHICS

A second aspect of ethical reasoning involves making ethical judgments, suggesting advice, and offering ethical evaluations. The type of ethical reasoning that most people associate with "ethics" is *normative ethics* (or "prescriptive," as opposed to "descriptive," ethics). Most ethical judgments that include an "ought" or "should" are normative claims. Normative judgments prescribe behavior; for example, "Endangered species ought to be protected," "Toxic wastes should not be dumped in less developed countries," and "Carbon dioxide emissions should be diminished." Normative judgments implicitly or explicitly appeal to some norm or standard of ethical behavior.

Many environmental controversies involve disputes of normative ethics. One side believes that people ought not kill endangered animals under any circumstances; the other believes that selective killing of some animals ("culling") is necessary to maintain an ecological balance. Both sides cite evidence and opinions in support of their judgments. No doubt much frustration that students experience with ethics arises because ethical discussions too often are left at this level, with disagreements and controversies abounding.

However, it is crucial that we not remain at the level of normative ethics. Resolving controversy requires us to step out of, or to *abstract* ourselves from, specific disagreements to examine the values in conflict and the competing reasons that underlie the conflict. Moving to this more abstract level of thinking is to move from normative to philosophical ethics.

The third aspect of ethical reasoning is *philosophical ethics*. Philosophical ethics is a higher level of generality and abstraction in which normative judgments and their supporting reasons are analyzed and evaluated. This is the level of the general concepts, principles, and theories to which one appeals in defending and explaining normative claims. And this is the level at which philosophers are most at home and have most to offer. Very generally, evaluating reasons that support or criticize a normative judgment, or seeking to clarify the concepts involved, is the essence of philosophical ethics. "Environmental ethics," in this sense, is a branch of philosophy involving the systematic study and evaluation of the normative judgments that are so much a part of environmentalism.

This framework of *descriptive*, *normative*, and *philosophical* ethics provides an initial answer to the question "What is environmental ethics?" and also introduces the general goals of this text. Environmental ethics trains us so that we can begin to understand environmental problems in all their complexity, and it challenges us to escape the limitations of an uncritical ethical perspective. Environmental ethics describes the varied ways in which different people understand the world (the different levels of "environmental consciousness"). In the study of environmental ethics, we are presented with a multitude of normative judgments and are asked to evaluate the evidence and reasons offered in support of these claims. In assessing this evidence, we typically must move to a more abstract and general level of analysis. At this more philosophical level, we are often asked to locate these specific normative claims in a more general philosophical context or theory. We examine and evaluate the philosophical assumptions that underlie these claims and perspectives. Finally, environmental ethics can involve "theory building" by articulating and defending a systematic and unified ethical perspective from which one then can generate and defend specific normative judgments. We will be engaged in these projects throughout this text.

1.7 SUMMARY AND CONCLUSION

A "story within the story" is told in this text. The primary emphasis of this book is to survey the wide variety of contributions that philosophers have been making to environmental debates. These represent the philosophical "visions" being offered to environmental scientists and policymakers. But within this story is a description of how philosophical ethics itself is challenged and extended by its encounter with the contemporary environmental and ecological crisis.

For many philosophers, traditional philosophical theories have proven inadequate to resolve environmental controversies. Thus, this book introduces philosophical ethics as an ongoing intellectual activity. It is an activity in which students are encouraged to become active participants, rather than passive observers.

Notes

1. For a discussion of cleanup technologies, including the use of hot water washing used during the *Exxon Valdez* cleanup, see "Soiled Shores," by Marguerite Holloway, *Scientific American* 265, no. 4 (October 1991): 102–116.
2. E. O. Wilson offers such estimates in a number of places. See, for example, "Threats to Biodiversity," in *Scientific American* 261, no. 3 (September 1989): 108–116.
3. Jane Mansbridge's *Beyond Self-Interest* (Chicago: University of Chicago Press, 1990) is a helpful collection of essays on this topic.
4. See, for example, Daniel Botkin, *Discordant Harmonies* (New York: Oxford University Press, 1990), for a critique of a mechanistic view of science from an ecological perspective.
5. Amory Lovins, "Technology Is the Answer (But What Was the Question?)," in G. Tyler Miller, ed., *Environmental Science*, 3d ed. (Belmont, CA: Wadsworth, 1991), pp. 56–57.
6. See, for example, John Rodman, "Four Forms of Ecological Consciousness Reconsidered," in Donald Scherer and Thomas Attig, eds., *Ethics and the Environment* (Englewood Cliffs, NJ: Prentice-Hall, 1983).
7. Aldo Leopold, *A Sand County Almanac with Essays on Conservation from Round River* (New York: Oxford University Press, 1949).

Discussion Questions

1. Reflect on some environmental controversy that recently has made news. Identify some of the ethical issues involved in this controversy. What makes an issue an *ethical* issue, anyhow?
2. Identify as many different uses of the words *natural* and *nature* as you can. Which, if any, have value connotations? Are all things that are "natural" also good? What about "human nature"? What is "natural" about human beings? What is not?
3. What makes "good" science? What is the difference between good science and bad science? What values distinguish good from bad science?
4. How should cleanup decisions, such as those made in the *Exxon Valdez* accident, be determined? Should the public be involved, or should these decisions be left to experts? Should local citizens have a direct voice, or is representation by such public agencies as the EPA sufficient? On what grounds do you defend your answers?
5. What sort of evidence is used to support controversial scientific claims? What sort of evidence is used to support controversial ethical claims? How is reasoning in science different from reasoning in ethics? How is it alike?

6. Should human behavior toward nonhuman natural objects be governed by ethical norms? Do we have any direct responsibility toward natural objects?

For Further Reading

The single best source for philosophical discussions of environmental issues is the journal *Environmental Ethics.*

James Rachels, *The Elements of Moral Philosophy* (New York: Random House, 1986), is a clearly written and philosophically substantive introduction to ethics.

G. Tyler Miller, *Living in the Environment*, 6th ed. (Belmont, CA: Wadsworth, 1990), is the single best introductory textbook to environmental science.

Daniel Botkin, *Discordant Harmonies* (New York: Oxford University Press, 1990), provides an insightful analysis by a scientist of how cultural myths and metaphors have shaped our understanding of the natural world.

Donald VanDeVeer and Christine Pierce, *People, Penguins, and Plastic Trees* (Belmont, CA: Wadsworth, 1986), and Tom Regan, ed., *Earthbound: New Introductory Essays in Environmental Ethics* (New York: Random House, 1984), are still among the best available collections of essays on environmental ethics, although they are slightly outdated given what has been written in the past few years.

Lynton Caldwell, *Between Two Worlds* (New York: Cambridge University Press, 1990), is a recent examination of the interplay of science, the environment, and public policy.

2

Ethical Theory and the Environment

Individual Rights and the Social Good

In 1962 the Atlantic Cement Company began operating a cement plant outside of Albany, New York. The company employed over 300 local residents and by 1970 had invested over $45 million in this plant. Part of this money was used to install the best available technology to reduce the discharge of dust and polluted air into the environment.

Nevertheless, the plant did emit large amounts of pollution as well as causing constant vibrations and loud noise. Local residents filed suit against the company claiming that the air pollution, the noise, and the vibrations were harming their health and property. The suit asked that the courts issue an injunction that would close down the plant until the pollution and the vibrations could be eliminated. Because the company already was using the best available technology, in effect the suit was asking that the company be closed down indefinitely.

To many observers, this case was a classic illustration of a conflict between individual rights and the overall good. The neighbors claimed that their rights to health and property were being violated by the air and noise pollution caused by the cement plant. Atlantic Cement argued that an injunction would cause serious economic harm to the entire community. The trial judge agreed that the plant had "created a nuisance insofar as the lands of the plaintiffs were concerned." However, he refused to issue the injunction because of the "defendant's immense investment in the Hudson River Valley and its contribution to the Capital District's economy."

The court reasoned that the costs of closing the plant outweighed the benefits to be gained by the residents. In the words of one judge, "the total damage to plaintiffs' [Boomers'] property is, however, relatively small in comparison with the value of defendant's operation and with the consequences of the injunction which the plaintiffs seek." Instead, the court ruled that the cement company should pay residents a one-time fee for damages that could be proven to exist already, and then pay them a monthly fee to compensate for ongoing harms. This fee, $535 per month for each household, was calculated to be a fair market price for what the residents would receive if they were inclined and able to rent their property.

To some critics, this case set a dangerous precedent. The decision seemed willing to treat health as deserving no greater legal protection than economic interests. It also ignored the environmental interests of the general public by considering only the claims of people living near the plant. The decision also effectively coerced the property owners by giving them the choice either to rent their property to the company at a price established by the court, or to suffer the consequences without any compensation. Finally, in the view of some critics, this decision amounts to granting the company a license to pollute with little or no incentive to improve its pollution control technology. As long as the company is willing to pay a fee established by the government, and as long as it uses the best technology available at the time the plant was built, it is free to pollute the air and harm its neighbors.

Construction of new nuclear power plants has come to a virtual standstill in the United States. No new plants have been ordered since the Three Mile Island accident in 1979. Significantly rising costs, due to a large extent to strong public opposition, and concerns about waste disposal continue to pose major obstacles to new construction. But earlier decisions to build, license, and locate nuclear power plants provide helpful examples of ordinary ethical decision making.

In order to be licensed to construct a nuclear plant, an electric power company must first demonstrate to government regulators that there is a need for more power. Typically, this would be done by demonstrating that there is a consumer demand for more electricity. The implicit assumption was that *social need* can be equated with *consumer demand*.

The next step in the process would require the company to show that nuclear energy, rather than coal or oil, should be the fuel used to meet the demand. Again, this typically was done by using cost–benefit analysis. The costs and benefits of the alternatives were compared and, if it was shown that a nuclear energy plant was more cost-effective than oil or coal, the company would have successfully met the second condition.

The third step in the process, done in consultation with various government bodies, involved choosing a location for the plant. Again various alternative sites would be proposed and a cost–benefit analysis would be conducted to decide between the alternatives. Such an analysis might proceed as follows.

One proposed site would be in a rural area some distance away from the major population center that was home to the increasing consumer demand for electricity. The costs for this site would include building and maintaining power lines as well as the small loss of electricity that occurs through transmission. On the other hand, land costs typically would be lower in a rural area, as would costs for labor and materials. And, of course, *if* there ever were an accident, a rural location would put a smaller number of people at risk.

In contrast, building the plant within a metropolitan area would save transmission costs and efficiencies. However, labor, land, and material costs would likely be higher in a metropolitan area. Finally, in the remote case of an accident, potentially hundreds of thousands of people would be put at risk. The actual location of nuclear power plants across this country is the best evidence we have for determining how and why government and industry made these decisions.

2.1 INTRODUCTION

Throughout history, philosophers have sought to develop systematic and comprehensive accounts of the ethical life. These ethical "theories" provide a basis from which to understand, evaluate, and guide ethical behavior. This chapter discusses the relevance of such

theories and briefly describes several that are important for much of
what follows in this text.

As used here, the term *ethical theory* refers to any attempt to provide systematic answers to the philosophical questions raised by
descriptive and normative approaches to ethics. These questions are
raised from both an individual moral viewpoint, and from the viewpoint of society or public policy. Individual moral questions include
"What should I do? What kind of person should I be? What do I
value?" and "How should I live?" Questions of social philosophy or
public policy include "What type of society is best? What policies
should we follow as a group? What social arrangements and practices will best protect and promote individual well-being?" and
"What should be done when individuals disagree?" Not only do
philosophers seek answers to these questions, but more importantly
they seek to provide a reasoned explanation and defense of these
answers. Thus, in this broad sense ethical theory includes philosophical analyses of moral, political, economic, legal, and social
questions.[1]

2.2 WHY ETHICAL THEORY?

Chapter 1 discussed in general terms why the study of ethics is
necessary for any complete evaluation of environmental controversies. This section considers why the study of ethical *theory* is also
relevant. Four general considerations make theory relevant to the
study of environmental ethics. First, ethical theories provide a common language to use in discussing and understanding ethical issues. Environmental ethics is characterized by deep and numerous
controversies. Clearly, a necessary first step in examining and resolving controversy requires us to understand these disputes fully
and accurately. The basic concepts and categories of ethics—
"rights" "responsibilities," "utility," "the common good," and the
relationships between these concepts—can provide a basis for mutual understanding and dialogue. Ethical theories make explicit and
systematize the common beliefs and shared values that are often
implicit in specific controversies. By learning the language of philosophical ethics, you become better able to understand, evaluate, and
communicate. This, in turn, can empower you to become full participants in environmental debates. Philosophical ethics can contribute
to the common language that is essential to reasoned dialogue.

Second, since various ethical theories have played a major role in
our own traditions they tend to be reflected in the ways in which
most of us think. By learning about ethical theories you become
more aware of the patterns and assumptions in your own ways of

thinking. You thus become better able to articulate your own views and better able to defend them. Of equal importance, you gain a philosophical perspective for a critical examination of your own ways of thinking. By making these patterns explicit, you also are in a position to better see and understand issues *as* ethical issues.

Third, one of the traditional functions of an ethical theory is to offer guidance and evaluation. Theories can be applied to specific situations and generate specific recommendations. The long history of ethics gives a reasonable basis from which to analyze and offer advice. As you work your way through environmental controversies, it will be helpful if you do not have to "reinvent the wheel" at every step. As it turns out, there are standard ways in which people reason about ethics, many of which match standard ethical theories. Because philosophers have spent considerable time thinking through these theories and uncovering their strengths and weaknesses, knowledge of theory is an important resource for the debates that follow.

Finally, familiarity with ethical theories is important, because some critics claim that these theories themselves, embedded as they are in standard ways of thinking, have been responsible for some of the environmental problems we face. That is, the practice of doing environmental ethics sometimes involves challenging the very theories of ethics that philosophers have been busy defending. Some argue that these theories are part of the problem, that people have been misled by these theories. Thus, an important part of doing environmental ethics includes examining philosophical theories about ethics. In this way, environmental ethics not only benefits from traditional ethical theory but also contributes to the development of this branch of philosophy.

2.3 ETHICAL RELATIVISM

Before we turn to a survey of traditional ethical theories, we need to confront a very common challenge to philosophical ethics. In the view of some people, studying ethics is futile because ethical values and judgments are, ultimately, a matter of mere opinion or personal feelings. As such, there are no objective and rational answers to ethical controversies. This skepticism about ethics—called "ethical relativism"—is often expressed in the rhetorical question "Who is to say what's right or wrong?"

Ethical relativism is the view that denies the possibility of making objective ethical judgments. The relativist holds that ethical standards depend on, or *are relative to*, an individual's feelings, culture, religion, and so forth. As such, there can be no objective, universal, or true ethical judgments. "It is all a matter of opinion," and therefore we are wasting our time trying to find the "correct" or "true" answers to environmental controversies.

There is, perhaps, no more serious challenge to teachers of ethics than relativism. This is not because we as teachers lack philosophical refutations of this view. Rather, relativism threatens our most important goal as teachers: to develop in students the skills of careful and informed thinking. Too often, the relativist challenge is raised at exactly the critical point of an ethical controversy when careful reasoning is called for. Unfortunately, many people turn to the relativist perspective more as a result of frustration and intellectual laziness than as the result of careful philosophical reasoning. Exactly when a controversy calls out for careful and reasoned analysis, the relativist shrugs his or her shoulders and dismisses the debate with the question "Who is to say what's right or wrong?"

The short answer to this rhetorical question is "Anyone who can offer good reasons to support their judgment of right or wrong." The chapters that follow provide evidence that good reasons can be given in support of ethical judgments. Doing philosophical ethics is just doing the hard work of reasoning through ethical controversies. This text invites you to participate fully in this hard work.

Of course, there are reasons for rejecting ethical relativism that go beyond its implications for teachers of ethics. First, we should not confuse the *fact* that people disagree about ethical issues with the philosophical claim that objective agreement is impossible. People in different cultures and from differing backgrounds hold different beliefs about many things, including but not limited to questions of ethics. But it would be a mistake to conclude that there is no right answer simply from the fact that two cultures hold different beliefs. For example, some people may believe the earth is flat and at the center of the universe. But we have no reason to conclude that there are no objective standards for evaluating these beliefs simply from the fact that people disagree. So, too, it is a mistake to reason from the fact that cultures disagree about values to the conclusion that no correct answer exists. Believing the earth is flat does not make it flat; believing murder is right does not make it right.

We should also be careful not to ask too much of ethical reasoning. Few of the controversies examined in this text can be resolved with moral certainty. It is tempting to think that if ethics cannot "prove" a conclusion beyond doubt, then no objective conclusion exists. But this standard of proof, which perhaps is applicable in mathematics and few other areas, is surely inappropriate in ethics. Just as sciences such as medicine, ecology, and meteorology offer rational and objective judgments without proving these judgments beyond any doubt, so too ethics involves standards of reasoning that are different from those found in mathematics.

Finally, I should point out the implications of relativism. A consistent relativist must believe there is no objective basis for praising friendship, love, freedom, and democracy, while condemning hatred, murder, slavery, and totalitarianism. The relativist must accept the conclusion that there are no objective grounds for denouncing Hitler or for praising Mother Teresa. To be a consistent ethical relativist, one must deny that rational persuasion and dialogue in ethics is impossible. Although some people may talk like ethical relativists, few of us could live our lives as consistent relativists. Perhaps this practical contradiction is the most telling refutation of the relativist position.

2.4 THE NATURAL LAW OR TELEOLOGICAL TRADITION

One of the oldest ethical traditions relevant to environmental ethics is the *natural law* or *teleological tradition*. The ethical views associated with this tradition can be traced to Aristotle (fourth century B.C.) and Thomas Aquinas (thirteenth century A.D.).

As mentioned in Chapter 1, in Aristotelian thought ethics and science were not as clearly distinguished as they sometimes are today. Further, Aristotle placed the biological sciences at the forefront of knowledge, whereas in the twentieth century physics and math seem to hold sway. This interesting blend of biology and ethics is one of the reasons that this ethical tradition can be relevant to environmental issues.

For Aristotle, to fully understand something is to understand the *causes* for its being the way it is. Science involves more than simply describing what exists; scientific knowledge requires that we be able to explain *why* something is what it is. To do this requires that we describe four aspects, what Aristotle calls the *four causes*, of an object's existence. The four causes are the *material, formal, efficient,* and *final* causes.

An account of an object's "material cause" is what an object is made from, its matter. The formal cause explains how that matter is organized or structured so that this material is what it is rather than something else made out of the same material. Thus, for example, a tree and a table have the same material cause, wood, which exists in two different forms. An "efficient cause" explains how something came to be what it is. A carpenter, for example, is the efficient cause for some wood becoming a table. Lastly, a "final cause" explains the purpose or characteristic activity of the object. The final cause of the table is to provide a place at which you can sit and eat.

Aristotle's science differs in part from a more modern version in holding that we don't fully understand an object until we understand its final cause, or its characteristic or "natural," activity. Given his observations of nature, Aristotle believed that all things did have a natural and distinctive activity. This activity (sometimes called its purpose, or function, or end), was identified in the Greek as the object's telos. Hence, Aristotle's science and his ethics are often called *teleological*. We have come to understand some object fully, according to Aristotle, only when we understand its natural function or activity.

An example might help. Suppose we seek a scientific explanation of a heart. In Aristotle's view, we don't fully understand the heart until we understand its characteristic activity. A teleological explanation of the heart answers the question "What is the distinctive activity of hearts?" or "What function do hearts perform that distinguish them from other bodily organs?" We understand the heart when we understand its function in the circulatory system. A teleological explanation describes the heart as an organ that pumps blood throughout the body.

A more modern explanation might instead explain the heart in terms of its composition (or matter): muscle tissue, cells, and so forth. A modern tendency is to reduce the object to be studied into more simple elements and investigate the physical, mechanical, and chemical forces (efficient causes) that make this object what it is (formal cause).[2]

Aristotle distinguishes two basic types of natural objects: those that are alive and those that are not. The characteristic activity of living things, what might be called the principle of life itself, is called the "psyche" or, as it was later translated, the *soul*. Thus to say some body is alive is to say it has a soul. Aristotle then goes on to describe three "powers" or fundamental activities of life: nutrition, sensation, and thinking. Some living things possess only one (the "nutritive soul"), while others possess two (the nutritive and "appetitive" or "sensitive"), and some possess all three types (the nutritive, appetitive, and thinking). Plants are living things that possess only the nutritive soul. This means that their characteristic activities include only the powers of nutrition, growth, and reproduction. Animals possess appetitive powers in addition to nutrition. This means that their natural activities also include the powers of sensation, desire, and motion. Finally, only humans possess the three life activities of nutrition, appetite, and thought.

With this admittedly brief characterization, we can now see how the distinction between scientific fact and ethical value was not as clear for Aristotle as it sometimes seems today. When we understand the characteristic activity of a heart, for example, we also come to understand what a *good* heart is. A good heart is one that pumps blood through the body in a regular, stable, and continuous manner and hopefully does so over a long period of time. A good heart is one that performs its characteristic activity well.

Aristotle believed that this teleological framework could be applied to all natural objects, including humans. All things have a natural activity or function. Things are good when they fulfill this function or, in terms more common to this tradition, when they actualize their potential.

In general terms, every living thing can be said to have a good of its own. The good for any living thing is to attain fully its natural activity (or fully actualize its "soul"). Thus, the good of a plant is to accomplish the nutritive functions of taking in nutrition, growth, and reproduction. The good of animals includes these functions as well as attaining its desires and fulfilling its appetites. The human good includes all these ends, as well as living a thoughtful and deliberative life.

This teleological system was further developed in the writings of Thomas Aquinas in the thirteenth century, and it is perhaps through Aquinas's writings that these views had the greatest impact on Western thought. Aquinas attempted to synthesize Aristotle's science and ethics with Christian theology. He interpreted the scientific and ethical teleology of Aristotle as evidence of a divine plan operating in nature. The characteristic activity of all natural objects resulted from God's plan and God's purposes. Because God was assumed to be supremely good and because the purposes discovered in nature were God's purposes, the natural order can be equated with the moral order. Nature itself has a purpose, and the harmonious functioning of nature reveals the goodness of God's plan. For an individual, fulfilling one's natural potential—a potential implicitly in harmony with the rest of nature—was the highest form of ethical activity.

Several themes in modern environmentalism are reminiscent of this ethical tradition. Some ecologists assume that natural ecosystems are in themselves well ordered and harmonious. All parts of an ecosystem, and especially all its biotic members, have their own distinctive place in the overall scheme. Each contributes to the natural order in its own way. Nature undisturbed is good. Ecological problems arise when humans interfere with the natural order and treat other natural objects as having value only in so far as they serve human purposes.

Other environmentalists emphasize the ethical status of all living things and base this status on the fact that every living thing has a good of its own. (A version of this view is presented in the examination of biocentric ethics in Chapter 7.) Although the Aristotelian system allows for a moral hierarchy with humans "higher" than animals and animals "higher" than plants, it nevertheless also allows for the possibility of seeing that all living things do have a good of their own. Thus they possess a good that was independent of human interests and uses.

Unfortunately, several major objections to this tradition can undermine its relevance to contemporary debates. The first objection denies that all natural objects do have some one definite and distinctive *telos*. It seems true that some objects have a definite purpose or function. Human artifacts, such as a chair or a computer, are obvious examples. Some *parts* of a natural whole, such as a heart, a chromosome, also seem to have natural functions. But these parts only have a purpose in the sense that they contribute to the function of the whole. It does not seem obvious that these wholes themselves have a purpose. What, for example, is the characteristic activity of a human being? What is the characteristic activity of a spotted owl? Philosophers and scientists in the modern era have thought they could fully understand and explain natural objects without having to assume some natural purpose or plan. (Interestingly enough, some ecologists are less reluctant to attribute characteristic functions to members of ecosystems.)

A second objection denies that we can conclude something is good simply from the fact that it is natural. A similar concern was already mentioned in the discussion of science and values in Chapter 1. Because some natural occurrences seem evil, such as death, disease, and natural disasters, some reason other than the appeal to "nature" must be given to show why something is good. Unfortunately, the answer most often given throughout the natural law tradition appeals to a divine plan. However, this appeal effectively ends the philosophical discussion because it provides a reason only to those people who already assume a divine creator. To people of other religious traditions or to people who do not believe in a supremely good creator, this reason carries little rational weight.

Finally, modern evolutionary science provides a significant, and perhaps insurmountable, challenge to the natural law tradition. The process of natural selection offers an account of the apparent design found in nature without appealing to any purpose or telos. The order found in nature comes not from divine plan but from the process of species adapting to their environment, typically through a process of random mutation and natural selection. For example, a defender of natural law might explain the long neck of the giraffe by claiming that the long neck exists (or was designed) to allow the giraffe to reach food high off the ground. The defender of natural selection, on the other hand, would claim that the giraffe did not develop a long neck to reach the leaves high up on a tree; rather, it survived because, having a long neck, it can reach these leaves and was thus better adapted to its environment than were competing organisms. The long neck is itself the result of random evolutionary change. Thus the purposive language of teleology can be reduced to the more mechanistic language of the physical sciences. In this view, "nature" as we find it today is the result of hundreds of millions of years of random evolutionary change. "Nature" is neither good nor bad; it just *is*.

Thus while the natural law tradition provides a framework for thinking and reasoning about relations between nature and ethics, it does not lack significant philosophical challenges. This brief review can help you to evaluate later occasions when you see various insights from this tradition applied to contemporary environmental issues.

2.5 THE UTILITARIAN TRADITION

A second ethical tradition helpful in studying environmental ethics is *utilitarianism*. The classical statements of this tradition are found in the writings of Jeremy Bentham and John Stuart Mill in the nineteenth century, but it continues to be a very influential theory today.[3] Utilitarian reasoning is especially influential in economics, public policy, and government regulation. Therefore utilitarianism has also played a significant role in environmental policy.

In general terms, utilitarianism tells us to "maximize the overall good," or to produce "the greatest good for the greatest number." Utilitarian theory thus rests on two elements: an account of the "good" and a rule for judging all acts and decisions in terms of that good. The rule tells us to look to the *consequences* of any particular act and to judge the ethical status of that act in terms of those consequences. If the act tends to maximize good consequences, it is an ethically right act; if it does not, the act is ethically wrong.

Consequently, utilitarians distinguish between two basic types of value: the "good," which is valued for its own sake, and all other things, which are valued because of their relation to the good. Thus, all acts or decisions are judged in terms of their "utility," or their usefulness in producing good consequences. This distinction is sometimes made in terms of *intrinsic* and *instrumental* value. Utilitarians defend some view of intrinsic value (for example, pleasure or happiness), and then judge the value of all other things and activities in terms of how well they serve as an instrument to achieve the optimal amount of that value.

The challenge to utilitarians, of course, is to successfully defend an account of the "good" that can serve as the basis of all other values. If this good is to function in this way, it should be *objective* (good independent of specific contexts) and *universal* (good for all people at all times). Different versions of utilitarianism can then be distinguished by how they describe the "good."

Two versions are important for what follows. One type of utilitarianism takes pleasure, or at least the absence of pain, to be the only good valued for its own sake. Pleasure and the absence of pain is something universally desired. People who desire pain or avoid pleasure typically are suspected of acting unreasonably. Pleasure seems to be a plausible candidate for something that is objectively good and universally valued. This version is called *hedonistic* utilitarianism.

A second version of utilitarianism understands the good as the happiness that results from the satisfaction of desires. In this view, people are happy when they have what they want, when their desires are satisfied. A world in which as many people had as much of what they desired as possible, would be the ethically best world. Contemporary defenders of this version often fine-tune this by adding the requirement that individuals are best left to choose and rank-order their own desires. Sometimes called *preference* utilitarianism, this version directs us to satisfy as many individual preferences as possible. As shown in the next chapter, this ethical theory is closely associated with the economic theory of the free market and in that way it has significant implications for environmental policy.

A number of standard challenges are raised against utilitarian thinking and, again, it proves helpful to review several of them at this early point. A set of challenges can be grouped together as *measurement* problems. Utilitarianism essentially involves a process of measurement and comparison. Phrases such as "maximize the overall good" and "the greatest good for the greatest number" necessarily require measuring, comparing, and quantifying. However, a tension exists when we try to quantify what is primarily qualitative. The "good" is taken by utilitarians to be what has intrinsic value, yet intrinsic value may not be the sort of thing that can easily be counted, measured, or compared.

These considerations lead to several serious philosophical problems. The first challenges the very possibility of quantifying such things as pleasure, happiness, and desires. Are we to assume that all pleasures or desires are qualitatively the same? Are all pleasures created equal? If not, how can they be measured? According to what scale? In part, preference utilitarianism seeks to overcome this problem because preferences, as opposed to desires, are rank-ordered. For example, I want both more time to finish my work and a vacation, but I *prefer* the vacation over work. However, while this may overcome some problems of comparing an individual's desires, it doesn't help in making comparisons between two different people with conflicting desires.

A second problem follows from this. Because the good is difficult to quantify, utilitarians tend to substitute for the good something that can be quantified. For example, suppose we took good health to be the social goal we seek to maximize. How can we measure and compare the health consequences of various policy decisions? In practice, it could become very easy to substitute for health some quantifiable considerations such as life expectancy, infant mortality, injury rate, or per capita expenditures on health care. Although such factors may well give us an indication of health, they surely do not give us the whole story. Moreover, in practice it becomes easy to forget the primary goal of health and simply identify these quantifiable factors as the final goal. This problem raises significant questions when we realize that the most easily quantifiable substitute for the good is dollars and cents.

Critics of the *Boomer v. Atlantic Cement* decision claim this is exactly what occurred there. Because the courts seemed unable to measure the value of health itself, they instead measured various economic factors associated with health and then proceeded to decide the case by comparing the "costs" of health to the costs of closing down the plant. The court also assumed that the value of a person's home could be expressed fully in economic terms. Thus, the value of the Boomers' home was equivalent to what they would receive if they rented it; that is, what they would receive as compensation for relinquishing the use of this home to someone else.

A final measurement problem arises when we consider the *scope* of the people to be considered and the *range* of what counts as a person. In theory, the utilitarian should be concerned with all the pleasure or happiness affected by the particular act. In practice, this is just about impossible. We can never know all the consequences of any act. The tendency among utilitarians is to restrict consideration only to the expected consequences to people in the immediate vicinity. Further, an act's effects on future generations, for example, or on people in other countries, or on animals (who do experience pleasure and pain after all) is often ignored. Each such limitation has significant environmental implications.

The criticisms raised so far could be countered by adjustments made in applying utilitarian principles. Other criticisms raise more direct challenges to the theory itself and call for abandoning rather than reforming utilitarianism. One such challenge begins from the provisional nature of utilitarian judgments. No particular act, in and of itself, is ever right or wrong, according to the utilitarian. The ethical status of any act always depends on something else: its consequences. Right and wrong always depend on the context, and therefore always depend on factors outside of one's control. But this seems to miss a very important area of ethical concern; namely, those occasions when the ethically correct decision is to act on principle, regardless of consequences. There can be times when we judge an act to be wrong in principle, even if the overall consequences turn out to be good. At times we judge an act to be ethically right in principle, even if the overall consequences turn out bad. Because utilitarianism seems unable to account for such notable cases, critics charge that this theory is at best incomplete.

Two examples may help illuminate this point. Imagine a situation in which significant and good consequences would result if only I would betray a friend. Imagine also that this friend would never know that I was responsible for the betrayal. In such a scenario, the utilitarian decision would be to betray the friend. However, critics would claim that this betrayal violates an important ethical principle ("Don't betray friends") and ought not to be done, even if the resulting consequences were bad.

A second example can be developed from a well-known environmental controversy. In recent years, many environmentalists have fought to prevent logging in the old-growth forests of the Pacific Northwest. Logging activities are threatening to destroy the habitat of the spotted owl, an endangered species. The spotted owl could become extinct if the logging continues. On the other hand, significant social benefits follow from growth in the logging industry. Because there is no known human *use* for the owl and because the owl does not contribute to human society in any obvious way, a utilitarian calculation might suggest that the logging be allowed. However, environmentalists charge that it is wrong in principle to cause the extinction of a species, even if doing so results in a net increase in beneficial social consequences.

At the beginning of this chapter, I suggested that ethical theory should be studied because, among other reasons, some of the standard theories are embedded in common ways of thinking and reasoning. This perhaps is most true of utilitarianism. In many ways it is the unofficial ethical theory of public policy in much of North America and western Europe. Time and time again, environmental debates are cast in utilitarian terms. *Boomer v. Atlantic Cement* is a case in point, as is the public policy decision making that surrounds nuclear power plants and protection of the spotted owl. I hope this brief introduction helps you recognize utilitarian reasoning, and sensitizes you to the implicit strengths and inherent dangers of this common public philosophy.

2.6 DEONTOLOGY: AN ETHICS OF DUTY AND RIGHTS

The final ethical tradition that we should consider emphasizes the notion of acting on principle rather than consequences. In this view, the central concepts of ethics involve duties and rights. (This approach to ethics is sometimes called "deontology," from the Greek word for "duty.") The classic philosophical defense of this view is found in the writings of the eighteenth century German philosopher Immanuel Kant.[4]

Remember one of the crucial concerns raised against utilitarianism: that view seemed to make the ethical status of our acts depend on factors over which we have no control. Our acts are judged by their consequences, yet surely we can neither anticipate nor control all the consequences of our actions. Thus, that ethical theory seems to hold people responsible for things they cannot control. This seems to violate the "ought implies can" condition described early in Chapter 1.

Kantian ethics begins with the claim that we can be held responsible only for those things we can control. This, argued Kant, means that the focus of ethics should be on those principles (what he called "maxims") on which we choose to act. We can think of these principles as expressing the intention of our action. Assuming that we are rational beings and do not act merely as a result of instinct or conditioning, we can be held responsible because we have freely chosen to act. Thus, Kant held that we are ethical beings because we are rational beings who can freely form intentions and deliberately choose to act on them. Our standing as moral beings is derived from our nature as free and rational beings.

But how do we determine which intentions are ethically correct and which are unethical? Kant argued that we are acting ethically whenever the principle or maxim on which we act is a rational one. A rational principle in ethics, like rationality in other areas, would be found acceptable and binding by all other actors. That is, a rational principle is one that is *categorical* and *universal*. The fundamental ethical duty, called by Kant the "categorical imperative," is to act only in those ways that could be acceptable by all rational beings.

Kant believed that this fundamental ethical duty could be expressed in a number of different ways. This categorical imperative also requires that we treat persons as *ends* and never simply as *means*, or as *subjects* and never simply as *objects*. Thus, we are ethically obligated to treat people as rational and autonomous beings. We should never treat a person as a mere thing to be used for our own purposes. People are subjects who have their own purposes and intentions.

Thus the categorical imperative establishes our fundamental ethical duties: treat persons as ends and never as mere means or as objects. However, because other people are equally obligated to treat you in this manner, the categorical imperative can also be seen as establishing your fundamental ethical *rights*. Like all persons, you have the right to be treated as an end, not as a means. You have the right to be treated as a free and rational being who has his or her own purposes and goals. You have the right to pursue those goals as long as you do not in turn treat others as a means to your ends. Following from these considerations, this ethical tradition places primary value on the duty to treat other persons with respect and on the rights of equality and freedom. These basic rights and duties all follow from our nature as beings capable of free and rational action.

This discussion of duties and rights gives us another way to understand the major deficiency in utilitarian thinking. Given its focus on consequences, utilitarianism neglects the important role that moral principles can play in ethical decision making. According to Kant, acting on principle just is to act in accordance with the categorical imperative. The principle of justice, for example, requires us to fulfill our duties to other persons. Justice requires that we respect the rights of other people. Utilitarianism requires us to fulfill our duties and respect others' rights *only when* doing so maximizes the overall good consequences. But this, argues the Kantian, is the perfect example of injustice: fulfilling duties and respecting rights only when doing so has beneficial consequences.

These ideas have had a profound influence on Western ethical and political thought. You can see them reflected in the central notions of democracy and civil liberties. An ethical theory that did not take seriously the dignity of each person as a free and rational agent would stand in need of significant philosophical defense. Nonetheless, several critical issues should be mentioned at this point.

Some critics claim that this ethical tradition offers little real basis for making normative value judgments. As long as you are treating other people correctly (which might be done simply by leaving other people alone), there would be no ethical basis for evaluating those choices that you do make. In that view, value becomes a matter of personal choice or preference. This deontological tradition, according to some critics, offers no account of what is good or worthy. A life of conspicuous consumption is, if autonomously chosen and if done without violating the dignity of other autonomous agents, ethically no better or worse than a more ecologically sound lifestyle. A life spent competing with others, or in solitude and loneliness, is ethically no worse than a life of friendships, caring, and community.

Other critics see a strong human-centered, or anthropocentric, bias implicit in this tradition. It seems a short step from treating humans as ends because they are rational, to treating nonrational things as mere means. There appears no basis in this tradition for ethical obligations to anything that is not free and rational. Thus it seems legitimate to treat other living beings and the environment simply as means to our ends. These things are, after all, the perfect example of objects, not subjects. Some of these criticisms are developed at greater length in later chapters.

2.7 PROPERTY RIGHTS

The ethical traditions of utilitarianism and Kantian deontology have had a significant influence on the development of modern political thinking. Indeed, it is fair to see these philosophical theories and the great democratic revolutions of the late eighteenth century as part of the same cultural and intellectual movement. Both classical utilitarianism and Kantian deontology seem to commit us to democratic forms of government with strong protections of individual freedoms and individual rights.

The political arrangements of a constitutional democracy are a useful example for seeing the connections between these ethical traditions and contemporary politics. A commitment to majority rule can be seen as serving the utilitarian goal of maximizing happiness.

If you seek to attain the greatest happiness for the greatest number, you would not go far wrong by taking a vote and following the will of the majority. Yet constitutional protections of civil rights and civil liberties can be seen as serving the Kantian goal of respecting individual autonomy. Thus constitutional rights serve as a check on and limit to the majoritarian decisions of legislature.

Few individual rights have played a more important role in Western political and philosophical traditions than the right of private property. Unquestionably, no right is more central to a wider variety of environmental issues than private property. Property, and the related concepts of ownership and land, are fundamental to many of the debates that we examine in this text. For this reason, it is helpful to present a brief introduction to the philosophy of property rights at this point.

Contemporary Western understanding of property rights is often traced to the seventeenth-century English philosopher John Locke.[5] Locke's political philosophy begins by speculating about a "state of nature," a condition in which humans would exist were there no government. In this original natural state, all land is unowned (or, more in line with seventeenth-century thinking, is owned by God). This unowned land becomes owned, becomes *private* property, when an individual "mixes his labor" with the unowned land. In essence, Locke's argument is as follows.

1. A person has exclusive rights over, "owns," his own body and its labor.
2. Land, in its natural state is unowned; that is, no one individual can rightfully claim exclusive control of it.
3. Therefore, when someone's labor, which is owned, comes to be "mixed" with land that is unowned, the exclusive rights over his or her labor are transferred to the land. That person comes to own the land.

For example, if a man travels into the wilderness, clears some land, builds a home, tills the soil, and grows crops on this land, he (Locke never would have thought this individual a "she") comes to have a legitimate claim to this land. This legitimate claim is the establishment of private property rights.

A number of powerful objections have been raised against this Lockean view of private property. Some of these problems stem from the vagueness of the "mixing" metaphor. If you do "mix" something owned with something unowned, why assume that you come to own what was previously unowned? Why not assume that you *lose* ownership of what was previously owned, your labor being lost in the mixing? Why not assume that you gain ownership only over the improvements that you make, so that you can own the crops you grow but not the land itself? Suppose that your labor makes the land worse, rather than improves it? What if the goal of the original person is to preserve the land, and therefore this person makes a conscious decision not to "mix" his or her labor with it? Must all land be developed to be valued and owned?

Other problems arise when we realize that Locke's seventeenth-century European image of some vast, unowned wilderness does an injustice to historical fact. The image of early American settlers mixing their labor with the Western frontier and laying claim to it ignores the fact that native peoples had already been using that land for millennia. In effect, the Lockean view of property presupposes an agricultural or industrial conception of property. Nomadic cultures, for example, might travel over broad expanses as they followed changing seasons or migrating herds. The idea of laying a private and exclusive claim on the land would be quite outlandish in such a culture.

Finally, on Locke's own grounds, private ownership can be justified only when "enough and as good" land remains for others. Lockean property rights are derived from a more fundamental right of personal liberty ("the exclusive rights over one's own body"). Thus, *your* ownership can be justified only when it does not violate the liberty of other people. This will not happen, according to Locke, as long as there is sufficient land left in common for others. In the modern world with a population of 5.5 billion people, it is difficult to see how this condition can be met.

Such difficulties have led more contemporary accounts to view private property as involving a bundle of associated rights. These include the right to possess, control, use, benefit from, dispose of, and exclude others from the property. The "bundle" view is thought necessary because of the complexity that follows from the attempt to specify the implications of property rights. For example, surely it won't do to say that your right to property means that you can do just anything you want with it. The rights of other people restrict your property rights in a number of ways. You cannot turn your backyard into a toxic waste dump, for example. Zoning laws restrict the type of building that you can construct on your property, as well as restricting the uses of that building. Owning stock in a corporation, for example, entitles you to receive certain benefits from that stock in the form of dividends and appreciation. However, stock owners may not have the right to manage nor exclude others from using the corporate property, nor in some case can they even sell the stock to just anyone they choose.

By viewing property rights as a "bundle" of rights, a property right no longer can be seen as an all-or-nothing thing. Just as zoning laws restrict but do not violate your property rights, much legislation aimed at protecting the environment restricts only some of the rights in the bundle. It is helpful to keep this in mind as we review contemporary environmental debates. The debate seldom if ever is phrased as "Either the environment is harmed or you lose your property rights." Rather, most debates involve the degree of control that property owners are allowed to exercise over the various aspects of their interests.

2.8 SUMMARY AND CONCLUSION

You might think of this text as presenting an ongoing conversation between philosophers, scientists, environmentalists, and citizens. The conversation has been going on for some time, but it clearly has a long way to go before reaching any conclusions. In this model, you can think of these initial chapters as introducing some of the main characters in this conversation and some of the motivation that initiated the conversation. You have also been introduced to some of the language used and some of what has been said in the past.

By no means have the philosophers had the final word. Don't think that the path is now open to go forward and simply apply these philosophical theories and concepts to environmental problems. Rather, now that the introductions have been made, see yourself as a participant in this conversation. Join in the conversation: learn as you go, contribute what and when you can—and don't end the discussion too soon.

Notes

1. For an insightful critique of a standard understanding of the role of ethical theory and principles in environmental ethics, see Ken Sayre, "An Alternative View of Environmental Ethics," *Environmental Ethics* 13, no. 3 (Fall 1991), pp. 195–213. Sayre argues against what he calls the "inferential" view of ethical theory, a view very similar to what I shall be calling "applied ethics." Like Sayre, this book suggests that the inferential-applied view of ethical theory is at best incomplete when addressing environmental issues.

2. For Aristotle's account of the four causes, see his *Physics*, Bk. II, ch. 3. For a critique of the abuse of the more mechanistic model in environmental science, see Botkin's *Discordant Harmonies*.

3. For the classic statements of utilitarianism, see Jeremy Bentham, *Introduction to the Principles of Morals and Legislation* (Oxford, England: Clarendon Press, 1823), and John Stuart Mill, *Utilitarianism*, ed. with an intro. by George Sher (Indianapolis: Hackett, 1979). For a contemporary defense of utilitarianism, see J. J. C. Smart and Bernard Williams, *Utilitarianism For and Against* (Cambridge, England: Cambridge University Press, 1973).
4. For Kant's views on ethics, see especially his *Groundwork for the Metaphysics of Morals*, trans. Lewis White Beck (New York: Macmillan, 1990).
5. For Locke's defense of private property, see his *Second Treatise on Government*, especially Chapter 5. A helpful collection of essays on property rights and economic justice is Virginia Held, *Property, Profits, and Economic Justice* (Belmont, CA: Wadsworth, 1980).

Discussion Questions

1. If you were a judge and the *Boomer v. Atlantic Cement* case was argued in your court, how would you decide this case and how would you defend your decision? What values would underlie your decision?
2. The NIMBY phenomenon is the practice of people who demand the social services that create environmental pollutants but who say "Not in my backyard!" when decisions must be made about storage of toxic wastes. If you were a rural resident and a nuclear plant were scheduled to be built in your neighborhood, could you argue against it in ways that were not an example of NIMBY?
3. How might a defender of natural law ethics analyze the relationship between predators and prey? It seems natural for some species to prey on others. Does that make it ethically right? In all cases? Are humans natural predators?
4. During the summer of 1992, President Bush refused to sign a treaty at the Earth Summit in Rio de Janeiro because he believed it would result in the loss of too many jobs in the United States. In reaching this decision, he seemed to be making a utilitarian tradeoff between jobs and pollution. Are such comparisons reasonable?
5. Kantian ethics claim that some ethical principles ought not be violated under any circumstances. Can you give examples of principles that you would never violate? What are the grounds for these principles? Why do you hold them so strongly?
6. Nomadic cultures on many continents travel across great distances following the seasons and following migrating herds of animals. They never settle permanently on one section of land. How might their understanding of ownership and property differ from yours? Can the concept of a "property right" exist in such a culture?

For Further Reading

The original sources mentioned in the footnotes within this chapter are the best places to begin a study of ethical theory, although perhaps only Mill and Bentham are accessible to undergraduate students on first reading.

Both Aristotle and Kant would require substantial background in philosophy to be understood by most undergraduates. There are, however, many very helpful secondary sources and introductory textbooks.

Louis Pojman, ed., *Ethical Theory: Classical and Contemporary Sources* (Belmont, CA: Wadsworth, 1989), is a comprehensive anthology. Pojman's *Ethics: Discovering Right and Wrong* (Belmont, CA: Wadsworth, 1990), contains helpful discussions of objectivity in ethics and ethical relativism.

C. E. Harris, *Applying Moral Theories* (Belmont, CA: Wadsworth, 1986), shows how ethical theories, including natural law, utilitarian, and Kantian ethics, might be applied to practical issues.

Virginia Held, *Property, Profits, and Economic Justice* (Belmont, CA: Wadsworth Publishing, 1980), contains classical and contemporary sources on property rights and justice.

ENVIRONMENTAL ETHICS AS APPLIED ETHICS

3

Forests, Pollution, and Economics

Development Versus Preservation

The U.S. Forest Service is charged with managing the national forestlands for "outdoor recreation, range, timber, watershed, and wildlife and fish purposes." This "multiple use" responsibility is the primary legal mission of the service. In practice, the most serious challenge facing the Forest Service lies in deciding exactly how to balance the competing interests of the timber industry, recreational users of various types, preservationists, developers, and farmers.

During the 1960s, the Forest Service began accepting bids to develop the Mineral King Valley, a wilderness area adjacent to California's Sequoia National Park, for recreational uses. In January 1969, the Forest Service gave approval to a plan submitted by Walt Disney Enterprises to develop Mineral King as a ski resort. The plan called for creating a complex of motels, restaurants, parking lots, and other structures to accommodate an estimated 14,000 daily visitors to the valley. Ski slopes, ski lifts, a cog-assisted railway, and utility lines would be built onto the mountainside itself. A 20-mile highway and a high-voltage power line crossing the Sequoia National Park would also be built.

The Sierra Club objected to these plans and filed suit in federal court seeking to prevent the commercial development of Mineral King Valley. The Sierra Club endorsed only those recreational uses that would be consistent with the preservation of this wilderness area in an undeveloped state. Critics of the Forest Service's decision offered many arguments to support their view. They claimed that the Forest Service failed to give aesthetic and ecological factors equal weight with economic considerations. They claimed that the well-being of the animals, plants, rivers, and the mountain itself were being ignored.

In defense of its decision, the Forest Service argued that more citizens would get more of what they wanted under the Walt Disney plan than under the Sierra Club's alternative. The 14,000 expected daily visitors to the resort would outnumber the small amount of people who use the area for hiking, camping, hunting, and fishing. Furthermore, the willingness of skiers to pay more for this activity than wilderness users are willing to pay, as evidenced by Disney's ability to make a greater profit from this use than the Sierra Club could ever hope to make from its proposed uses, shows that the desire for skiing is more intense and widespread than is the desire for wilderness. For an agency of a democratic government, the economic market is a convenient measure of the desires of its citizens.

Water pollution is one of the most visible environmental problems. In 1969 the Cuyahoga River in Cleveland was so saturated with petrochemical pollutants that it caught fire and burned. During the summer of 1988, numerous beaches along New Jersey's Atlantic Ocean shore were closed when human feces, hospital wastes, and other toxic substances washed ashore. In March 1989, the *Exxon Valdez* ran aground in Prince William Sound, Alaska, spilling approximately 11 million gallons of oil. The final toll on wildlife, the fishing industry, and recreation is still being counted. According to the World Health Organization, five million people, mostly children, die every year as a result of water-related diseases. These diseases are easily eliminated with proper sanitation and clean drinking water.

Like water pollution, air pollution is one of the first environmental issues that the average citizen confronts in daily life. Airborne acidic chemicals, commonly called acid rain, have caused tremendous environmental destruction through North America and Europe. Forests, lakes and rivers, and soil have become so acidified that they can no longer support life. During the record heat in the summer of 1988, seventy-six cities in the United States registered ozone pollution levels of at least 25 percent higher than the maximum safe limit set by the Environmental Protection Agency (EPA). Airborne pollutants continue to destroy the earth's upper-atmosphere ozone layer. This results in an increase of harmful ultraviolet radiation reaching the earth's surface. Other airborne pollutants, generally called "greenhouse gases," can result in a global warming effect that threatens significant climatic upheaval.

3.1 INTRODUCTION

The philosophical skills introduced in the previous chapters—identifying ethical problems, clarifying and classifying concepts, analyzing arguments—have been applied to a wide variety of public policy issues in the past two decades. "Applied ethics" has contributed to public debates in such fields as medical and business ethics, and to such issues as affirmative action, economic justice, abortion, and the nuclear arms race. It is not surprising, then, that much of the philosophical work on environmental issues has followed the applied ethics format of identifying and clarifying ethical issues, and analyzing them in terms of ethical theories and principles. At least initially, the application of ethics to specific issues was not seen to affect ethics itself. The theory and principles that were applied remained relatively unchanged by the application.[1]

Applied ethics has frequently focused on the use of economic and market analyses in public policy debates. Economics is without question the most common tool of policy analysts, government decision makers, and private-sector experts. This chapter examines the contributions that philosophers can make to environmental debates by applying philosophical ethics to economic analysis. Specifically, we examine how economic analysis plays a central role in debates concerning the conservation of national forests and pollution of air and water. My philosophical evaluation suggests that there are deep problems with the uncritical use of economic analysis in resolving environmental debates.

It is not surprising that economics plays a major role in environmental debates. For example, many environmental problems appear to be, fundamentally, economic problems. Many of these problems are easily cast in economic terms: the distribution of scarce resources, allocation of risks and benefits, competing interests, production of desired goods, and so forth. Furthermore, much environmental destruction can be traced to economic factors. To recognize this, one need only review the terrible environmental destruction that took place under the central-state command economies of central and eastern Europe during the past generation.[2]

The relevance of economics to the environment is nicely summarized in the foreword to a book of economic analyses of U.S. environmental policy:

> A significant social development of the past decade has been the general realization that important damage may be done to the environment if the economy is permitted to operate in an unfettered way. . . . This certainty of "market failure" has long been known by economists. . . . It is appropriate that economists concern themselves with this general group of problems. Just as the awareness of environmental problems becomes more general, it is now also becoming known more generally that environmental improvement requires more resources and greater sacrifices. Thus an economic problem exists whether lawmakers decide to protect the environment through direct regulation or whether they choose to modify economic incentives that affect the behavior of millions of decision makers in the economic system.[3]

Thus, environmental problems are often understood as economic problems requiring the skills and expertise of economists.

The following two sections show how economic analysis is applied to two major issues, forest conservation and pollution. Following this, I emulate the standard technique of applied ethics by identifying and analyzing the ethical commitments implicit in economic analysis.

3.2 FORESTS: CONSERVATION OR PRESERVATION?

A pivotal moment in the history of American environmentalism occurred during the first decade of the twentieth century. The specific debates concerned a proposal to build a dam and reservoir in the Hetch Hetchy Valley adjacent to California's Yosemite National Park. Demand for water in San Francisco led to the plan that would result in flooding the Hetch Hetchy. Two of the most prominent early American environmentalists, Gifford Pinchot and John Muir, were at the center of these debates, which have come to symbolize two major competing environmental worldviews.

Gifford Pinchot was head of the U.S. Forest Service, one of the first professionally trained foresters in the United States, and close friend and adviser to President Theodore Roosevelt. Pinchot was a founder and leader of the *conservation* movement, which held that forestlands are to be conserved so that they might be wisely used and controlled by people. He was an early defender of the scientific management of national forestlands. His guiding principle was that public lands exist to serve the needs and uses of the public:

> The object of our forest policy is not to preserve the forests because they are beautiful . . . or because they are refuges for the wild creatures of the wilderness . . . but . . . the making of prosperous homes.[4]

He said, further, that

> Forestry is the knowledge of the forest. In particular, it is the art of handling the forest so that it will render whatever service is required of it without being impoverished or destroyed. . . . Forestry is the art of producing from the forest whatever it can yield for the service of man.[5]

Pinchot supported San Francisco's plan to build the reservoir. Damming the Hetch Hetchy would provide much-needed water to millions of people. It would represent the most efficient use of this natural resource.

John Muir was the founder of the Sierra Club and the best-known spokesperson for the *preservation* movement. Muir argued to preserve the Hetch Hetchy. He thought that the conservationist view of treating natural resources as mere commodities to be used for human consumption was a serious mistake. Muir defended the spiritual and aesthetic value of wilderness, as well as the inherent worth of other living things.[6] In his view, the Hetch Hetchy should be preserved as it was, and protected from human activity that would degrade and spoil it.

Thus, this early debate symbolizes the worldviews of two dominant strains of American environmentalism. The conservationists sought to protect the natural environment from exploitation so that humans would receive greater long-term benefits from it. The preservationists sought to protect the environment from any human activity that would disrupt or degrade it. Their goal was to preserve the wilderness in its natural, unspoiled state.

The ethical justification for the conservationist program was fairly straightforward. The natural environment is valuable as a means for serving human interests. Thus, natural resources were said to have instrumental value. Preservationists, in contrast, appeal to two different types of reasons to support their goals. One type cites the instrumental value of wilderness as a source of religious inspiration, a refuge from modern life, a location for aesthetic experience, and so on. But some preservationists also argued that the wilderness should be recognized as having intrinsic value in itself. Thus, we ought to preserve the wilderness not only for its human uses but also for its own sake.

It's easy for contemporary observers to cast Muir as the environmentalist and Pinchot as the environmental villain in this dispute. But this would be a mistake. Pinchot's position was quite progressive at the time, and it is helpful to consider this claim briefly.

For much of U.S. history, the forests and wilderness areas of this country represented a threat to be overcome, an enemy to be conquered. The images are common throughout the first four hundred years of European settlement of North America. Man against nature. The frontier is to be pushed back, the wilderness to be conquered. Life in the wilderness was difficult, and if humans were to survive they needed to fight and defeat the forces of nature. Nature was seen as the enemy to be subdued and exploited.

By the mid to late nineteenth century, the United States had pretty much succeeded in these tasks and most of the American landscape lay open for use. During this period of tremendous industrial growth and urbanization, nature was generally thought to be less an enemy to be conquered and more an inexhaustible resource to fuel the U.S. economy. In practice, this often meant that natural resources contributed to the extraordinary wealth of the privileged few who monopolized much of U.S. industry.

Pinchot's conservation movement was part of a more general progressive movement that was fighting the laissez-faire, monopolistic Social Darwinism characteristic of much nineteenth-century U.S. economic life.[7] The progressives held that natural resources should benefit all citizens, not just the wealthy few who privately owned vast amounts of property. Government policy should serve this goal by preventing waste, limiting monopolistic control, providing economic opportunity for the many, and by keeping prices low.

Pinchot's progressive conservation was in line with the progressivism of nineteenth-century utilitarians such as Bentham and Mill. Government policy, including economic policy, should aim to provide maximum benefit to all citizens, not just to a privileged few. In Pinchot's own words,

> The central idea of the Forester, in handling the forest, is to promote and perpetuate its greatest use to men. His purpose is to make it serve the greatest good of the greatest number for the longest time. . . . The idea of applying foresight and common-sense to the other natural resources as well as to the forest was natural and inevitable. . . . It was foreseen from the beginning by those who were responsible for inaugurating the Conservation movement that its natural development would in time work out into a planned and orderly scheme for national

efficiency, based on the elimination of waste, and directed toward the best use of all we have for the greatest good of the greatest number for the longest time.[8]

Thus, Pinchot's conservation movement fits squarely within the utilitarian tradition. Public policy should be directed to "serve the greatest good of the greatest number for the longest time." Consistent with much in the utilitarian tradition, Pinchot encouraged the use of experts who could manage policy so that it might attain this goal. Utilitarian thinking promotes reliance on experts, especially social scientists, who can calculate, measure, compare, predict, and influence the consequences of various policy options. The goal of maximally satisfying public welfare is accepted. Decision makers then rely on professional managers to determine which policy options will result in consequences most closely approaching this goal. This is precisely the role Pinchot saw for the professional forester. This is fundamentally the same role played by economists and other social scientists in many of today's environmental policy debates. To expand on this, let us now turn to a more contemporary version of this practice.

3.3 MANAGING THE NATIONAL FORESTS

Today, Pinchot's Forest Service manages 156 different national forests containing over 191 million acres of land. It is the largest agency in the U.S. Department of Agriculture, employing over 30,000 people.[9] In the hundred years of its existence, the Forest Service has gone through a number of changes. The 1897 Organic Administration Act established the purpose of national forest reserves "to furnish a continuous supply of timber." For fifty years, this mission was satisfied primarily through fire suppression, research, and other custodial duties. In the years following World War II, an increase in housing and a decrease in the supply of privately owned timber lands led to a greater focus on managing forests for timber sales. Later in 1960, Congress passed the Multiple-Use Sustained Yield Act to require that the Forest Service manage the forests for "outdoor recreation, range, timber, watershed, and wildlife and fish purposes." Although "multiple use" remains the primary legal mission of the service, in practice most of the activity of the Forest Service today is concerned with timber production, harvesting, and sales.

One controversial activity that follows from this mission is the construction of roads into wilderness areas to provide access to that timber. Although the Forest Service often defends these construction projects on "multiple use" grounds (they provide access for recreational uses as well as for timber companies), critics charge that the roads and the timber harvesting that they promote are responsible for significant environmental damage.[10] These critics fault the Forest Service for widespread destruction of wilderness areas, loss of old-growth forests, degradation of wildlife habitat, and threatening endangered species with extinction.

Perhaps it is not surprising to find a government bureaucracy that is responsible for administering a multiple-use policy to be the focus of criticism from its competing constituencies. The timber industry believes that not enough high-quality forests are open for its use. Environmentalists argue that too much wilderness is being sacrificed to timber interests. Ranchers would like to see more forestland open for grazing. Sportsmen decry the loss of hunting and fishing resources. And, as if to add insult to these injuries, despite the fact that the Forest Service manages assets estimated by some to be in excess of $42 billion, the agency costs taxpayers over $1 billion a year. In the words of one critic,

> In terms of assets, the agency would rank in the top five in *Fortune* magazine's list of the nation's 500 largest corporations. In terms of operating revenues, however, the agency would be only number 290. In terms of net income, the Forest Service would be classified as bankrupt.[11]

The purpose of this section is not to develop a detailed criticism of the Forest Service, however. It is enough to recognize that serious environmental controversies surround the management of the national forests. Our immediate interest in seeing the relevance of applied ethics lies instead with the evaluation of present policies and the recommendations for alternatives offered by some environmental critics.

Economist Randal O'Toole has written a sustained critique of Forest Service management. In his book, *Reforming the Forest Service*, O'Toole summarizes his five years of analyzing the activities of the Forest Service:

> I've visited national forests in every part of the country and have seen costly environmental destruction on a grand scale. Money-losing timber sales are costing taxpayers at least $250 to $500 million dollars per year. Many of these sales are reducing scarce recreation opportunities, driving wildlife species toward extinction, and polluting waters and fish habitat.[12]

Nevertheless, despite these troubles O'Toole remains optimistic in offering his recommendations:

> My economic research has convinced me that Americans can have all the wilderness, timber, wildlife, fish, and other forest resources they want. Apparent shortages of any of these resources are due solely to the Forest Service's failure to sell them at market prices.[13]

O'Toole's diagnosis of the Forest Service's problems is consistent with much economic analysis, and he can be used as an example of how economic analysis is used in environmental debates. The Forest Service is a large government bureaucracy with little or no incentive to balance revenues and expenses. Economic and environmental problems created by the policies of the Forest Service are due "not to ignorance or maliciousness but rather to a lack of incentive to be concerned." O'Toole attempts to show that "inefficient management and environmental controversies are not problems in themselves but are merely symptoms of major institutional defects within the Forest Service."[14] In general, the "major institutional defects" all stem from the fact that the Forest Service does not operate according to the economic laws that guide a private, for-profit business.

O'Toole's analysis is based on "the fundamental economic assumption that people's decisions are strongly influenced by the incentives affecting the decision makers."[15] The present structure of the Forest Service provides incentives only to "maximize its budget" and provides little or no incentive to supply Americans with "all the wilderness, timber, wildlife, fish, and other forest resources they want." The laws of economics tell us that if we "change the incentives, the decisions change."

What are the sources of Forest Service mismanagement? Essentially there are two. First, the Forest Service is primarily responsible to Congress. Like Congress, its decisions reflect an attempt to balance the demands of competing and sometimes contradictory interest groups. Recent debates concerning protection of the spotted owl in the Pacific Northwest demonstrate the type of controversial decisions that the Forest Service faces. Thus, the primary incentive for the Forest Service is to satisfy these interest groups as much as possible, even if this comes at the expense of consistently enforcing a long-range, rational, and efficient policy. Like Congress, which measures its success not in terms of the quality of legislation but in terms of re-election rates, the Forest Service is left with no measure of its success other than its budgetary retention rates. If its budget is maintained or increased, the Forest Service must be properly balancing the demands of its constituencies.[16]

The second source of Forest Service mismanagement lies in the fact that much of its budget comes from revenues retained from timber sales. An example is the Knutson-Vandenberg Act of 1930, which allows the Forest Service to retain money collected from timber sales to fund reforestation. Congressional thinking seems to have been that this would accomplish desired goals without costing taxpayers any money. However, because this made the service's budget dependent on any timber revenues collected, including those collected from below-cost sales of timber, this practice provides an incentive to sell timber at any price. There is no incentive to balance either revenues and costs, or timber sales against other uses of the forests.

Thus, in O'Toole's view, classical economic analysis has uncovered the underlying cause of the Forest Service's inability to manage national forests in an ecologically sound manner. The bureaucracy is organized in such a way that managers have incentives only to maximize their own budgets.

This is the diagnosis of Forest Service ills. Now, what is the cure? The recommendation of classical economics calls for the "marketization of the Forest Service." That is, the decisions of the Forest Service should mimic those decisions that would be made by private-sector business managers seeking profits in a competitive market. The economic laws of the marketplace lead to decisions that would best satisfy the diverse demands of the public. The market would "ensure efficient production of most forest resources and an efficient allocation of forestlands." The market would give Americans "all the wilderness, timber, wildlife, fish, and other forest resources they want."

It is interesting to contrast this recommendation with Pinchot's own views of the Forest Service. Both approaches agree on the desirable outcome: using forestlands to provide the greatest good for the greatest number of people. In this way, both accept the utilitarian goal of maximally satisfying individual preferences. The forests should be used to give people as much of what they want as possible. These approaches differ, however, on the correct means for attaining this goal. While Pinchot left it to scientific foresters and other experts to determine the correct policy, O'Toole trusts the workings of a competitive, free, and open market to achieve this goal. In this view, the role of the economist is not to make substantive policy decisions, but to help eliminate barriers to the operation of the market. The economic marketplace is the most appropriate means for attaining the utilitarian goal of maximum satisfaction of wants.

O'Toole cites the work of the new resource economists, especially John Baden and Richard Stroup, to support his recommendations.[17] According to these economists, it is a mistake to treat natural resources as "public goods" to be managed for the public welfare by experts. Instead, we should recognize that not "every citizen benefits from his share of the public lands and the resources found thereon." In leaving resource decisions to government bureaucrats and asking them to make decisions for the public good, we assume "that culture can 'rewire' people so that the public interest becomes self-interest."[18]

These economists argue that a market is the most equitable and reasonable means for making these decisions. The market requires only those people affected by a decision to participate in it, and therefore it is more equitable. It is more reasonable in assuming that every person is motivated by his or her own self-interest. Ignoring the laws of the market has "caused most of the environmental destruction the United States has seen in this century."[19]

Specifically, how should Forest Service decisions mimic the market? The Forest Service should manage resources the way a private owner would seek to manage private property. Private owners use their property to maximize their own self-interest. Baden and Stroup explain:

> If the buffalo is not mine until I kill it and I cannot sell my interest in the living animal to another, I have no incentive—beyond altruism—to investigate others' interest in it. I will do with it as I wish. But if the buffalo is mine and I may sell it, I am motivated to consider others' value estimate of the animal. I will misuse the buffalo only at my own economic peril.[20]

The Forest Service should seek to make a profit from its use of the national forests. According to the laws of economics, a profit is evidence that a decision is satisfying demand in the most efficient manner. Maximum profit reflects the fact that those people who most value a resource, those who are most willing to pay for it, have control of that resource. Thus, O'Toole recommends that all Forest Service activities should be funded out of the profits, not gross receipts, generated by those activities.

This would imply, first, that timber no longer will be offered for sale below cost. Selling timber rights to national forests on the open market would increase the costs of those rights. According to the economic law of supply and demand, this would decrease demand for timber, thereby increasing the amount of forestland available for wilderness, wildlife preservation, and recreation uses. Individuals who wish to use the national forests as wilderness areas or for recreational use will, of course, be required to pay for that use. These "user fees," in effect, will mean that competing users of the forests—timber, wilderness, recreation—will be bidding against each other for access rights. By seeking to maximize the profits generated by the forests, the Forest Service will attain an equilibrium between these competing interests. The group who most values the resource will be willing to pay most for it, thereby achieving the most efficient use of it. The market optimally satisfies competing consumer demand. It provides Americans with "all the wilderness, timber, wildlife, fish, and other forest resources they want."

Before we examine the ethical implications of this view, let's consider a similar economic analysis offered of air and water pollution. I will be highlighting types of reasoning similar to those found in the foregoing evaluation of the Forest Service.

3.4 POLLUTION AND ECONOMICS

As the case description that opened this chapter suggests, water and air pollution are among the most pressing environmental problems we face. Few people anywhere in the world have not, at least at one point in their lives, been adversely affected by polluted water or air. But although there is wide agreement about the problem, there is also wide disagreement about the solution.

Part of the challenge in meeting pollution issues lies with specifying the goal. Everyone wants clean water and clean air, but what exactly counts as *clean* and what would we need to give up in order to attain it? Pure water, with absolutely no contaminants, exists in laboratories, but exists nowhere in nature. What is clean air? The atmosphere contains nitrogen (78 percent) and oxygen (21 percent) and trace amounts of many other gases, water, and solids. How clean is "clean"?

Perhaps the only answer to these questions is to say that water and air are clean if they are safe for human consumption. But safety is not an all-or-nothing proposition. To determine safety, we need to identify, describe, and assess risks. To determine safety, we need to balance risks with benefits, something we do in many contexts every day. Is crossing a busy street safe? Is driving a car? Is it safe to eat food containing chemical preservatives?

It would seem that something is judged to be safe if its risks are judged acceptable, if its benefits outweigh its potential costs. When the equation is phrased this way, you can see why it is tempting to treat pollution problems as economic problems. How should resources be allocated so that maximum benefits are received from minimum costs? What are the costs and benefits of various levels of pollution?

William Baxter's *People or Penguins: The Case for Optimal Pollution*, develops an economic analysis of pollution that parallels O'Toole's analysis of forest conservation.[21] In Baxter's words,

> To assert that there is a pollution problem or an environmental problem is to assert, at least implicitly, that one or more resources is not being used so as to maximize human satisfactions. In this respect at least environmental problems are economics problems, and better insight can be gained by application of economic analysis.[22]

Baxter begins his analysis by reviewing some of its basic assumptions. He values individual freedom to do whatever one wishes as long as those actions "do not interfere with the interests of other human beings." He assumes that "waste is a bad thing" and therefore any resources that are "employed so as to yield less than they might yield in human satisfactions" are wasted. He also assumes that human beings are the source of all value and that environmental policies ought to be "people oriented." He explains this point while discussing the threat posed to penguins by use of the pesticide DDT:

> My criteria are oriented to people, not penguins. Damage to penguins, or sugar pines, or geological marvels is, without more, simply irrelevant. One must go further, by my criteria, and say: Penguins are important because people enjoy seeing them walk about rocks. . . . I have no interest in preserving penguins for their own sake.[23]

With these assumptions, Baxter turns to an economic analysis of pollution. Denying that there is any "naturally good" state of air or water, he explains that "there is no normative definition of clean air or pure water—hence no definition of polluted air—or of pollution—except by reference to the needs of man." In a similar vein to the preceding discussion of risks, Baxter argues that "clean" air and water is whatever level is judged acceptable by human beings. Too much pollution would be judged unacceptable by society, but so too would too little pollution. Air and water that were totally free from any contaminants *could* be desired, but their costs would be too high. In essence, society aims at a proper balance of risks, an "optimal level of pollution." This optimal level is "Just those amounts that attend a sensible organized society thoughtfully and knowledgeably pursuing the greatest possible satisfaction for its human members."[24] Baxter believes, consistently with much economic thinking, that the functioning of a free and competitive market is the mechanism that will yield this "maximum possible amount of human satisfaction." How is this to work?

Baxter reminds us that most decisions that we make involve tradeoffs. If I choose to do one thing, I give up something else. Every opportunity pursued involves other opportunities forgone. This captures the classic economic meaning of "costs." The cost of something is equivalent to what must be given up to attain it. In Baxter's example, if we choose to build a dam, then the resources used in building the dam cannot be used to build hospitals, fishing poles, schools, or electric can openers. Thus, the "cost" of the dam is equivalent to alternative uses of those resources—labor, building materials, technological skills, capital, energy—that have been forgone.

Accordingly, the costs of reducing water and air pollution should be understood in terms of those other goods that we would need to give up to accomplish this goal. In short, we need to make tradeoffs. Every resource devoted to reducing pollution is a resource not devoted to washing machines, hospitals, schools, B-1 bombers, and so forth. We continue to make these tradeoffs as long as the result is a net increase in human satisfaction; that is, as long as the benefits gained outweigh the additional costs. The optimal level of pollution is that point of equilibrium at which the next tradeoff made to reduce pollution results in a *decrease* of overall satisfaction. This is the point at which the resources used to fight pollution would have a higher value to society if used elsewhere.

Let us consider an example of how this process might work. Suppose a community's drinking water showed contamination levels slightly above those recommended by health officials. Lowering the contamination below recommended levels would involve certain costs; for example, tax monies diverted to this project could not be used to build a new school, fund road construction, and so on. Assume that this community decides that the benefits outweigh the costs. They would rather have cleaner drinking water than newly paved roads, and decide to make this tradeoff. This decision results in a greater satisfaction of the community's desires than either the status quo or other alternatives.

Now, this community might also desire to have drinking water that is absolutely pure, totally free of any contaminants. The costs for this goal would be much higher; that is, still other community projects would have to be sacrificed and taxes raised further. Eventually the community must decide when to stop making these trade-offs. This is the point at which slightly improved water quality is not worth the costs, not worth those other goods that would have to be given up to achieve this goal. At that point any decision to obtain cleaner water would result in a net decrease in community satisfaction.

According to classical economics, this point of equilibrium between diverse and competing community desires should be the goal of public policy decisions. This would be the point at which optimal satisfaction is achieved. People have more of what they want than would occur under any other allocation of resources. This is the "optimal level of pollution."

Baxter admits that this may sound "so general and abstract as to be unhelpful." However, this abstraction has just accurately described what results, at least in theory, from the workings of a free, open, and competitive marketplace. Economic analysis tells us that when people have the opportunity to freely exchange goods and service, when competition ensures that alternative choices exist, and when these individuals seek to maximize their own welfare, the result is an optimal satisfaction of desires. More people get more of what they most want through this process than they would under any other economic arrangement:

> If individuals in a society are free to engage in whatever exchanges of resources are mutually satisfactory for themselves then, at least in theory, every resource in society will be deployed in the way that yields the greatest possible human satisfaction.[25]

Thus Baxter's solution to the pollution problem, like O'Toole's solution to forest conservation problems, rests in the working of the free market. In both these cases, economic analysis and methodology has offered a diagnosis of environmental ills. In each case, a particular economic prescription is offered to cure those ills. A society that structures its economy to follow the principles of the free market will successfully meet all its environmental challenges.

3.5 ETHICAL ISSUES IN ECONOMIC ANALYSIS

Before we can analyze these claims, we need to clarify the issues involved. A first step in applied ethics is to identify and clarify the ethical issues at stake.

As discussed in Chapter 1, turning to technical and objective disciplines such as economics can be an attractive option when we face controversial environmental problems. Part of the reason for this lies in the myth of objectivity that often surrounds scientific and technical disciplines. According to this myth, the scientific method offers precise and objective answers to our problems. Sciences such as economics are, in this view, value-neutral. A helpful starting point for our ethical analysis, therefore, is to show how these economic analyses are heavily influenced by value assumptions. The first step is to show that economic analysis is value-laden.

The ethical framework of classical economic analysis can be understood in terms of *ends* and *means*. The end of economic policy is the maximum satisfaction of individual desires or maximum happiness. The functioning of a free and competitive market is believed to be the ethically best means for attaining that end.

Economic analysis of environmental problems, as represented by the work of such people as O'Toole and Baxter, thus assumes an essentially *utilitarian* ethics. The ultimate policy goal implicitly or explicitly assumed throughout these analyses is the utilitarian goal of maximizing the overall good. The specific understanding of that good, and the specific means defended to attain that goal, locates these views as a version of *preference utilitarianism*. Let us examine these claims more closely.

Perhaps Gifford Pinchot was most explicit in stating the utilitarian goals of his policies. Forest management sought "the greatest good for the greatest number for the longest time." O'Toole is less explicit but no less utilitarian. His recommendations aim to give the U.S. people maximum satisfaction of their wants. Baxter's recommendations seek to ensure that resources are "used so as to maximize human satisfactions." Thus, they all judge environmental policies in terms of their ability to produce certain beneficial consequences.

Pinchot believed that scientific management techniques could best lead us to this goal. O'Toole and Baxter argue that the workings of the economic market are the most efficient means available. Their reasons for relying on the market suggest further value assumptions. Markets give priority to the wants that people actually express themselves, as opposed to those interests that other people (such as professional foresters) determine or assume that they have. That is, the market version of utilitarianism assumes the best way to determine what someone wants is to see what they are willing to pay for in the marketplace.

To say that the market is the "best way to determine" what people want is not only the claim that it is the most efficient (although for economists it certainly is that!), but it is also the "best" way ethically. Why *should* public policy give priority to those preferences expressed in the market? We can discover at least three philosophical answers to this question in O'Toole and Baxter.

First, market utilitarianism is thought to promote individual freedom. Baxter takes it as a "basic tenet of our civilization" that "every person should be free to do whatever he wishes in contexts where his actions do not interfere with the interests of other human beings."[26] By his own admission, his market solution to environmental problems "stems from" this criterion. O'Toole explains that the market "preserves individual freedom since those who support and wish to participate in each activity may do so on the basis of willing consent."[27] The market is preferable to government regulation, for example, because the government "is based on coercive activity." Thus, O'Toole and Baxter would reject Pinchot's reliance on experts as a threat to individual freedom of choice.

A second reason for supporting market solutions rests with a commitment to the value of private property rights. O'Toole tells us that "The marketplace is centered around the notion of private property. . . . For the market to work, private property rights to resources must be easily transferable. . . . The market works when rights are both privately held and easily transferable." Indeed, "most environmental problems, such as lack of protection for wildlife, air pollution, and poor water quality, are due to the lack of transferable property rights."[28] Market solutions to public policy questions will be reasonable therefore only within a society that recognizes and values private property rights.

Finally, market solutions are consistent with certain philosophical assumptions about human nature. O'Toole identifies a major problem with the Forest Service as the "lack of incentive to be concerned." "The fundamental economic assumption," he tells us, is "that people's decisions are strongly influenced by the incentives affecting the decision makers" and that if we "change the incentives, the decisions change." As it stands, this seems trivially true. But what are these incentives? The answer can be found when O'Toole quotes the reasons offered by the new resource economists, Baden and Stroup, for rejecting Pinchot's nonmarket version:

> The national forests, for example, were created with the idea that "scientific foresters" employed by the public could objectively determine the method of management that best meets the public interest. But to assume that managers will be altruistic, say Stroup and Baden, it must be assumed "that culture can rewire people so that the public interest becomes self-interest." Instead, "Property rights theorists assume that

the decision maker will maximize his own utility . . . in whatever situation he finds himself."[29]

The fundamental assumption about human nature is that human beings act, primarily if not solely, on the basis of self-interest. Self-interest then is understood in the classic utilitarian sense of maximizing one's own satisfactions, or "utilities." Altruism, or acting for the best interests of others, would require that human nature be "rewired." In Baxter's words,

> It may be said by way of objection to this position, that it is very selfish of people to act as if each person represented one unit of importance and nothing else was of importance. It is undeniably selfish. Nevertheless I think it is the only tenable starting place for analysis for several reasons. First, no other position corresponds to the way most people really think and act—i.e., corresponds to reality.[30]

Thus underlying the economic analyses described in this chapter, we find commitments to the values of individual freedom and private property rights, and to philosophical assumptions about human nature. Along with the clear utilitarian goal of providing the greatest good for the greatest number, these commitments clearly show the ethical and philosophical nature of economic analysis. Despite common opinion, economic analysis and methodology does not claim to offer us ethically neutral answers to environmental controversies. These recommendations clearly make philosophical assumptions concerning several value issues. Thus, this type of analysis lies within the domain of philosophical ethics. Following the applied ethics model, we now need to ask, Do these analyses offer justifiable answers and recommendations?

3.6 ETHICAL ANALYSIS AND ENVIRONMENTAL ECONOMICS

To the degree that contemporary economic analyses of environmental problems reflect a utilitarian ethics, philosophers have much to offer in the evaluation of this ethical theory.[31] Several standard criticisms that were mentioned briefly in the last chapter are a useful starting point for this evaluation.

As mentioned in Chapter 2, utilitarians face several problems when they try to quantify and measure consequences. One problem involves attempting to quantify qualitative goods. So we see, for example, the challenge posed by determining "clean" or "safe" water and air quality. These qualitative goods find no place in the economic approach because there simply is no way to easily quantify them. A second problem was the tendency therefore to translate qualitative goods into categories that can be measured. Thus, we found Baxter translating discussions of "clean" and "safe" into a discussion of risks, the probabilities of which can be quantified and calculated. And we found O'Toole following the more standard practice of translating qualitative goods into economic terms. The value of wilderness or recreation areas is understood as capable of being measured by the willingness of users to pay for them. A final measurement problem involved the tendency to artificially restrict the range of relevant subjects. As shown in the following chapters, some critics claim this tendency systematically ignores the well-being of animals, future generations, trees, the biosphere, and so forth. The charge that the economic approach is overly *anthropocentric*, or human-centered, is examined in greater detail in what follows.

The general point of these measurement problems is to raise the possibility that economic analysis seriously distorts or ignores important environmental issues. Now let's turn to a more comprehensive examination of the use of economic analysis.

In a series of articles culminating in the book *The Economy of the Earth*, Mark Sagoff develops an insightful and convincing case against the use of economic analysis as the dominant tool of environmental policy makers.[32] In the remainder of this chapter, I use Sagoff's evaluation as an example of the best that applied ethics has offered. Although his book offers a variety of subtle and powerful arguments, we can concentrate on three major challenges to the use of economic analysis.

Sagoff argues that much economic analysis rests on a serious confusion between wants or preferences on the one hand, and beliefs and values on the other. Economics deals only with wants and preferences, because these are what get expressed in an economic market. The market can measure the intensity of our wants by our willingness to pay (by price), can measure and compare individual wants (through cost–benefit analysis), and can discover efficient means for optimally fulfilling wants. But markets cannot measure or quantify people's beliefs or values. Because many environmental issues involve beliefs and our values, economic analysis is beside the point. When economics is involved in environmental policy, it treats beliefs as if they were mere wants and thereby seriously distorts the issue. In the words of an early article, Sagoff claims,

> Economic methods cannot supply the information necessary to jus-
> tify public policy. Economics can measure the intensity with which we
> hold our beliefs; it cannot evaluate those beliefs on their merits. Yet such
> evaluation is essential to political decision making. This is my greatest
> single criticism of cost–benefit analysis.[33]

What exactly is the distinction between wants and beliefs, and why
is it important?

When I express a want or personal preference, I am stating something that is purely personal and subjective. There are no grounds
for another person to challenge, rebut, or support my wants. Wants
are neither true nor false. If I express my preference for chocolate ice
cream, there is no room for someone to challenge that and claim,
"No, you don't like that flavor best." I have a certain privileged
status with regards to my own wants. In the public sphere, they are
taken as a *given*. Thus do economists treat human interests. Willingness to pay measures the intensity with which I hold my wants (I
won't pay more than a few dollars for a dish of chocolate ice cream),
but it says nothing about the legitimacy or validity of that want.

Beliefs, in contrast, are subject to rational evaluation. They are
objective in the sense that *reasons* are called for to support them.
Beliefs can be true or false. It would be a serious mistake (a "category mistake" in Sagoff's terms) to judge the validity of a belief by a
person's willingness to pay for it. Putting a price on beliefs misun-
derstands seriously the nature of belief.

Sagoff reminds us that when environmentalists argue that we
ought to preserve a national forest for its aesthetic or symbolic
meaning, they are not merely expressing a personal want. They are
stating a *conviction* about a public good that should be accepted or
rejected by others on the basis of reasons not on the basis of who is
most willing to pay for it. Because economics has no way to factor
them into its analysis, beliefs and convictions are either ignored or
treated as if they were mere wants.

Essentially, O'Toole's "marketization" solution to environmental
problems does exactly this. You'll remember that O'Toole's goal is to
provide all the wilderness, and so on, that the U.S. people "want."
But this goal is equated with what the people, in their roles as
timber users, hikers, hunters, and so forth, are willing to pay. If
recreational users are unwilling to pay a "user fee" that is economically competitive with the fees paid by the timber industry, then by
definition they must not "want" recreation as much as timber users
"want" the lumber.

Returning to the cases at the beginning of this chapter, if pre-servationists in the Sierra Club were not willing to pay as much for Mineral King Valley as Walt Disney, then they must not want the wilderness area as much as skiers want a new ski resort. Likewise, if a community is unwilling to spend any more tax monies on reduc-ing air and water pollution, then they must not want cleaner air and water as much as they want lower taxes or other public projects.

This tendency to reduce all beliefs and values to wants and prefer-ences also seriously distorts the nature of the human person. It is to treat people at all times as *consumers*. People, at least in so far as the economist as policymaker is concerned, are simply the locations of a given collection of wants. They care only about satisfying these personal wants and the role of the economist is to discover means of maximally attaining this end.

The alternative that is ignored by economic analysis treats hu-mans as thinking and reasoning beings. The market leaves no room for debate, discussion, or dialogue in which people's beliefs are defended by reasons. It ignores the fact that people are active think-ers, not merely passive "wanters." Most importantly, by ignoring the distinction between wants and beliefs, economic analysis re-duces the most meaningful elements of human life—beliefs and val-ues—to matters of mere personal taste or opinion. To the degree that they are held with equal intensity, all desires equally deserve to be satisfied; no matter what is desired.

This leads to a second major challenge to economic analysis. By ignoring the distinction between wants and beliefs, market analysis threatens our democratic political process. By treating us as always and only *consumers*, market analysis ignores our lives as *citizens*. As consumers, we may seek to satisfy personal wants; as citizens we may have goals and aspirations that give meaning to our lives, that determine our nature as a people and culture, that define what we stand for as a people. Ours is a *liberal-democratic* society. Liberal in the sense that we value personal liberty to pursue our own indi-vidual goals, but democratic in the sense that collectively we seek agreement about public goods and shared goals. Thus our political system leaves room for both personal *and* public interests. We are all, at one and the same time, both private individuals and public citizens. Market analysis ignores this public realm and thereby un-dermines our democratic political institutions. According to Sagoff,

> Our environmental goals—cleaner air and water, the preservation of
> the wilderness and wildlife, and the like—are not to be construed, then,
> simply as personal wants or preferences; they are not interests to be

"priced" by markets or by cost–benefit analysis, but are views or beliefs that may find their way, as public values, into legislation. These goals stem from our character as a people, which is not something we choose, as we might choose a necktie or a cigarette, but something we recognize, something we are. These goals presuppose the reality of public or shared values that we recognize together, values that are discussed and criticized on their merits and are not to be confused with preferences that are appropriately priced in markets. Our democratic political processes allow us to argue our beliefs on their merits.[34]

Economic analysis seems to assume a particular view of democracy wherein representatives passively follow the demands of the electorate, seeking to balance competing demands in a manner that satisfies the majority. The role of the politician in this model is to read the public opinion polls and act accordingly. But this neglects the more participatory nature of democracy in which citizens exchange views, debate their merits, learn from each other, and reach agreement.[35] The model encourages a view of elected officials as active leaders rather than passive followers. Constitutional democracies are committed not only to the personal freedom that Baxter's analysis assumes, but also to a system in which we mutually define and pursue a vision of the good life. A healthy, beautiful, undeveloped, and inspiring environment may not benefit me as a consumer, but it may be quite valuable to me as a citizen. This participatory model of democracy would reject the views of the new resource economists that O'Toole approvingly quotes: "It is a common misconception that every citizen benefits from his share of the public lands and resources found thereon."[36]

Many economists reject the notion of a "public" welfare or "public" good because they view people solely as consumers. Not every citizen "consumes" Mineral King Valley, for example. But this fails to recognize that we are citizens as well as consumers and that we can benefit from the environment as citizens. Mineral King Valley can be valuable to us as citizens because of what it means to us, because of what it says about our self-image, our self-respect. These benefits are not and cannot be priced in the market, and therefore are ignored by the type of economic analysis offered by O'Toole, the new resource economists, and Baxter.

A final challenge denies that economic analysis has any ethical basis at all. Despite the appearance that markets are committed to utilitarian ends, in actuality the goal of efficiency lacks any coherent and substantive ethical basis at all. Let us remember the role that economic analysis plays in many contemporary environmental issues. Economic analysis is unquestionably the major public policy methodology in reaching environmental decisions. Economics tells us as individuals, as a society, and as a government what we should do. Why should we follow this advice? Presumably because by doing so we will be led to a better state of affairs. At first glance, this better state of affairs—economic efficiency—appears to be the utilitarian goal of providing the greatest good for the greatest number. But does economic efficiency provide the greatest good for the greatest number? Again, Sagoff is persuasive in claiming that it does not.

What is the goal of economic efficiency? As suggested earlier, efficiency implies optimal satisfaction of consumer preferences. (Preferences are wants that the individual has rank-ordered.) But why should we, as a society and especially when we are concerned with environmental issues, take the satisfaction of individual preferences as our overriding goal? It is unclear why this should be the goal of public policy when we recognize the obvious and admit that many individual preferences are silly, foolish, vulgar, dangerous, immoral, criminal, and so on. Why should we think it would be good if the preferences of a racist, a criminal, a fool, or a sadist are satisfied?

What is so good about satisfying preferences? The only options seem to be that satisfying preferences is good in itself, or that it is a means to something else that is. In terms used in describing utilitarianism in Chapter 2, preference satisfaction is either intrinsically good or instrumentally good. Given the wide variety of harmful, decadent, and trivial preferences that exist, surely no one could claim that satisfying preferences is good in itself. Surely it is not good in itself that a child molester or rapist has his preferences satisfied. If not good in itself, what other good is brought about instrumentally by satisfying preferences?

This economic approach typically uses such terms as "utility" or "welfare" or "well-being" or "happiness" to explain this goal. However, if these terms are simply *defined* as the satisfaction of preferences, then this answer is trivial and begs the question. For example, sometimes happiness is defined as "getting what you want." But if some more substantive account is given of utility, welfare, happiness, or well-being, then the claim that preference satisfaction always leads to these goods is false. Satisfying my preference for a cigarette does not always make me happy in a nontrivial sense. Sometimes having my preferences frustrated can be in my own best interests, teaching me patience, or diligence, or modesty. Sometimes satisfying preferences is disappointing. Sometimes I might have all that the market can supply, but I might still lack what is more important. ("What good does it benefit a man if he gains a kingdom but loses his soul?") The economic methodology assumes that all other things being equal, it is good for people to get what they want. A more realistic and honest answer to the question "Is it good for me to get what I want?" seems to be "It depends on what I want."

Thus, even if (and it is a big "if"), economic analysis could overcome the measurement problems, all the problems associated with the application of market analyses to the real world, even if the market did succeed in attaining its goal, we still would have no reason for accepting this as an ethical goal. An efficient allocation of resources is not itself an ethical goal at all.

3.7 SUMMARY AND CONCLUSION

As we struggle with great environmental controversies, we must look beyond the economic market for a vision to guide policy decisions. Economic analysis cannot answer the fundamental ethical and philosophical questions raised by these controversies. The solution, according to Sagoff, is to

> recognize that utopian capitalism is dead; that the concepts of resource and welfare economics, as a result, are largely obsolete and irrelevant; and that we must look to other concepts and cultural traditions to set priorities in solving environmental and social problems. To set these priorities, we need to distinguish the pure from the polluted, the natural from the artificial, the noble from the mundane, good from bad, and right from wrong. These are scientific, cultural, aesthetic, historical, and ethical—not primarily economic—distinctions.[37]

Sagoff encourages us to do the hard thinking required to explain and justify environmental policy. We must explain why we value clean air and water, we must justify why we value the preservation of wilderness areas. We must move beyond simply saying that these are things we "want" or "prefer," and must offer reasons that show their value and meaning.

But even Sagoff's alternative is restricted to the important interests of presently living human beings. These "scientific, cultural, aesthetic, historical, and ethical" values and beliefs tends to keep the environmental debate focused on the claims of present-generation humans. The following chapter shows how environmental concerns lead us away from this narrow focus. We turn next to those ethical concerns for future generations raised by various environmental issues.

Notes

1. See Richard Momeyer, "Philosophers and the Public Policy Process," *Journal of Medical Philosophy* 15, no. 4 (August 1990): 391–409, and Loretta Kopelman, "What Is Applied About 'Applied Philosophy?' " *Journal of Medical Philosophy* 15, no. 2, (April 1990): 199–218. Momeyer argues that beside simply identifying and clarifying concepts and analyzing arguments, philosophers engaged in applied ethics should also become active participants in the public policy debates by arguing for specific normative conclusions. Kopelman argues that whenever principles and theories get applied to specific issues, they get changed in the process. Hence, she argues that applied ethics should not be viewed as being derived from other more theoretical approaches to ethics.

2. For a thorough description of the environmental destruction of the former Soviet Union, see Murray Feshbach and Alfred Friendly, *Ecocide in the U.S.S.R.* (New York: Basic Books, 1992).

3. Paul Portney, A. Myrick Freeman, and others, *Current Issues in U.S. Environmental Policy* (Baltimore, MD: Johns Hopkins University Press, 1978).

4. As quoted in Samuel Hays, *Conservation and the Gospel of Efficiency* (Cambridge, MA: Harvard University Press, 1959), pp. 41–42.

5. Gifford Pinchot, *The Training of a Forester* (Philadelphia: Lippincott, 1914), p. 13.

6. See Michael Cohen's book, *The Pathless Way* (Madison: University of Wisconsin Press, 1984), for a helpful study of John Muir. Chapters 6 and 7 especially provide an insightful introduction to many of the ethical aspects of Muir's thinking.

7. This may be too simple an interpretation of this conservation movement. An alternative view is defended by Samuel Hays in *Conservation and the Gospel of Efficiency*. Hays argues that U. S. business supported rather than fought the conservation movement, recognizing in it a more enlightened, long-term economic self-interest. Pinchot's own writings seem to me to suggest a strong anticorporate sentiment. For an interpretation supporting my reading, see James Bates "Fulfilling American Democracy: The Conservation Movement, 1907–1921," *Mississippi Valley Historical Review* 44 (June 1957). Whether or not early twentieth century corporate America supported the conservation movement is irrelevant to the more general point, however. Pinchot's progressivism was directed against a common nineteenth-century view that resources are there for the benefit of immediate economic exploitation.

8. Pinchot, pp. 23–25.

9. USDA Forest Service, "1987 Budget Explanatory Notes" (Washington, DC: U.S. Forest Service, 1986), p. 2.

10. See USDA Forest Service, *National Forest Roads for All Uses* (Milwaukee, WI: Forest Service, 1985), p. 2, for a defense of the claim that roads support a policy of multiple uses.

11. Randal O'Toole, *Reforming the Forest Service* (Washington, DC: Island Press, 1988), p. 14.

12. Ibid., p. xi.

13. Ibid., p. xii.

14. Ibid., p. xi, 7.

15. Ibid., p. 101.

16. O'Toole quotes a more detailed study to support this claim. See Ronald Johnson, "US Forest Service Policy and Its Budget," in *Forestlands: Public and Private* (San Francisco, CA: Pacific Institute for Public Policy Research, 1985), pp. 103–133.

17. See especially Richard Stroup and John Baden, *Natural Resources: Bureaucratic Myths and Environmental Management* (San Francisco, CA: Pacific Institute for Public Policy Research, 1983).

18. Ibid., p. 7, p. 29.   •

19. O'Toole, p. 190.

20. Stroup and Baden, p. 14.

21. William F. Baxter, *People or Penguins: The Case for Optimal Pollution* (New York: Columbia University Press, 1974).

22. Ibid., p. 17.

23. Ibid., p. 5.

24. Ibid., p. 8.

25. Ibid., p. 27.

26. Ibid., p. 2.

27. O'Toole, p. 189.

28. Ibid., pp. 188–190.

29. Ibid., p. 190.

30. Baxter, p. 5.

31. See Bernard Williams, *Morality: An Introduction to Ethics* (New York: Harper Torchbooks, 1972), for a useful introductory evaluation of utilitarianism.

32. Mark Sagoff, *Economy of the Earth* (New York: Cambridge University Press, 1990).

33. Mark Sagoff, "Economic Theory and Environmental Law," *Michigan Law Review* 79 (1981): 1393–1419.

34. Sagoff, *Economy*, pp. 28–29.

35. For an examination of representative and participatory democracy, see Jane Mansbridge, *Beyond Adversarial Democracy* (New York: Basic Books, 1980).

36. O'Toole, p. 189.

37. Sagoff, *Economy*, p. 22.

Discussion Questions

1. If a Disney-like ski resort was built in a wilderness area near you, would you be willing to pay money to visit it? If so, would that be evidence that you preferred development over wilderness preservation? Do citizens always "vote with their pocketbooks"?

2. Review the distinction between *conservation* and *preservation*. In the debate concerning the Hetch Hetchy Valley, would you support Pinchot's

conservationist or Muir's preservationist policy? Why? What values underlie your decision?

3. The Rolling Stones once sang, "You can't always get what you want." Is
that always a bad thing? Should government always seek to provide citizens with what they want? Should government play a role in teaching citizens what wants are good and valuable, or should government remain
neutral on such questions?

4. Should government agencies such as the Forest Service aim to make a
profit? Why or why not? If you were director of the Forest Service, how
would you understand your role in serving the public?

5. It has been suggested that one way to protect endangered species like
the blue whale would be to sell them to the highest bidder. In this view,
only unowned species such as whales and spotted owls are threatened
with extinction. Species that are owned, such as chickens and cows, seldom face extinction. Property rights would ensure that humans have an incentive to protect endangered species. How would this work, exactly? Do
you think that it is a good idea to sell exclusive whaling rights to Norwegian, or Russian, or Japanese whalers?

6. Baxter claims that "Penguins are important because people enjoy seeing
them." Do you agree? Is this the only reason why penguins should be protected?

7. Is human nature "undeniably selfish" as Baxter claims? Can you think of
any situations in which people do not act selfishly? In answering this question, be careful to distinguish between a *reason* for acting from the *feelings*
that follow from acting.

For Further Reading

Garrett Hardin and John Baden, eds., *Managing the Commons* (San Francisco: Freeman, 1977), details the classical economic approach to environmental issues.

   A. Freeman, R. Haveman, and A. Kneese, *The Economics of Environmental
Policy* (Baltimore, MD: Johns Hopkins University Press, 1973), presents and
defends the reform economics approach.

   E. F. Schumacher, *Small Is Beautiful* (New York: Harper & Row, 1973), is
the well-known defense of "economics as if people mattered."

   Lester W. Milbrath, *Envisioning a Sustainable Society* (Albany, NY: SUNY
Press, 1989), is a more recent account of the role of economics in public policy decision making concerning the environment. Also contains a very
helpful bibliography.

4

Ethics, Energy, and Future Generations

Greenhouse Gases and Nuclear Wastes

At no time in the past has human activity been capable of so directly and so significantly affecting the earth's atmosphere and climate as it is today. Minor fluctuations in climate and in the composition of the atmosphere of course have been a normal part of earth history. One need only think of the great ice ages to recognize that fact. However, the magnitude and especially the *rate* of climatic and atmospheric change that humans can now produce is unprecedented in history. Two related problems, the greenhouse effect and depletion of the ozone layer, are the most visible examples of these changes.

A variety of "greenhouse gases"—carbon dioxide, methane, nitrous oxides, and chlorofluorocarbons—act in much the same way that glass panes function in a greenhouse. These gases allow solar radiation to enter the atmosphere and warm the earth but prevent the radiated heat from escaping back into space. If some heat were not trapped in the earth's atmosphere, of course, life as we know it could not survive. Earth's temperature would be too cold. But if too much heat is trapped life is also threatened. Global warming, or the "greenhouse effect," would be the result.

Some natural events, such as volcanic eruptions and changes in the energy output from the sun, for example, contribute to a buildup in greenhouse gases, as they have for eons. But human activity in the past few centuries, especially burning fossil fuels such as oil, gas, and coal, and the widespread cutting and burning of forests, has greatly increased the amounts of these gases in the atmosphere.[1]

There is little serious scientific dispute about the "greenhouse" effect in theory. Various gases can and do trap heat within the earth's atmosphere and an increase in these gases can lead to global warming. It is also beyond dispute that humans are dumping an immense amount of these gases into the atmosphere. What is disputed, however, is the extent, the degree, and the specific effects of global warming. The potential harms include serious loss of agricultural crops, drought, plant and animal extinctions, and massive flooding caused by a rise in ocean water level due to polar ice melting.

Much of this scientific dispute is due to the fact that measurements of global temperature change have been recorded for only a relatively short period of time (one hundred years or so). Thus, any changes in global temperature have fallen within a normal range of fluctuation. We do not yet have a trend sufficiently long enough to show that the temperature change is beyond the normal fluctuations, and we will not have such a long-term trend established in the near future. In climatic time, the "long term" is measured in millennia. Therefore, when the temperature rise predicted by the theory is confirmed, it may be too late to do anything about it. But, of course, by that time none of us (that is, no one presently alive) will be around to suffer the consequences.

Radioactive wastes are generated at each step in the production of nuclear energy, from mining uranium to decommissioning nuclear plants. These wastes are classified either as *low-level* or *high-level* radioactive wastes. Low-level wastes, which might include everything from uniforms worn by uranium miners to the tools used in decommissioning a nuclear plant, give off relatively small amounts of radiation. High-level nuclear wastes, typically the spent fuel rods from the plants themselves, give off very high levels of radiation.

Virtually all electric power plants generate electricity by boiling water. The steam generated by the boiling water turns giant turbine engines, which generate electricity. Plants differ in the fuel they use to boil the water. Coal plants burn coal, and oil-fired plants burn oil. Nuclear power plants rely on the heat energy generated from nuclear fission, the process of splitting the nucleus of uranium atoms.

Several things occur in this process. Heat energy to boil water is generated. Neutrons break free from the uranium atom and go on to split further atoms of uranium (the "chain reaction" of nuclear fission). Certain other elements—for example, cesium, krypton, plutonium, iodine—are created as by-products of this fission. Finally, radiation is given off, in the form of alpha particles, beta particles, and gamma rays. This radiation is the focus of the nuclear waste problem.

Certain elements, including uranium and the by-products of fission mentioned earlier, give off radiation over a long period of time in a process of spontaneous decay. The "unstable isotopes" give off alpha and beta particles and gamma radiation until they attain a more stable atomic form. This radiation causes harm to human and other life-forms ranging from burns and tissue damage to chromosomal damage. The rate of this radioactive decay is measured in terms of its "half-life." The half-life is the time it takes for one-half of the original isotope to decay into a stable, and therefore nonradioactive, form. The half-life of radioactive waste materials generated by nuclear power plants range from a fraction of a second to millions of years.

Thus, nuclear wastes pose dangers to untold generations of humans. Plutonium-239, for example, a major by-product of nuclear fission, has a half-life of 24,000 years. Even a small amount of plutonium will remain highly toxic for 250,000 years. Plutonium also, of course, is the principal component in nuclear weapons. As this plutonium decays, it becomes uranium-235, itself a radioactive isotope with a half-life of 710,000 years.[2]

4.1 INTRODUCTION

Understandably much early philosophical thinking about the environment fit the "applied ethics" model. As philosophers came to recognize the seriousness of environmental challenges, they tended to turn to standard ethical theories and principles for guidance. "Ethics" was seen as a given, an area wherein philosophers independently developed their theories and, as the need or interest arose, applied these theories to more practical matters. This implied an essentially negative and conservative function for ethics. The role of theory was to evaluate and analyze issues with less thought given to constructing a positive environmental ethic. It was conservative in the sense that applying standard theories tended to reinforce the philosophical status quo. The theories applied were those presently accepted, which, by being applied to new issues, tended to define these issues in standard ways.

The next three chapters show how these standard approaches to ethics were expanded by the interaction with environmental issues. In this chapter we look at how a variety of energy-related issues raise ethical questions concerning our duties to future generations of people. This is an issue that had not received much attention among philosophers until this time. Chapter 5 considers the question of moral standing and examines early efforts to extend standard ethical theories to include new environmental rights for both humans and nonhumans. Again, these were topics seldom before considered by philosophers. Chapter 6 examines in detail more systematic attempts to extend moral standing to animals.

4.2 ENERGY AND FUTURE GENERATIONS

No other single issue has as great an environmental impact as the production and use of energy. A cluster of environmental and ethical issues are grouped around the energy choices that the world now confronts. A brief survey of some of these issues provides a helpful introduction to the application of ethical analysis to questions concerning future generations.

In general, we have only four energy choices available. First, we can continue our heavy reliance on fossil fuels. According to most estimates, oil, coal, and natural gas presently account for more than 80 percent of the energy used throughout the world. Second, we can increase our reliance on nuclear energy. In 1988, nuclear power accounted for less than 10 percent of the world's energy consumption.[3] Third, we can seek to develop alternative energy sources for meeting our present demand. Fourth, we can reduce the demand for energy, thus conserving resources and minimizing the environmental impact of energy production.

Each of these alternatives has major environmental and ethical implications. In what follows, I focus on those consequences that raise particular questions about our duties to future people.

Continued heavy reliance on fossil fuels raises two major questions about the future. First, fossil fuels are nonrenewable (at least in any practical sense). Every barrel of oil and ton of coal that we burn is forever lost for use by future generations. Every mountain mined and wilderness developed in the search for coal and oil is also lost for future people. Second, combustion of fossil fuels will continue to dump billions of tons of carbon dioxide into the atmosphere. We are only beginning to understand the potential risks to future generations posed by global warming. What are our duties, if any, to preserve resources for and minimize risks to future generations of people?

Reliance on nuclear power, in contrast, would be one means for conserving fossil fuels and minimizing carbon dioxide emissions while still meeting the present demand for energy. However, as we have seen, nuclear power generates toxic wastes that remain dangerous to humans for tens of thousands of generations. Is it just to subject future people to such dangers in order to satisfy present consumer demands for electricity?[4]

Alternative energy sources are still in their infancy. It is difficult to predict what environmental or ethical implications might follow from as yet undeveloped technologies. The most optimistic predictions, of course, envision a future with plentiful, renewable, and environmentally benign energy. With history as our guide, we should be very skeptical of such predictions. In the early days of nuclear power, for example, consumers were promised energy so plentiful that we could abandon electric meters on our homes. But even if (and this is an ideal future!) energy is abundant and clean, its social implications would be far from clear. Would plentiful energy lead to growing demand for consumer products and materialistic lifestyles? Would it lead to an even greater population explosion, which would lead to even further environmental destruction?

Finally, the alternative of conservation and decreased demand also raises questions about our obligations to the future. First, for this choice to represent a true alternative to fossil fuels or nuclear power, a significant decrease in energy demand would be required. We would need to do more than merely turn off the lights as we leave a room. But there seem to be only two ways to accomplish such a major goal over the long term. Either we greatly reduce demand, in which case future people would have a significantly different lifestyle from the one we now enjoy, or we greatly reduce the number of people demanding energy.

The first option again raises questions about our responsibilities to posterity. Is it fair that we enjoy a standard of living that requires them to lower their expectations? The second alternative raises ethical questions about population policy. What are our responsibilities toward the size and makeup of the future population? Should population size, and therefore procreation, be limited? Do people have a *right* to have children? Should they be prohibited from having more than one or two? Do unborn generations have a right to be born?

In part because of the energy crisis and oil embargos of the 1970s, some philosophers turned their attention to questions concerning future generations. These questions virtually were never asked within the frameworks of traditional ethical theories. Yet they have far-reaching ethical implications for the present generation. To a very large degree, this new ethical concern was due to a new environmental consciousness.

As these energy issues suggest, decisions that we make today will have profound implications for the lives and life prospects of future generations. Although it is trivially true that the same can be said for the decisions of all past generations, at no time in the past have the causal connection between present decisions and future consequences been so direct and predictable as they are today. As philosophers addressed issues of environmental ethics, questions concerning our responsibilities to future generations received their first significant philosophical attention.

In considering duties to future generations, philosophers have sometimes distinguished two general issues: "What are our duties to produce, or not to produce, future people?" and "What, if anything, do we owe to those future people whom we assume will exist?" The first set of issues, what we might call *population policy*, is concerned with questions of future population size, population growth, and population control. The second set of issues, sometimes called our *duty to posterity*, focuses on the content and type of world that future generations will inherit from us.[5] This is a rough distinction in that there is obvious overlap between them. For example, ethically responsible decisions about reproduction should take into consideration the state of the world that will be inherited by our ancestors. Nevertheless, this is a helpful way for organizing the many ethical and philosophical issues raised by the general topic of our duties to future generations. This distinction structures the discussion that follows.

Let's return to the environmental issues mentioned earlier to consider what questions they raise concerning duties to future generations. To organize the discussion, we can use the issue of population growth to illustrate ethical issues of population policy and the issues of climatic change and nuclear wastes to examine duties to posterity. Although each issue raises many other ethical questions, this limiting structure will help to keep us focused.

4.3 POPULATION POLICY AND POPULATION GROWTH

For many people, population growth is the key to the most serious environmental problems.[6] In some obvious ways, overpopulation increases the human harms caused by environmental damage. The more people who exist, the more people will suffer from pollution, global warming, and so on. Even now, in the late twentieth century, environmental problems such as drought, erosion, urban development, the loss of farmlands, and pollution have produced 10 million "environmental refugees," the world's single largest class of homeless and landless people.[7]

More directly, perhaps, overpopulation places a tremendous strain on the environment. An increasing *number* of people obviously requires us to provide more energy, homes, food, and jobs, and also creates more trash, pollution, and development. One need only consider the world's large urban centers, such as New York, New Delhi, and Mexico City, to understand the environmental devastation that follows from human overpopulation.

Further devastation comes when the economic growth and development sought by these populations leads to excessive consumption due to overpopulation.[8] In industrialized countries such as the United States, environmental damage *per capita* is much higher than many less developed countries. For example, with less than 5 percent of the world's population, the United States uses 33 percent of the world's nonrenewable energy and mineral resources. As less developed countries pursue the "higher standard of living" (as economists might say) attained by the industrialized countries, threats to the environment increase almost inconceivably.[9]

These considerations have wide-ranging ethical implications. Is there some ethically preferable population goal? If so, what are the philosophical grounds for establishing this goal and what policies should be promoted to attain this goal? Do humans have an obligation to procreate? An obligation to refrain from having babies? Is it ethically responsible for families to have more than two children? Do generations not yet conceived have a right to be born?

Let us use the issue of population growth to explore the philosophical and ethical issues that concern the population size and makeup of future generations. What, if any, future population goal ought present-generation humans aim for? For a start, imagine for a moment that scientists determine that a certain threshold of ozone depletion has been reached and surpassed. Suppose also that we discover that certain genes that control reproduction are particularly susceptible to damage from ultraviolet radiation. As a result, the entire human race will no longer be capable of reproducing. Within the next 100–125 years, the species Homo sapiens will become extinct. Let us ignore for now the unhappiness that present-generation people would suffer when they discovered this fact—for example, the mostly psychological harm of not being able to have (more) children, and the increasing loneliness of later survivors. What, if anything, would be wrong with the extinction of human beings? Is there any ethical reason why there should be future generations? Are there ethical reasons why we should propagate our species?

(To avoid questions about the harms done to living humans by such prospects, and perhaps to imagine a more idealized scenario, we could change the example. Imagine that the living generations decide, willingly and thoughtfully, to adopt a policy of universal celibacy. Perhaps they recognize the environmental destruction caused by humans and conclude that the world would be better off if this particular species became extinct.)

How might we even begin to answer such questions? Perhaps we could begin to sketch answers to these questions by returning to the ethical traditions outlined in Chapter 2. Philosophers in the *natural law* tradition might well argue that we do have ethical reasons for the continuation of our species. Perhaps arguing from both biological (the natural function of our reproductive organs) and philosophical grounds (the nature of human beings as social beings who live in families and communities), a case might be made that a real moral tragedy would occur if humans became extinct. (When the natural law tradition in philosophy is joined with Christian sources—for example, the biblical injunction to "go forth and multiply"—further arguments would also be made.) The *utilitarians* might suggest that we have a duty to perpetuate our species, because doing so will maximize human happiness. The *deontologists* might argue that future generations have rights, and among those are the right to life—understood as the right to be conceived and born.

As even this brief thought experiment suggests, thinking about responsibilities to future generations can quickly become puzzling. First, any discussion of future happiness or the rights of future people forces us to consider who those "future people" might be and what they will be like. Yet because future people do not exist and because we don't know that they will exist, it is difficult to understand how we can even talk about responsibilities to them.

There are several ways in which one could argue against the view that we do have obligations to future generations. Because many

environmental issues assume it is meaningful to talk about obligations to future generations, it is helpful to consider some of these
challenges.

The first, what can be called the "argument from ignorance,"
stresses the fact that we know very little about future people.[10] We
do not know *who* they will be, *that* they will be, or *what* they will be
like, or what their needs, wants, or interests will be. Thus, because
we know so very little about them, it makes little sense to try to
specify any obligations to them that we might have.

It is difficult to see why we should draw this conclusion, however.
Surely we have a fairly good idea about what future people will
need and what their interests will be if they are to have a reasonably good life. Minimally, this would include an adequate supply of
clean air and water, a moderate climate, protection from poisons
and disease, and so forth. Furthermore, we already acknowledge
responsibilities that parallel those to future generations. In civil law,
we hold people responsible for actions that result in unintended but
foreseeable harms to others. For example, imagine someone establishes a toxic waste dump on his or her property. Imagine that a few
years later neighbors living adjacent to the dump are poisoned by
the escaping toxins. Imagine the polluter offering a defense based
on the argument from ignorance. "I did not know who would be
hurt, I did not even know for certain that anyone would be hurt, and
I surely did not know that these people would have a particular
interest in health. How can I be said to have had an obligation to
them?" Just as in cases of legal negligence where we hold people lia-
ble for unintended but foreseeable and avoidable harms that occur
in the future, it is meaningful to talk about foreseeable but unknown
harms to future generations.

Another view, perhaps the most extreme one, argues that we have
no obligations to future generations. From this perspective, not only
have we no responsibility to bring future generations into existence,
but also it is meaningless even to talk about ethical obligations to
future generations.[11] The short version of this claim holds that we
can have no obligation (based on either the maximum happiness
principle or the rights of future people) to bring a future generation
into existence because there is no particular people to whom that
responsibility is directed. Let us call this the "disappearing beneficiaries" argument and examine it in a bit more detail.[12]

During the summer of 1992, most of the world's nations met in
Rio de Janeiro, Brazil for the United Nations Conference on Environment and Development. Among other things, the "Earth Summit"
considered a proposal that would significantly limit the amount of

greenhouse gases discharged into the atmosphere. President Bush and the United States pressured the conference to accept a significantly weakened version of this proposal. The United States argued that a significant reduction of greenhouse gases would have disastrous economic repercussions. Many environmentalists argued that we ought to accept these short-term consequences in order to protect the interests of future generations. These people argued that we need to reduce our reliance on fossil fuels to ensure a future world protected from global warming. (See the case that opens this chapter for a description of the connection between global warming and fossil fuel use.)

Intuitively we might say that this decision is ethically preferable because those future people born into that world will be better off than they would have been had we maintained the status quo and continued our heavy reliance on fossil fuels. But wait a minute. "Better off than they would have been" assumes that these very same people would exist if we had chosen the alternative. That is, the moral intuition underlying this decision is that one set of future people will either be harmed or benefited by our decisions. But alternative policy decisions, especially those as significant as would be required to achieve major reductions in carbon dioxide emissions, will surely result in *different* people being born. According to this view, the existence of any one person depends on a remarkable number of contingencies. (Imagine all the possible events that might have prevented your parents, or great-grandparents, from meeting; or caused them to postpone the moment of conception by a year, or a month, or even a minute.) Thus, alternative policy decisions will result in two, not one, sets of future people; those who will be born if we choose policy A, and those who will be born if we choose policy B. (Of course, this simplifies the issue. Alternative policies adopted at Rio would be only one of many factors determining who gets born.) Because the group who would be harmed by one choice would not exist unless we made that choice, it makes little sense to say that they would be "better off" if we had made the other choice. Because different policy decisions result in different future generations, there simply is no one future generation that would be made better or worse off by either of those decisions.

Let's consider two responses to the "disappearing beneficiaries" argument. The first was developed by Annette Baier.[13] Baier argues that we can make sense of the claim that someone is made "worse off" by our actions even if, under the alternative action, that person would not have existed at all. On the one hand, we can acknowledge the significance of a "wrongful life"; that is, a life in which the person can say, "I would have been better off not being born."[14] We can imagine a world so polluted and so miserable that a population would acknowledge that it would have been better had its members not lived, and suffered, at all. Further, the concept of moral rights provides us with a way of explaining "worse off" even when the alternative is nonexistence.

If we acknowledge that all humans have, and will continue to have, rights to certain goods or to having certain interests protected, then our actions today may violate the rights of future people. Thus if we continue to dump massive amounts of pollutants into the atmosphere, we harm future people not by making them worse off than they would have been, but by violating their rights. That is, we have failed in our duty to provide future people, whoever they turn out to be, with a certain moral minimum. These people can say they were harmed, not because *they* would have been better off in some other possible future, but because in the future in which they do exist certain central interests of theirs (such as health) were jeopardized by our actions. In this sense our obligations are not to any particular future people, but to the interests that future people, whoever they turn out to be, will have. These interests do not "disappear" with alternative decisions.

A somewhat different response is developed by Mary Anne Warren.[15] Warren distinguishes between *possible people*, those people who could, but do not necessarily, exist, and *future people*, those people who *will* exist in the future. Warren admits it is absurd to suggest we have obligations to merely "possible" people. Because there is an infinite number of possible people, that view makes little sense. But we can meaningfully compare the happiness or suffering of "future" people. We can do this because we can compare "types of human life" and recognize that a life of suffering is worse than a life of happiness. Thus while any one particular possible beneficiary may "disappear" under alternative decisions, the relative amount of suffering or happiness does not. Our obligations to future generations, in this view, are not obligations to specific possible people, but are obligations to "recognize certain *minimal requirements of moral responsibility*." As Warren sees it,

> It is irresponsible, and contemptuous of the welfare of future persons, to deliberately bring into being persons who will almost certainly be unhappy. It is wrong because it results in unnecessary suffering in the future, suffering on the part of individuals [future people] who in the timeless perspective are no less real than we are.[16]

Thus, following Baier and Warren, it can be meaningful to talk about duties to future generations of people. We have good grounds for believing that our present actions can be restricted by ethical obligations we owe to people not yet born. But we have not yet considered the content of those obligations. Assuming that it is meaningful to talk about our duties to them, what do we owe them? To consider this concern, let us turn to the second environmental issue mentioned earlier.

4.4 CLIMATE CHANGE AND DUTIES TO POSTERITY

As mentioned at the beginning of this chapter, human activity is affecting climatic and atmospheric change at a rate unprecedented in earth's history. Two related problems, the greenhouse effect and depletion of the ozone layer, are the most visible examples of these changes.

In addition to the potential for global warming that results from the emission of billions of tons of greenhouse gases into the atmosphere, a second atmospheric problem concerns the depletion of the high-level atmospheric ozone. A number of chemicals, especially a group of chlorofluorocarbons (CFCs), have the ability to react chemically with and break down ozone. When such chemicals, used as coolants in air-conditioning and refrigerators, propellants in aerosol cans, and in polystyrene (Styrofoam) insulation and packaging, rise into the stratosphere they destroy the ozone layer that acts to filter out harmful ultraviolet radiation. Among the consequences of an increased exposure to ultraviolet radiation would be an increase in a variety of cancers and damage to DNA molecules in humans, plants, and animals.

Again, although scientists accept the reality of ozone-destroying CFCs and acknowledge the potential harms, disagreement remains about the range and significance of the effects of ozone depletion. Besides, why should we be overly concerned with cancer rates or genetic defects in the future? Perhaps future generations will smoke fewer cigarettes, and therefore there might actually be an overall reduction in future cancers. Perhaps medical research will by that time discover a cure for cancer. Perhaps genetic research and genetic counseling will eliminate genetic defects or at least allow individuals with chromosomal damage to refrain from having children. There is just no way to calculate the long-term consequences of our acts because we cannot foretell the future.

Assuming that we can meaningfully be said to have responsibilities to future generations, how do we decide where those responsibilities lie? What is the ethical basis of these responsibilities? As shown earlier in the discussion of Warren's position, one way to answer these questions is to focus on minimizing suffering. A utilitarian—and intuitively plausible—view suggests that minimally we have an obligation to reduce the suffering and optimally to maximize the happiness of future generations. The attempt to specify this obligation further has led to some problems, however.

Suppose we adopt a utilitarian view and argue that we have an obligation to maximize the happiness of future generations. Should that "maximal happiness" commit us to increasing the *total overall* happiness, or the *average* happiness?[17] This distinction is not as important when we restrict our concerns to the present. Given a constant population, the total and average happiness amounts to the same thing. However, when we recognize that one of our decisions regarding future generations concerns *how many* future people there will be, we see that the total versus average distinction is very important.

For example, we might decide that it is preferable to increase future population size, thereby increasing the overall *total* future happiness, although the *average* amount of happiness might remain constant. Is it ethically preferable to increase the overall total happiness of the future population, or to increase the average happiness of individual future people? The answer to this question has significant implications for population and environmental policies.

Suppose we adopt the *total happiness* view and adopt environmental policies that aim at increasing the total future happiness. One implication of this view may well commit us to *increasing* future population size. This seems to commit us to what Derek Parfit has called the "repugnant conclusion."[18] As long as overall world happiness is increased, we ought to create as many people as possible. Thus we might be obligated to create a world with billions and billions of marginally happy people rather than a world with a much smaller population of much happier people. (Or, suppose we were committed to a world in which *total* suffering was minimized. Might such a future world contain *no* human beings? Might our obligation under this view be to refrain from having any children?)

The total happiness alternative does not appear very attractive. It seems to commit us to sacrificing the happiness of individual future people to an abstract notion of some "overall total" happiness. Is it permissible to cause to exist countless people who will suffer as long as the overall amount of world happiness is increased?

But suppose we adopt a population policy aimed at increasing the average future happiness. This seems to avoid the problem raised against the total view. Environmental and population policy ought to aim to increase the happiness on average of those individual people who will exist in the future. Will the average person living in the future be happier if we reduce carbon dioxide emissions or if we continue the present rate of CO_2 emissions?

The average happiness view also faces serious problems. It places an unreasonable ethical restriction on the birth of future people. In effect, it commits us to saying that future people ought not to be born unless they will enjoy a life at least as happy as the average person today enjoys. This discounts the happiness of future people. Their happiness is important only compared to ours. Even if a future person would be, on balance, happy with her life, the average happiness view would say that this person ought not to be born if she will not be as happy as the average person today.

This view, too, might place us on a slippery slope to a particularly repugnant conclusion. It might be argued that because people living in impoverished nonindustrialized countries will produce future generations that would likely not increase average happiness, population policy ought to aim to restrict the reproductive freedom of the world's poor. Those countries with relatively high standards of living, with access to plentiful and affordable food, health care, education, resources, and energy would have an ethical claim to reproductive priority. Those countries in which a person's life prospects are relatively low (even if still moderately happy), should be required to lower birthrates. Minimally, this appears to imply an unfair priority to the status quo. The rich get richer, and the poor get contraception.

It would seem that defenders of the average happiness view need to say more about the *distribution* of both happiness, and the resources necessary to achieve happiness. Also, note that this problem is a version of the "justice" criticism raised against utilitarianism in Chapter 2. Now let's turn to another issue to pursue the question of the distribution of environmental risks across generations.

4.5 NUCLEAR WASTES AND THE RIGHTS OF FUTURE GENERATIONS

Some of the best ethical analyses of the nuclear issue can be found in the writing of Richard Sylvan and Val Plumwood.[19] They ask us to imagine a trip on a crowded long-distance train. As the train leaves one station, someone places a package aboard that contains a highly toxic and explosive gas. The gas is packaged in a container that the sender knows is not very strong and may well leak before the package arrives at its destination. It will certainly leak if the train is involved in an accident or derails or if some passenger accidently or intentionally interferes with, mishandles, or attempts to steal the gas. All these events have happened with packages on past trips. Any leak will probably kill those people close by and seriously harm others. Some but not all of the passengers know about the container; none have consented to its accompanying them.

Sylvan and Plumwood suggest that most people would seriously condemn the person who placed the package aboard the train. Even if this sender hopes and believes that no accident will occur, or even if the sender had no other alternative means of sending the package and could not afford a safer container, we would seriously criticize this person for jeopardizing the lives and health of many innocent people.

Our present policy of creating and storing nuclear wastes is, according to Sylvan and Plumwood, exactly analogous to this example. The present generation is sending extremely toxic wastes on a train ride into the future with the world's future populations, perhaps as many as 40,000 generations, as passengers. The present generation is guilty of a great injustice by placing innocent future people in grave risk, all because we wish to avoid making changes in our comfortable consumer lifestyle. In their words,

> Like the consignor in the train parable, contemporary industrial society proposes, in order to get itself out of a mess arising from its own life-style—the creation of economies dependent on an abundance of non-renewable energy, which is in limited supply—to pass on costs and risks of serious harm to others who will obtain no corresponding benefits. . . . If we apply to the nuclear situation standards of behavior and moral principles generally acknowledged (in principle if not so often in fact) in the contemporary world, it is not easy to avoid the conclusion that nuclear development involves *injustice with respect to the future* on a grand scale.[20]

The authors suggest that there are but two possible ways to avoid this conclusion: either we try to deny that we owe future people any consideration at all, or we must argue that present concerns override our responsibilities to the future generations. I use this structure in what follows.

As noted earlier, we are usually quite willing to hold people responsible for actions that cause harms at some future date. I am responsible for poisoning you even if the effects of my poison do not occur for some time. Thus, it is not the fact that harms happen in the *future* that can defeat our responsibilities. Perhaps the issue centers on the fact that in one case I harm presently existing people in the future, and in the other I harm future existing people in the future. Does this make a difference?

Philosopher Gregory Kavka argues that it does not. His analysis of what he calls the "futurity problem" rejects three arguments that might be given to support the claim that present generations have no obligations to future people. These arguments are based on temporal location, our ignorance of future people, and the contingency of future people.[21] Since we have seen these claims before, we can review them briefly here.

Does the fact that people who are harmed by our actions exist at a future time (a different "temporal location") excuse us from our responsibility to them? Kavka offers two reasons for thinking it does not. First, arguing by analogy with our own future desires, he claims that just as it is unreasonable for any individual to favor his or her present desires over future desires, so it is unreasonable to favor satisfying the desires of present people over those of future people. Consider the following example. We normally think it unreasonable of someone who sacrifices his or her future well-being simply to satisfy some present desire. It would be irrational for me to spend my life savings right now simply because the specific desires that I will have during retirement are desires that will occur only in the future. It is because future desires are as important as present desires that the rational person saves for the future. Likewise, we should treat the desires of future people as deserving equal consideration as the desires of present people.

Kavka denies that temporal location is a morally relevant feature of a person. Just as we have good reasons to believe that living people will be harmed by my dumping of toxic wastes in my yard, we have good reasons for thinking that there will be future people harmed by long-term toxic wastes. The burden of proof is on those who would claim otherwise, and it is a burden not easily dismissed.

The "argument from ignorance" we have seen, and rejected, before. Just as we hold polluters responsible despite their ignorance of who would be harmed by their actions, we can hold present generations responsible despite their ignorance of who their victims will be.

The "contingency argument" we have also seen previously. It is true that given the immense control that the present generation has over the makeup of future generations, it is likely that the particular possible people who would be harmed by a policy of creating massive amounts of nuclear waste are not the same possible people who would be benefited by avoiding that policy. Thus, there are no specific future people to whom we could owe the duty to refrain from creating nuclear waste. Nevertheless, we have very strong reasons to believe that there will be some future people, that they will be the types of beings who would be harmed by radiation poisoning, and that our present actions will lead to such harms. We therefore have equally strong reasons for saying that we have duties to these people.

Might someone now argue that while we do have duties to future people, those duties are overridden by more pressing present interests? Since we are concerned with the interests in life and health of future people, interests that we normally would not override for reasons of convenience or comfort, this argument needs to involve a process of *discounting* the interests of future people.

The idea of discounting the interests of future people has roots in the classical utilitarianism of Jeremy Bentham. Bentham developed a "hedonistic calculus" as a means of measuring pleasure to aid in calculating the utilitarian consequences of our acts. According to Bentham, the amount of pleasure and pain produced by our actions varies along several dimensions, including the *certainty or uncertainty* that they will occur and their *propinquity or remoteness*. Thus uncertain or remote pleasures count for less than certain and immediate ones. But is it reasonable to do this? We can find reasons for rejecting this practice on both utilitarian and human rights grounds.

The practice of discounting future interests finds a contemporary expression in the economic concept of discounted present value of future payments. In this view, a dollar held now is worth more than a dollar held at some time in the future, because the present dollar could be invested, earn interest, and therefore be worth more than a dollar at that future date. Thus, future dollars must be "discounted" to be equivalent to present value. As a result, the practice of discounting future interests is common in economic analyses of environmental issues. As we saw in the last chapter, economic analysis is the most commonly used methodology of public policy decision making. Thus, what may seem like a very abstract and arcane concept ends up playing a significant role in environmental policy. One implication of this practice, for example, might require us to maximize present value of our resources and discount their future value to later generations.[22]

Two immediate considerations cast doubt on the plausibility of this practice. First, no matter how small the discount rate, any discounting eventually reduces future values to nothing. Second, it would seem that some values such as health and life should not be discounted at all. A single dollar possessed by my great-great-grandchild may be worth less (in purchasing power) than a single dollar that I possess, but it would be peculiar to claim that my great-great-grandchild's life (assuming that my children and their children's children have children) will be worth less than my life.

Another strong case against the discounting of future interests can be made on utilitarian grounds. An interesting version of such an argument is developed by Mary Williams.[23] Williams argues that discounting the future value of resources can be consistent with utilitarian goals as long as those resources stay around to produce value in the future. In that case, maximizing present value also maximizes the total overall value because in the future these resources will continue to produce value. However, when resources with future value can be removed from production, as happens when present generations deplete nonrenewable resources (or renewable resources at a rate below sustainability), then the total overall good is not maximized.

The essential point of this argument, for our purposes, seems to be this: in calculating the future consequences of our present environmental policies, policymakers tend to rely on the economic practice of discounting future values (costs and benefits). As noted in Chapter 3, the ethical basis of this approach is a version of utilitarianism. However, Williams claims that even on utilitarian grounds discounting social value in environmental cases often frustrates rather than promotes maximization of total happiness. This occurs because those resources that would produce the future value are being depleted to the point of extinction by our present policies. Williams's image is that rather than living off the interest of our "investments," we too often are spending our savings so that eventually there will be no savings left to generate interest payments.

Her alternative is to defend an environmental policy of "maximum sustainable yield." That is, we should seek to maximize the return on our investments (for example, our environmental and agricultural resources) without jeopardizing the investments themselves. We should, to use the economists' language, live off our interest and not our capital. To use an agricultural image, we should seek to maximize the yield of our croplands in a manner that guarantees that the cropland will continue to be productive into the indefinite future. By discounting future values, we make it easy for the present generation to spend its capital as well as its interest.

4.6 THE RIGHTS OF FUTURE GENERATIONS

Perhaps a more direct critical response to the practice of discounting future values can be developed from a deontological approach to the rights of future people. As we have seen, discounting the interests of future people allows us to override their interests in life and health with our own interests in a comfortable lifestyle. Ordinarily, we would think that life and health "trump" mere comfort. Philosophers who take seriously the rights of future generations (or our obligations to them[24]) deny that we can override the central interests of future people.

We already have seen some of the strategies employed by philosophers who would defend the rights of future generations. Many of these strategies seek to show that no sound argument can be given to deny rights to future generations. Thus, neither their temporal location, nor our ignorance of them, nor their contingency justifies the denial of our obligations to future people.

Other philosophers have argued that while we do have obligations to future generations, these obligations extend only into the near future. We have duties to our children's and our grandchildren's generations perhaps, but we have no duties to the distant future; for example, ten, twenty, one hundred generations into the future. These claims can be defended on a variety of grounds. Some argue that rights and duties are fundamentally contractual, that they arise out of a social contract between people. Although a plausible case can be made for interpreting the relationship between immediate generations on a contractual model (we continue to be bound by the social contract established by the U.S. Constitution), it is less plausible to think that generations separated by thousands of years could be so bound.

A slightly different view argues that rights and responsibilities are relative to one's "moral community." Minimally, a moral community consists of those people with a shared moral understanding, a recognition of mutual and reciprocal moral relations, and so on. Thus our rights and responsibilities end at the boundaries of our moral community, be those boundaries conceptual, spatial, or temporal.[25] Still others might argue that our responsibilities are a function of other moral relations such as caring, love, or sympathy. Since these affections can extend into the immediate future but not the distant future, our responsibilities also only extend into the immediate future.

The next chapter considers some of these issues in more depth. Indeed, we will see how some philosophers have pushed the notion of "moral considerability" well beyond the question of future generations of humans. For now, let's focus on two fundamental philosophical questions: "Can future generations be said to have rights?" and "What rights do (would?) future generations have?"

Is it meaningful to say that future generations have rights *now*? If we tend to think of rights as some sort of attribute that belongs to people and exists "out there" in the world to be discovered, it is difficult to see how that claim could be defended. Since the right-holders do not exist, how could their rights? But if we think of rights in terms of their *function*, it is more plausible. Rights function to limit the behavior of other people. My rights limit your behavior by imposing certain obligations on you. Rights limit behavior in order to protect certain central interests of the right-holder. Further, there should be some socially recognized means for enforcing my rights.[26] Thus, the existence of rights depends on what the moral community acknowledges central interests to be. Future generations might be said to have rights to the degree that we acknowledge, and accept limitations on our own behavior for the sake of, their interests.

Do we have good reasons to accept such limitations on our own behavior? It seems to me that we do have such good reasons, to the degree that we have good reasons for believing that future genera-tions will exist, and that they will have central interests that we can now understand and predict. That is, we have extremely strong reasons for attributing rights to future generations. The burden of proof surely rests with those who claim either that future genera-tions likely will not exist, or that their needs and interests will be so different from ours that we cannot predict what they might be.

If we accept something like this account, the rights we should attribute to future generations will depend on the needs and inter-ests we assume those future generations will have. Let us return to the question of nuclear energy and nuclear wastes. We can be fairly certain that future generations will have an interest in being pro-tected from the dangers of nuclear radiation. But what will their energy needs and interests be? If we forgo nuclear energy to protect the interests of future generations, the only plausible alternative for us (at least into the immediate future and assuming the demand remains constant) will involve greater reliance on nonrenewable en-ergy sources like oil, gas, and coal. Ignoring for the moment the present pollution problems that follow from burning these fossil fuels, our greater reliance on fossil fuels implies both that less of these resources will be available for future generations and that we are putting them at risk of global warming. How, then, should we balance our responsibilities to future generations regarding limiting nuclear wastes, against our own interests in and needs for energy, and the energy interests and needs of future generations? Do we have obligations to conserve nonrenewable energy resources so that future people will have access to these resources? How should we balance the risks of nuclear wastes against the risks of global warming?

It would seem that any attempt to specify the rights of future people will encounter serious difficulties. By definition, any use of nonrenewable resources means that others will have less available for their use. If we have a duty to conserve out of respect for the rights of the near future generations, shouldn't they conserve out of a respect for the rights of distant future generations? If the near future generation has the right to use these resources, why don't we?

An interesting response to these problems is defended by Brian Barry.[27] Barry's position is to allow present generations to continue to use nonrenewable energy resources, even if this means placing future generations at a relative disadvantage, as long as we compensate those future people for causing them this disadvantage. Barry holds that, at a minimum, justice requires equal treatment. When we use nonrenewable energy resources, we are denying future generations the equal opportunity to use those resources. Justice demands that denials of equality be compensated. We cannot compensate future generations for the loss of energy resources by returning that energy to them, but we can compensate them for the loss of those opportunities and choices that require energy resources. The central human interest lies not in the resources themselves (such as oil, gas, coal), but in those uses for which we employ energy resources. We, and they, use energy to produce the goods and services that we need. It is the loss of an equal opportunity to these goods (to this "productive capacity") that requires compensation:

> We can now venture a statement of what is required by justice toward future generations. As far as natural resources are concerned, depletion should be compensated for in the sense that later generations should be left no worse off (in terms of productive capacity) than they would have been without the depletion.[28]

Barry admits that there are many practical difficulties involved in specifying what would be required to offset the loss of productive capacity. Nevertheless, we can infer some implications. Since the resources that we are using are relatively accessible, we owe future generations capital and technological investments that will pay future dividends in terms of their ability to find and extract energy resources. Presumably, we also owe to them an investment in research and development of alternative energy sources. It would also seem reasonable to say that we owe them as large an inheritance of energy resources as practical. Wasting energy resources is a particularly callous violation of their rights.

What conclusions might we draw from this discussion of our duties to future generations? I offer three: First, we have the obligation to make a sincere and serious effort to develop alternative energy sources. The risks of continued reliance on fossil fuels and nuclear power are real and serious. We can reasonably foresee the dangers that follow from these energy sources, and it is within our power to minimize them. Failing to take steps to avoid them is on a par with criminal negligence.

Second, we have the duty to conserve energy resources. At present rates, we will use up the known reserves of fossil fuels and uranium within two hundred years. Wasting these resources, especially when known technology can increase efficiencies so that we can conserve without significant sacrifice of convenience, denies future people a fair opportunity to attain a lifestyle commensurate with our own.

Finally, we owe these people a reasonable chance for happiness. The earth cannot continue to support an exploding population. We need to limit population growth so that we do not bring people into the world who will have little chance of a minimally decent life. In addition, we need to recognize that poverty is a major factor that both contributes to and results from overpopulation.

4.7 CONSERVING RESOURCES AND CARING FOR FUTURE GENERATIONS

If we understand rights as protecting central interests and if we accept the reasonableness of attributing rights to future people, then future generations would seem to have strong claims on our use of a variety of resources. Clean air and water, agricultural lands, and energy are all tied in obvious ways to the central interests of future people. But what about other, less essential, resources? Do future generations have a right to undeveloped shorelines, wilderness areas, wetlands, mountainsides? Do we have a duty to preserve animal and plant species for future generations? Or is the preservation of these resources more akin to acting out of charity than acting from a duty?

Do future generations have a *right* to such resources? We can understand that future generations, like us, might enjoy such resources. But then again, they might not. This issue is even more difficult when we recognize that what future generations will enjoy or desire depends in large part on the type of world they inherit from us. Will a world without the blue whale miss it? Will future generations that have never experienced a wilderness area, a rain forest, or a grizzly bear care about such things? Do we miss the dodo bird? the passenger pigeon? Would we really miss the snail darter or the California condor?

There are several ways in which it could be argued that we have a duty to preserve wilderness areas and plant and animal species. It might be argued that the biological diversity protected in wilderness areas and represented by plant and animal species has a potential for great future benefit to humans. The agricultural and medical potential of biological diversity provides strong prudential reasons for their preservation.

As the following chapters show, a number of philosophers have argued that animals, plants, and ecosystems themselves should be the direct beneficiaries of our responsibilities. In this view, we should preserve them for their own sake. Before turning to these questions, consider a nonprudential defense of preservation: We should preserve such natural resources because we *care* about future generations. We care about the type of people they will become, and we believe that a life lived in a world in which wilderness areas and rare species are preserved is a better life than the alternative.

Can we care about people who do not exist? To answer this question, we need to say something about what is implied by "caring for" someone. Just a brief consideration suggests that "care" is a more complex concept than we might initially think. Let us overlook most of the complexity to focus on just a few central ideas.

In one sense, "care" can refer to the responsibility to attend to someone's needs or interests. An elderly parent may be in the care of an adult child, or a nurse may be charged with the care of a patient. This meaning is relevant for our concerns. In part, we are asking if present generations can be charged with the care of future people.

But there is more to care than simply this. Just as an adult child may be charged with the care of an elderly parent yet never visit that parent in a nursing home, so too we might be charged with the care of future people yet do nothing more than the barest minimum to render that care. A more interesting notion of care involves a motivational or emotional engagement with the subject.

Care is more than a mere feeling or a fleeting recognition of an interest in another person. (The way that most of us, when it is brought to our attention, acknowledge that we "care" about the victims of some foreign war or natural disaster.) If care about future generations involved only this feeling, it would be of little interest for us. For our purposes, "care" is something closer to "love" or altruism in that it involves our being engaged with and motivated by the well-being of others. Can our concern for the interests of future people—for the type of life they will face, the type of people they will become—provide a reason for us to act in the present? Can it provide a reason that can override our own personal interests?

Put this way, the question would seem easily answered. Reasonably strong empirical evidence suggests that people are often motivated to act out of a concern for the interests of future people. On the political level, decisions to protect wilderness areas; to establish national and state parks, forests, and shorelines; to build museums and libraries; and to fund research and development in medicine, industry, and national defense—all make sense only if we recognize that the beneficiaries of these decisions will be generations as yet unborn. On a private level, decisions to endow charitable and educational foundations, to fund artistic, cultural, and social organizations also seem obviously motivated, at least in part, by a concern to provide future people with a decent and humane world. On a personal level, a decision as simple as planting an oak tree—one of countless varieties of plants that mature over long periods of time—suggests that individuals are motivated by a concern for the distant future.

Against this empirical evidence, however, lies a strong philosophical tradition holding that humans are motivated solely by self-interest. This view, called "psychological egoism," is associated with a tradition of thought running from the Greek Sophists through Hobbes and contemporary economics. That philosophical tradition holds that rational people act only when they believe that doing so is in their own self-interest. (Remember the economists, mentioned in Chapter 3, who suggest the alternative demands that we "rewire" human nature.)

Of course, this tradition does not deny that people act in ways that benefit or manifest concern for others. It does not claim that all people are narrowly selfish. It only claims that our ultimate reason for acting to benefit others lies in self-interest. In this view, I help others because by doing so I will benefit in turn. When I donate to charity or contribute to posterity, I am seeking the esteem, status, or tax deduction that follows from such gifts.

Thus, egoism interprets altruism or friendship on a contractual model: "I will benefit you if you will benefit me." Accordingly, because people in the distant future can do nothing that serves my self-interest, it makes little sense to talk about caring for future people.

But surely this is an impoverished understanding of caring for another. If we discover that someone "cares" for us only because doing so is in that person's own self-interest, we would be justified in denying that any caring actually exists. Caring for others seems to exclude, rather than be a form of, self-interest. Care requires that we take, as much as possible, the other person's viewpoint.

In an insightful analysis of the role of caring in ethics and education, feminist writer Nel Noddings suggests that:

> Apprehending the other's reality, feeling what he feels as nearly as possible, is the essential part of caring from the point of view of the one caring. For if I take on the other's reality as possibility and begin to feel its reality, I feel, also, that I must act accordingly; that is, I am impelled to act as though on my own behalf, but in behalf of the other.[29]

To care for another is to take the other's point of view. It is to ask, not "What would *I* do if I were in that position?" but, as far as possible, "What would be best for this other person from her own perspective?" As Noddings says, "When my caring is directed to living things, I must consider their natures, ways of life, needs, and desires. And, although I can never accomplish it entirely, I try to apprehend the reality of the other."[30]

Thus, the question of whether we can care about future generations asks whether we can view the world from their perspective. Can we replace our interests, needs, and desires with the interests, needs, and desires of future people?

On first glance, it would seem we can. Friendship and parenting seem the two most obvious and widespread situations in which people restrain their own self-interests for the interests of others. If it were not possible to be motivated by the interests of others, neither friendship nor parenting could exist. Rational egoism, as we can call it, would make loyalty, love, sacrifice, honesty, and a whole range of other virtues and attitudes rationally impossible.

But friends and children are actual people who have real interests and needs. Future people do not exist, and perhaps this is a relevant difference. But why should this matter?

Perhaps it could be argued that we can only take the point of view of, and care for, people who are actually living. Yet many people (possibly more often in other cultures) seem to care deeply about their ancestors. People seem able to act in ways that would make their ancestors proud, that would honor their ancestors, that show respect for or pay homage to, their ancestors.

Perhaps, instead, it would be argued that since the interests and desires of future people will depend, in part, on the type of world they inherit from us, we have no way of knowing in advance what those interests and desires will be. But if we do not know this, it is impossible for us to view the world from their perspective and hence impossible to be motivated by their interests and desires. We cannot care about them because we cannot know what would count as their "behalf."

However, this argument fails to appreciate the true nature of the motivation to preserve nonessential resources for future people. We do not seek to preserve a wilderness area or an endangered species because we believe future people will desire these things. The objection is correct in holding that if future people do not know of these things they cannot desire (or miss) them. But the motivation to preserve for the future does not rest on the content of their desires; it rests with our judgment that a life lived with the possibility of knowing and desiring these things is fuller and more meaningful than one lived without them.

A parallel argument can be made with the example of distinguished works of art. If we failed to preserve all Renaissance paintings, for example, and all records of this art were lost to future generations, then surely they could not be said to miss them. If future generations knew nothing of these paintings, then they could not feel their loss. But their lives would be impoverished by this loss nonetheless. And it is our concern for this, our caring that they not live impoverished lives, that motivates us to preserve great artwork for the future.

Thus it does seem meaningful to care about future people. To the degree that we can imagine ourselves in their position, we can recognize that such lives would be missing much were they not to know the wilderness or the rich complexity of biological diversity. We can care about the type of people future generations become and the types of lives they can lead. And this care, I suggest, can and does motivate us to act.

4.8 SUMMARY AND CONCLUSION

As philosophers turned their attention to environmental issues, it became clear that simply applying standard ethical theories does not produce satisfactory analyses of these issues. As this chapter shows, some of the most pressing environmental challenges force us to consider in detail the ethical impact of our actions on future people. Yet this issue was often ignored in much traditional philosophy, and new, ground-breaking work was required. Philosophical ethics needed to be extended beyond traditional boundaries.

The next chapter shows how these boundaries were extended even further. Most of the issues so far considered have focused on the effects that various environmental policies have on humans. The next chapter makes a fundamental shift in philosophical perspective, asking, "Do we have direct responsibilities to *non*humans?" Although many philosophers had considered this question, almost all had rejected the possibility that anything other than humans, perhaps even future humans, had moral standing. Primarily in response to environmental concerns, philosophers have in recent years sought to extend ethical consideration beyond human beings. We now turn to these further extensions of ethics.

Notes

1. For this explanation and the data that follow, I am especially indebted to *Environmental Science*, by G. Tyler Miller, 3d ed. (Belmont, CA: Wadsworth, 1991). I have found no better single sourcebook for explaining the science of environmental issues to the nonscientist.

2. The figures quoted are from Nicholas Lenssen, *Nuclear Waste: The Problem That Won't Go Away*, Worldwatch Paper 106 (Washington, DC: Worldwatch Institute, December 1991) p. 9.

3. For a scientifically sound yet readable discussion of these issues, see Jonathan Piel, ed., *Energy for Planet Earth: Readings from Scientific American* (New York: Freeman, 1991). These readings were originally published in *Scientific American* (September 1990).

4. This, of course, ignores the equally pressing question of justice to present generations. Some of the biggest ethical challenges facing storage of any toxic wastes involve the possibility that those people in the least advantaged position in society will be asked to support the greatest burden. Those people lacking political influence will be unlikely to compete with more powerful NIMBY (not in my backyard) advocates. Questions of fairness and coercion can also be raised against proposals to store toxic wastes on Native American reservations.

5. As far as I can determine, this distinction first occurs in Jan Narveson, "Future People and Us," in R. I. Sikora and Brian Barry, eds., *Obligations to Future Generations* (Philadelphia: Temple University Press, 1978). It is also used in Ernest Partridge, ed., *Responsibilities to Future Generations* (Buffalo, NY: Prometheus Books, 1980), and Mary Anne Warren, "Future Generations," in Tom Regan and Donald VanDeVeer, eds., *And Justice for All* (Totowa, NJ: Rowman and Allanheld, 1982). The Sikora and Barry book, along with Michael Bayles's *Ethics and Population* (Cambridge, MA: Schenkman, 1976), are primarily focused on population policy issues. Partridge's book, along with Douglas MacLean and Peter Brown, eds.,

Energy and the Future (Totowa, NJ: Rowman and Littlefield, 1983), focus primarily on duties to posterity.

6. Perhaps the most influential defenders of this view are Paul and Anne Ehrlich. See Paul Ehrlich's classic *The Population Bomb* (New York: Ballantine, 1968) and the more recent book *The Population Explosion* (New York: Doubleday, 1990). For a well-known criticism of the view that population growth is the key to environmental devastation, see Barry Commoner, *The Closing Circle* (New York: Knopf, 1971).

7. As reported in Miller, p. 11. Miller cites, without further reference, the Worldwatch Institute as the source of these figures. "Environmental refugees" are people who have been displaced or exiled by environmental or ecological emergencies.

8. Miller, pp. 13–15, refers to these two issues as "people overpopulation" and "consumption overpopulation."

9. For a development of these claims, see Anne Ehrlich and Paul Ehrlich, *The Population Explosion* (New York: Doubleday, 1990).

10. See Gregory Kavka, "The Futurity Problem," in R. I. Sikora and Brian Barry, eds., *Obligations to Future Generations* (Philadelphia: Temple University Press, 1978), for a full analysis of this argument. Kavka cites Martin Golding, "Obligations to Future Generations," *Monist* 56 (1972): 97–98, as an "interesting variant" of the argument from ignorance.

11. For versions of this argument, see Derek Parfit, "On Doing the Best for Our Children," in Michael Bayles, *Ethics and Population* (Cambridge, MA: Schenkman, 1976); and Thomas Schwartz, "Obligations to Posterity," in R. I. Sikora and Brian Barry, eds., *Obligations to Future Generations* (Philadelphia: Temple University Press, 1978).

12. The phrase is from Schwartz.

13. Annette Baier, "For the Sake of Future Generations," in Tom Regan, ed., *Earthbound: New Introductory Essays in Environmental Ethics* (New York: Random House, 1984).

14. Compare this with the legal notion of "wrongful life" in, for example, *Curlender v. Bioscience Laboratories*, 106 Cal. App. 3rd 811 (1980) in which a California court allowed a tort suit on behalf of a child born with Tay-Sachs disease after the parents had been told that they were not carriers of the Tay-Sachs gene.

15. Warren, "Future Generations," in Tom Regan and Donald VanDeVeer, eds., *And Justice for All* (Totowa, NJ: Rowman and Allanheld, 1982).

16. Ibid., p. 154.

17. I rely here primarily on Warren, although further discussion can be found in several papers of the Barry and Sikora collection. See especially the papers by Narveson, Bennett, Scott, Sumner, and Sikora: See Ian Narveson, "Future People and Us"; Jonathan Bennett, "On Maximizing Happiness"; Robert Scott, "Environmental Ethics and Obligations to Future Generations"; L. W. Sumner, "Classical Utilitarianism and the Population Optimum"; and R. I. Sikora, "Is It Wrong to Prevent the Existence of Future Generations?" Warren herself engages most of these authors in her discussion.

18. Parfit, "On Doing the Best for Our Children."

19. Richard and Val Routley, "Nuclear Power," in Tom Regan and Donald VanDeVeer, eds., *And Justice for All* (Totowa, NJ: Rowman and Allanheld, 1982), pp. 116–138.

20. Ibid., pp. 118–119.

21. Kavka, pp. 186–203.

22. For a discussion of this economic approach, see Colin Clark, *Mathematical Bioeconomics: The Optimal Management of Renewable Resources* (New York: Wiley, 1976).

23. Mary Williams, "Discounting Versus Maximum Sustainable Yield" in R. I. Sikora and Brian Barry, eds. (Philadephia: Temple University Press, 1978), pp. 169–185. Another more general review of criticisms of social discounting can be found in Derek Parfit, "Energy Policy and the Further Future: The Social Discount Rate," in Douglas MacLean and Peter Brown, eds. (Totowa, NJ: Rowman and Littlefield, 1983), pp. 31–37.

24. This qualification is necessary since some philosophers argue that while it does not make sense to attribute rights to people who do not exist to claim them, it still makes sense to say that *we* have obligations to the future. See "The Environment, Rights, and Future Generations," by Richard DeGeorge and "Can Future Generations Correctly Be Said to Have Rights?" by Ruth Macklin in Ernest Partridge, ed., *Responsibilities to Future Generations* (Buffalo, NY: Prometheus Books, 1980).

25. See Golding for an example of this position.

26. Versions of this familiar understanding are used by Annette Baier, "The Rights of Past and Future Persons" in Ernest Partridge, ed., *Responsibilities to Future Generations* (Buffalo, NY: Prometheus Books, 1980), and in Joel Feinberg, "The Rights of Animals and Unborn Generations," in William Blackstone, ed., *Philosophy and the Environmental Crisis* (Athens, GA: University of Georgia Press, 1974), and elsewhere throughout Feinberg's writings.

27. Brian Barry, "Intergenerational Justice in Energy Policy" in Douglas MacLean and R. I. Brown, eds., *Energy and the Future* (Buffalo, NY: Prometheus Books, 1980), pp. 15–30.

28. Ibid., p. 23.

29. Nel Noddings, *Caring: A Feminine Approach to Ethics and Moral Education* (University of California Press, 1984), p. 16.

30. Ibid., p. 14.

Discussion Questions

1. Controversies such as those surrounding global warming and ozone depletion involve long-term predictions and therefore are undecidable in the short term. In light of this uncertainty, is there one reasonable course of action? What does reason tell us when we must make a decision without full or accurate information?

2. Native Americans maintain significant sovereignty over reservation lands. Some tribes have considered selling tribal lands for use as nuclear waste storage sites. What ethical concerns are raised by this issue?

3. Strong moral relations exist between parents and children, and between grandparents and grandchildren. But can moral relations such as care and love exist between people separated by more than one or two generations?
4. Is procreation a natural right? What if any restrictions should be placed on having children? Do humans have a duty to procreate? What goods does "having a child of one's own" attain that cannot be attained through adoption?
5. Is population growth itself the major environmental problem? Or is the poverty and resource use that accompanies overpopulation the key? Which problems would you address first?
6. Numerous indigenous cultures were destroyed when Europeans conquered the Americas. We can only guess at what has been lost to present generations by these conquests. Have present generations been hurt by this loss? Can people be harmed by the loss of opportunities and the loss of knowledge of which they will never be aware? Will future generations be harmed if they never know about the blue whale or wilderness areas?

For Further Reading

The best collections of essays on ethical issues and future generations are those edited by Sikora and Barry, Partridge, and MacLean and Brown (see Note 5 in this chapter).

Michael Bayles, *Ethics and Population* (Cambridge, MA: Schenkman, 1976), and Philip Wagaman, *The Population Crisis and Moral Responsibility* (Washington, DC: Public Affairs Press, 1973), are slightly dated but still helpful discussions of population issues and ethics.

Beside the works referenced in Note 6, see Anne and Paul Ehrlich, *Earth* (New York: Franklin Watts, 1987), and Paul Ehrlich and John Holdren, eds., *The Cassandra Conference: Resources for the Human Predicament* (Texas Station: Texas A & M University Press, 1988), for detailed discussions of the interplay of population and resource use.

Julian Simon and Herman Kahn, eds., *The Resourceful Earth* (New York: Blackwell, 1984), presents the more optimistic view on resource use and the future.

Susan Weber, ed., *USA by the Numbers: A Statistical Portrait of the United States* (Washington, DC: Zero Population Growth, 1988), is a useful overview of population trends in the United States.

5

Duties to the Natural World

Killing Rivers and Species

On July 14, 1991, a Southern Pacific freight train derailed as it was crossing a bridge over the Sacramento River in northern California. One of its tank cars was carrying metam sodium, a liquid herbicide. The derailment punctured the tank car and spilled 20,000 gallons of this chemical into the Sacramento River. As the resulting 10-mile-long spill drifted slowly downstream, it killed virtually every living thing in its path. Nearly a 40-mile stretch of the river's ecosystem was destroyed by this spill. Aquatic plants, flies, nymphs, small fish, and more than 100,000 trout were killed. In effect, the spill killed the river itself.

Since the Sacramento is a fast-flowing river, it soon flushed itself clean of the toxin. By the end of the summer, the river was clean enough to support life once again. The spill also posed little danger to humans. The river flows into Lake Shasta, the state's largest man-made reservoir. The spill was so dispersed throughout the 550 billion gallons of water in the lake, that health officials determined that the water remained safe to drink. Humans were affected by the spill, however, in that fishing, boating, and other recreational uses of the river—along with a strong tourism business that depends on these activities—were devastated.

But what of the river itself? Had it been harmed in any morally significant way? What of the fish and plant life destroyed by the spill? Society has worked out fairly straightforward ways to determine when humans have been harmed by acts of negligence. We also have well-established ways for determining compensation. We might, for example, require the railroad to compensate merchants for lost revenues. Property owners might require compensation for cleanup costs. But has the railroad incurred a debt to the river, or to any of the life-forms destroyed by the spill?

Imagine also that the railroad did seek to restore the river as a means of compensation. What would count as restoration? To some wildlife officials, the river could be restored by stocking the area with fish raised in hatcheries. This would result in the immediate repopulation of trout. But other wildlife experts worried that restocking the river with hatchery fish would further harm the river's ecosystem. Nonnative and nonnatural species might make it more difficult for the native species of plants and animals to repopulate the river. Interbreeding of native with hatchery fish would be an artificial manipulation of the gene pool with unknown results. Rather, these experts argue that the river ought to be left alone to restore itself. Wild fish and plants will return, coming downstream from tributaries and upstream from Lake Shasta. The problem is that this solution may require many years, and it looks more like disregarding than helping the river.

In 1914 a passenger pigeon named Martha died in the Cincinnati Zoo. Her stuffed body is displayed in the National Museum of Natural History in Washington, D.C. Martha was the last known surviving member of her species. Only sixty years earlier, one observer estimated the population of a single flock of passenger pigeons at more than 2 billion birds.[1]

Before European settlers arrived in North America, upward of 125 million bison ranged across the Great Plains from Mexico to Canada. Native Americans enjoyed an ecologically stable and balanced relation with the bison, relying on these animals for food, clothing, shelter, heat, and tools. As anyone who has ever watched a television or movie "western" knows, these huge herds were subjected to overhunting, habitat loss, and simply slaughtered for sport by the newly arriving settlers. By 1892, the last remaining bison herd, 85 individual animals, was moved into the protected refuge of Yellowstone National Park. Today, there are approximately 75,000 bison in the United States.

The blue whale is the world's largest animal, reaching lengths of over 100 feet and weights of 150 tons. Estimates in the early years of the twentieth century suggested a population of over 200,000 blue whales in the Antarctic Ocean. Today the population is estimated at less than 1,000. With a very low reproduction rate, this population may not be large enough to guarantee the survival of the blue whale.

These three examples—one species extinct, one that has recovered from near extinction, and one still threatened with extinction—symbolize the choices that humans face in the coming decades. We can continue past practices and witness the extinction of millions of plant and animal species, or we can take aggressive steps to preserve and protect other life-forms.

It is estimated by some scientists that as many as 99 percent of the plant and animal species that have ever existed on earth are now extinct. Extinction, then, is a common occurrence in nature. All species eventually become extinct. What is uncommon about the extinction occurring at present, however, is its *rate* and its causes.

The biologist Edward O. Wilson estimates that the naturally occurring "background" extinction rate, the rate of extinction that would exist independently of human activity, is approximately one species every few years.[2] At the present time, he estimates that from 4,000 to 6,000 species a year are now becoming extinct, or slightly more than 10 species a day. This rate of extinction in the presence of humans is perhaps 10,000 times greater than what would otherwise occur. Without question, human activity is causing the single greatest episode of mass extinction since at least the end of the dinosaur age some 65 million years ago.

These estimates include both plant and animal species. As the three examples just used suggest, extinctions of animal species tend to be best known. Nevertheless, because humans and other animals depend, directly or indirectly, on plants for food (as well as clothing, shelter, and other necessities), a strong case could be made that plant extinctions are the more immediate issue. Some scientists have estimated that by the year 2000, human activity may account for the extinction of as many as 25 percent of all plant species.[3]

It was estimated that during the late 1980s an area of tropical rain forest the size of two football fields was destroyed every second of every day. If the burning and clearing of tropical rain forests continue at this rate, almost all of them will be completely destroyed within the next few decades. Since 1960 about half of all the earth's forestlands have been destroyed.[4]

Apart from prudential reasons that might show how biodiversity benefits humans, do we have any reason to be concerned with this loss of diverse life-forms? Do we have direct ethical responsibilities to other forms of life?

5.1 INTRODUCTION

As philosophers began to apply various ethical traditions to environmental issues, two fundamental questions guided their work. First, what is the ethically proper relationship between humans and the natural environment? Second, what is the philosophical basis for this relationship? In seeking to answer these questions, many philosophers discovered that the appeal to standard ethical theories was highly ambiguous. Traditional philosophical (and theological) views on the human relationship with nature seemed in many cases to have contributed to environmental destruction and degradation.

For the most part, the Western philosophical tradition denied that any direct moral relationship existed between humans and the natural environment. According to most ethical theories within this tradition, only human beings had moral standing; all other things had ethical value only in so far as they served human interests. Thus when considering some environmental decision, the ethical person needed only ask, "How will this decision affect humans?" To the degree that it could be said to exist, "environmental ethics" on these views were all *consequentialist* ethics: environmental right or wrong depended on the consequences to humans. As we saw in the previous chapter, this perspective was later extended to include future generations of humans.

But with this chapter we begin to see a more radical shift in the philosophical perspective. Paralleling the deontological critique of the utilitarian concern with consequences, some philosophers began to argue that we have direct ethical responsibilities to the natural world. In this view, we have responsibilities to the natural environment that do not depend on the consequences to humans. This shift can be identified as a shift from *anthropocentric* to *nonanthropocentric* theories of value.

5.2 EARLY ENVIRONMENTAL ETHICS: WHITE, PASSMORE, AND BLACKSTONE

These older traditions are represented symbolically by the passage from the book of Genesis in which the Judeo-Christian God creates all the living creatures and then says,

> Let us make man in our image and likeness to rule the fish in the sea, the birds in the sky, the cattle, all the wild animals on earth and all the reptiles that crawl upon the earth. So God created them in his own image and blessed them and said to them, "Be fruitful and multiply, and fill the earth and subdue it; and have dominion over the fish of the sea and over the birds of the air and over every living thing that moves upon the earth."[5]

The possibility that our own Western philosophical and theological traditions were at the root of our present environmental crisis is the focus of a classic essay by Lynn White, Jr.[6] In "The Historical Roots of Our Ecological Crisis," White argues that many of our contemporary scientific and technological approaches to nature have their roots in a particular Judeo-Christian perspective. That perspective, developing from biblical sources like the preceding passage taken from Genesis, is especially anthropocentric. In this view, humans occupy a privileged position in all creation. Being created in the "image and likeness of God," they have a moral and metaphysical uniqueness. Humans are separate from, and transcend, nature. God has created a moral hierarchy in which humans are superior to nature and have been commanded by God to subdue and dominate it.

White's claim is not that this is the only or the most reasonable interpretation of Christian theology. Indeed, he goes on to suggest an "alternative Christian view" that would support a much more harmonious relationship with nature. What is crucial is that this is the interpretation that many Jews and Christians *have given* to the biblical story of creation. Much of contemporary science and technology developed in a context in which this anthropocentric view of nature held sway. And this, according to White, lies at the root of our present ecological crisis.

At the same time these very traditions contributed much to philosophical theories that were being applied to solve environmental problems. In a very real sense, the tension between these two developments of mainstream Western philosophy creates the biggest challenge to traditional ethical theories. Can the dominant ethical traditions provide the resources to resolve environmental controversies? A good example of this ambiguity can be found in one of the first book-length philosophical examinations of environmental issues, John Passmore's *Man's Responsibility for Nature*.[7]

With an image that characterizes much of applied ethics, Passmore understood his own philosophical role in terms first used by John Locke. In identifying issues and clarifying and analyzing arguments, the ethicist is "employed as an under-labourer in clearing ground a little and removing some of the rubbish that lies in the way to knowledge." The first role of the philosopher was to dispose of unhelpful, unreasonable, or dangerous alternatives. Among the "rubbish" to be removed, Passmore placed all views that call for the abandonment of the "Western tradition," including "mysticism," the "nature as sacred" view, and animal rights.

Nevertheless, Passmore recognized the paradoxical character of his appeal to Western traditions. On the one hand, he acknowledges that the dominant Western tradition "denied that man's relationship with nature is governed by any moral considerations whatsoever." In this tradition, man was the "despot" who ruled over nature with "arrogance" and "hubris" and who treated nature as mere wax to be molded in whatever manner man desired (see Chapter 11 for a discussion of the sexist language). On the other hand, Passmore believed that the Western tradition contained the "seeds" for an ethically appropriate relationship with nature:

> The traditional moral teaching of the west, Christian or utilitarian, has always taught men, however, that they ought not so to act as to injure their neighbors. And we have now discovered that the disposal of wastes into sea or air, the destruction of ecosystems, the procreation of large families, the depletion of resources, constitute injury to fellow-men, present and future. To that extent, conventional morality, without any supplementation whatsoever, suffices to justify our ecological concern.[8]

Thus the call for a "new set of moral principles" was "not entirely wrong-headed." However, what is needed is "not so much a 'new ethic' as a more general adherence to a perfectly familiar ethic." For example, Passmore concluded that the ethical problems associated with pollution were not "overwhelming" but involved applying the generally accepted principle that "nobody ought to poison his neighbor." He also believed that the primary causes of our ecological disasters are "greed and short-sightedness," problems that can be overcome with an "old-fashioned procedure, thoughtful action."

For the most part, Passmore's work followed the standard applied ethics model. Careful philosophical analysis had much to offer to environmental controversies. However, one aspect of his analysis did call for a major extension of modern Western ethics. Lamenting the materialistic greed of consumerist societies, Passmore calls for a more "sensuous" attitude toward the world. The "puritan attack" on sensuousness, which he traces from Plato through Augustine and the Protestant Church to the modern Western world, leads to a denial of the beauty and love of nature. The "new ethic" demanded by the environmental crisis must be one in which aesthetic value plays a prominent role. The denial of sensuousness contributes to the environmental threats caused by the population explosion by "restricting the publicizing of birth control methods and condemning all sexual relationships which do not have procreation as their aim." It also fosters an easy acceptance of environmental degradation:

> A more sensuous society could never have endured the desolate towns, the dreary and dirty houses, the uniquely ugly chapels, the slag heaps, the filthy rivers, the junk yards which constitute the 'scenery' of the post-industrial West. . . . Only if men can first learn to look sensuously at the world will they learn to care for it.[9]

To many philosophers like Passmore, standard ethical theory did contain the resources for articulating new environmental rights. Another early attempt at extending standard ethical theories was developed by William Blackstone.[10] Contrasting those things that we merely *desire* with those things to which we have *rights*, Blackstone argued for recognition of a new human right, the "right to a livable environment."

To provide a context for this discussion, let us return to the framework presented in Chapter 3. One way to look at environmental problems is to view them as involving conflicting interests. One side (for example, Walt Disney Enterprises) prefers one thing while another side (for example, the Sierra Club) prefers something else. The challenge to public policymakers is to resolve these conflicts in fair and impartial ways.

The economic model resolves the conflict by treating all the competing preferences as equally deserving to be satisfied. The goal therefore is to satisfy an optimal number of these preferences. That is, the resolution of conflict is accomplished on quantitative grounds—more is better.

On the other hand, someone like Mark Sagoff would argue that environmental conflicts should be settled on qualitative grounds.

We need to make a political and ethical judgment that some preferences are more worthy of being satisfied than others. Not all interests are equal, and some deserve special consideration.

Unfortunately, as Sagoff admits, it is notoriously difficult to articulate and defend such value judgments. The relativist challenge
remains in the background: "Who are you to say that what you want
is more valuable than what I want?"

Traditionally, the concept of a moral "right" functions to protect
certain important interests from being sacrificed for a net increase in
the overall good. When my wants conflict with your wants, the
market goal of seeking the optimal satisfaction of wants is attractive
as long as the conflict does not involve rights. For example, if you
want to dump toxic wastes on your property that is adjacent to my
home we have more than merely a conflict of wants. In this case,
what you *want* conflicts with my *rights*. On this view, rights "trump"
mere desires and should not be sacrificed, even if doing so would
maximize the overall good.

In Passmore's view, standard ethical theory has the resources to
handle such situations. But to other philosophers the changing environmental conditions of our world make certain interests that were
not previously recognized as centrally important, now crucially important. The interest in clean air and water, in preserving dwindling
wilderness areas, may be important today in a way that they were
not a generation ago. They may have become so important that they
now deserve protection by moral rights.

Blackstone's approach adopted a standard *deontological* defense of
human rights similar to the Kantian view described in Chapter 2. He
defended the general view that there are universal and inalienable
human rights. These rights entail a "correlative duty or obligation"
on the part of other people either to act or refrain from acting in
certain ways. Our moral duties, in turn, limit our own liberties and
the exercise of certain other rights. Thus, to use a well-worn example, the liberties that follow from my property rights to a hunting
knife are restricted by those duties that I owe you as a result of your
right to life; that is, I cannot stab you with this knife.

The question that arose from this general framework was "Is there
a human right to a livable environment?" Blackstone argued that
there was. In this view, human rights are possessed by each person
"in virtue of the fact that he is human and in virtue of the fact that
those rights are essential in permitting him to live a human life (that
is, in permitting him to fulfill his capacities as a rational and free
being)."[11]

Blackstone further argued that none of those basic human rights that follow from our nature as free and rational beings—equality, liberty, happiness, life, and property—can be realized without a safe, healthy, and livable environment. Thus, a right to a livable environment can be defended as necessary to fulfilling a human life. And since a livable environment is equally necessary to all humans, there is "no relevant grounds for excluding any human the opportunity" to live this life.

Accordingly, we have a fairly standard philosophical framework. Human rights follow from basic interests that we have in virtue of our nature as free and rational agents. They are defended as being necessary for fulfilling our natural human capacities and on the grounds that there is no relevant basis for denying these rights to anyone; that is, they can be universalized. But how is this a new human right? Blackstone reasoned that "changing environmental conditions" require us to restrict traditional freedoms and rights, especially property rights, in the name of both the public welfare and equality. Thus "what in the past had been properly regarded as freedoms and rights (given what seemed to be unlimited natural resources and no serious pollution problems) can no longer be so construed."[12] When the traditional ethical and political framework of natural rights is applied to the new environmental reality, some traditional rights must be modified and some new ones created.

Several challenges can be raised to Blackstone's position, however. It can be argued that talk of a "new right" is not very useful and is true only in a trivial sense. At best, this right to a livable environment is a shorthand way of talking about more fundamental rights such as life, liberty, or property. If I dump toxic wastes into a river I have caused harms to, or violated the rights of, people living downstream from me. Standard property rights would seem sufficient to handle this issue. If I pollute the groundwater you drink or the air you breathe, I have harmed you in fairly standard sorts of ways. The generally accepted principle of which Passmore spoke, that "nobody ought to be allowed to poison his neighbor," suggests that talk of a right to a livable environment is unnecessary. In fact, this new right might even be detrimental to the environmental cause by creating a new layer of rights that hides the real harms caused by pollution and environmental destruction. An expansion of the number of rights might make it more rather than less difficult to specify the ethical and legal harms of pollution.

Another criticism holds that when properly understood, rights entail only *negative* and not *positive* duties. My duty that follows from your right to life involves only the negative duty not to kill you, it does not entail the positive duty that I supply you with all that you need to live, for example. From this perspective, the "right" to a livable environment is either unnecessary or it requires too much of others. If it is understood as a *negative* right—for example, the right not to be harmed by pollution or more generally the right not to have my well-being threatened by your environmental actions—then it does nothing ethically or legally that is not already done by standard ethical and legal concepts. If it is understood as a *positive* right, implying a duty on the part of others to provide or produce a clean environment, then, like education or health care perhaps, it is a desirable state of affairs but not a right. Serious challenges could be raised about the extent of other people's duties that would follow from the positive right to a livable environment. Are my rights violated whenever anyone drives a car and thereby pollutes the air for example? Or whenever anyone uses pesticides to grow vegetables? Or disposes sewerage sludge in the ocean? Surely this would result in a proliferation of rights and duties so great as to paralyze much of modern life.

There are of course responses to these concerns. A defender of the right to a livable environment might argue that this right involves only certain minimal and basic duties on the part of others. A parallel might be drawn to education or health care for example. The right to health care need not imply a universal right to any and all medical procedures, such as cosmetic surgery, but it should include a right to emergency care. A right to education need not imply a right to free tuition for a graduate degree at a private university, but it might imply free public education through high school. So, too, a right to a livable environment need not imply a right to pristine and pure air and water, but it would prohibit a laissez-faire policy toward dumping of toxic wastes, polluting the oceans with municipal garbage and sewerage, the burning of high-sulfur coal, and so forth.

A deeper criticism of this approach is reflected in the work of some philosophers who reject as meaningless the very notion of rights. Jeremy Bentham, for example, claimed that talk of rights was "nonsense" and of natural rights as "nonsense on stilts." The contemporary philosopher Alasdair MacIntyre suggests that we have as little reason for believing in rights as we have for believing in witches and unicorns.[13] Examining this debate is far beyond our concerns here. Nevertheless, these challenges can provide the opportunity to reflect on the implication of claiming new environmental rights.

Critics who reject rights seem to miss one of the most important functions that rights perform. By identifying something as a right, we are giving it a status as a centrally important human interest. Rights *are* distinct from merely desirable states of affairs in that they are more central and more important to human well-being. We should not think of rights, even "natural rights," as something "out there" to be discovered or recognized (as "self-evident"). Rights are human creations that function to protect certain human interests from being sacrificed too easily, if at all.[14] In this way, Blackstone's call for a "new right" is a summons for us to recognize how very important a clean environment is to human well-being. It is a proclamation that past practices that pollute, exploit, and degrade the environment can no longer be tolerated if we value human well-being. In this sense, environmental challenges have extended ethics into new areas.

5.3 MORAL STANDING

As we witnessed in the last chapter, environmental issues provoked philosophers to extend ethical concepts beyond their traditional boundaries. To develop a philosophically adequate account of energy or population policy, for example, philosophers were required to consider the moral status of something other than presently living human beings. The remainder of this chapter examines further extensions of ethics that require consideration not only of our duties *regarding* objects in our natural environment, but also of our duties *to* these objects.

Consider the issue of carbon dioxide pollution. In standard ethical views, this would be wrong if it harmed other human beings, perhaps by threatening their health or property. If standard ethical practice did not adequately capture the harms caused by pollution, we could argue, as William Blackstone did, for a recognition of some new environmental rights. When we discover that some of the harmful effects of carbon dioxide pollution might not occur for generations, ethical concepts such as duties and rights were extended to include future generations. This extension gave future people a *moral standing* that they did not have under more traditional ethical theories. We can identify the practice of extending moral standing to include future humans or to develop new human rights as *anthropocentric extensionism*. Ethics was extended beyond traditional boundaries, but only human beings continued to possess moral standing. Our duties—for example, not to pollute—were duties *regarding* the environment, but they were not duties *to* the environment.

In this respect, Lynn White's interpretation of the Genesis story of creation also describes an anthropocentric view of moral standing. Human beings, and only human beings, have moral standing because they were created in the image and likeness of God.

I now begin to consider nonanthropocentric extensions of ethics. That is, I examine attempts to extend ethics and give moral standing to things other than human beings. Candidates for moral standing include animals, plants, species, nonliving natural objects such as mountains, rivers, wilderness areas, and even the earth itself. Throughout these debates, two fundamental positions emerge: (1) a defense of the extension of moral standing to include animals and other natural objects; and (2) the belief that these extensions are too outlandish and that traditional ethical concepts are sufficient to address environmental concerns.

One final preliminary comment concerning terminology should be made at this point. The general concern in this chapter is with our duties *to* the natural environment. As you will see, much of the discussion is in terms of the "rights" of animals, trees, wilderness, and so on. However, not every philosopher is willing to attribute rights in every case where we have duties. For example, some philosophers say that although we have duties to future generations, it makes little sense to say of people who do not exist that they possess rights or anything else for that matter. More generally, utilitarians reject talk of rights, although they too are willing to talk about duties. For this reason although many philosophers speak in terms of rights, it is preferable to think in terms of "moral standing" and "moral considerability" when we examine our duties to the natural environment. These more general terms include, but are not limited to, cases in which animals or trees are said to have rights. The general philosophical question is "What things have a moral claim on us such that we have a duty to consider them in our moral deliberations?" Who and what *counts*, morally? On what grounds do we recognize (or attribute) moral standing?

With the question phrased in this way, we can recognize that many other contemporary moral problems and public policy debates are located at the boundaries of moral standing. The abortion debate is often focused on the moral status of the fetus: "Is a fetus a moral person? Does it have rights?" Many debates in medical ethics concern euthanasia and treatment of seriously impaired patients. These issues force us to consider the moral status of patients in irreversible comas, patients who are brain-dead, frozen embryos, and severely impaired infants. We also have seen how these boundaries are further stretched by concerns for future generations. Thus, in pursuing the question of our duties to the natural environment, it is helpful to begin by examining a more fundamental philosophical issue: Where do we draw the boundaries of moral consideration? Who and what should have moral standing? On what grounds do we make these decisions?

5.4 PHILOSOPHERS AND MORAL STANDING

It is useful to set a historical context for these discussions, to remind us how far traditional ethics is being extended. Chapter 2 suggested that the natural law tradition possessed resources that could make it particularly relevant to environmental issues. Nevertheless, the two philosophers most associated with this tradition defended views that exhibited little sympathy to the moral status of natural objects. Aristotle tells us that

> plants exist for the sake of animals . . . all other animals exist for the sake of man, tame animals for the use he can make of them as well as for the food they provide; and as for wild animals, most though not all of these can be used for food and are useful in other ways; clothing and tools can be made out of them. If then we are right in believing that nature makes nothing without some end in view, nothing to no purpose, it must be that nature has made all things specifically for the sake of man.[15]

Sixteen centuries later, Thomas Aquinas picked up this issue and placed it in a theological context.

> We refute the error of those who claim that it is a sin for man to kill brute animals. For animals are ordered to man's use in the natural course of things, according to divine providence. Consequently, man uses them without any injustice, either by killing them or employing them in any other way. For this reason, God said to Noah: "As the green herbs, I have delivered all flesh to you."[16]

Aristotle and Aquinas could hold these positions because they believed that only human beings (and perhaps angels and gods) had moral standing. Human beings had moral standing because they possessed an intellect (or "soul") capable of thinking and choosing. Since animals and other living beings lacked this capacity, they could not be considered morally relevant in themselves. Any duties we had regarding nature were explainable in terms of the needs or interests of human beings.

Kantian ethical theory is only a little less restricted. There is some evidence that Kant himself was sympathetic to duties to future generations, and the categorical imperative itself seems relevant to several environmental issues.[17] Nonetheless, in his *Lectures on Ethics*, Kant is quite clear in saying that our duties regarding nature are indirect; for example, duties *to* other humans. More generally, the Kantian analysis that limits rights and moral standing to "subjects" and "ends," as distinct from "objects" and "means," strongly reinforces the view that only humans have moral standing. In this view, only autonomous beings, beings capable of free and rational action, are moral beings. Again, because it was believed that other living things lacked this capacity, they could be excluded from moral consideration. Nonhuman animals and plants were the clearest example of "objects."

Another view that proved quite influential is traceable to the seventeenth-century philosopher René Descartes. Descartes argued that all reality was reducible to two fundamental types of substances, "minds" and "bodies." The realm of the mental included all thinking, sensation, and consciousness. The realm of the body included all things physical and spatial. This physical realm was seen as purely mechanistic and devoid of consciousness. While not denying the animals and plants were alive, Descartes nonetheless denied that they were anything other than machines, or "thoughtless brutes." In the Cartesian view, therefore, consciousness is the criterion of moral standing. Anything not conscious is a mere physical thing and can be treated without concern for its own well-being.

One of the few philosophers who does not unquestioningly exclude animals from moral consideration is Jeremy Bentham. In a passage famous because it is such an exception to the mainstream of Western philosophy, Bentham suggests that

> The day *may come*, when the rest of the animal creation may acquire those rights which never could have been withholden from them but by the hand of tyranny. The French have already discovered that the blackness of the skin is no reason why a human being should be abandoned without redress to the caprice of a tormentor. It may come one day to be recognized that the number of the legs, the villosity of the skin, or the termination of the *os sacrum*, are reasons equally insufficient for abandoning a sensitive being to the same fate. What else is it that could trace the insuperable line? Is it the faculty of reason, or perhaps the faculty of discourse? But a full-grown horse or dog is beyond comparison a more rational, as well as more conversable animal, than an infant of a day, or a week, or even a month old. But suppose they were otherwise, what would it avail? The question is not, Can they *reason*? nor Can they *talk*? but Can they *suffer*?[18]

True to his utilitarian views, Bentham expanded the realm of moral considerability to include all things that have the capacity to feel pleasure and pain. We will see a view very similar to Bentham's developed and defended when we consider the writing of Peter Singer.

To summarize, for most philosophers in the Western tradition human beings and only human beings have moral standing. Most often, the criteria used to draw the boundaries of the moral realm are in some sense *intellectual*; for example, the ability to think or reason in some particular way. As a result, there are two strategies open to critics. One could reject the *philosophical* basis for the exclusion of animals by arguing, for example, that rationality is an inappropriate criterion for moral standing. One might argue instead, following Bentham's suggestion, that sensation should be the criterion for moral standing. Or, one could accept the philosophical basis but deny the conclusions drawn from it. With this approach, one could argue that rationality is an appropriate criterion but that animals, at least certain "higher" mammals, do in fact have this capacity. Examples of both strategies are seen in the following pages.

5.5 THE RECENT DEBATE

What, then, is the proper relationship between humans and other living things? One of the earliest contemporary discussions of the moral standing of animals and other living beings was Joel Feinberg's "The Rights of Animals and Unborn Generations."[19] Feinberg's essay was quite influential, and a brief review of his argument provides a valuable introduction to the more recent debates.

Feinberg begins with a common understanding of rights as involving a claim *to* some good, *against* some other person (who would therefore have some duty), and as being socially recognized in some way, such as by legal rules or an "enlightened conscience." Feinberg's strategy is to begin with clear and unproblematic cases of moral standing and seek to pull from these clear cases a criterion that best explains our intuitions. We then can apply this criterion to more problematic cases:

> In the familiar cases of rights, the claimant is a competent adult human being. . . . Normal adult human beings, then, are obviously the sorts of beings of whom rights can meaningfully be predicated. . . . On the other hand, it is absurd to say that rocks can have rights, not because rocks are morally inferior things unworthy of rights (that statement makes no sense either), but because rocks belong to a category of

entities of whom rights cannot be meaningfully predicated. . . . In between the clear cases of rocks and normal human beings, however, is a
spectrum of less obvious cases, including some bewildering borderline
ones. Is it meaningful or conceptually possible to ascribe rights to our
dead ancestors? to individual animals? to whole species of animals? to
planets? to idiots and madmen? to fetuses? to generations yet unborn?[20]

Turning to the case of individual animals, Feinberg recognizes
that most people acknowledge that we have a duty not to mistreat
or be cruel to animals. Some might argue that this duty derives from
a duty to other humans; that is, to those who are offended by the
mistreatment of animals. Others might argue that this duty is derived from a duty to ourselves; that is, a duty to avoid situations in
which we might develop such character traits as callousness or cruelty. Feinberg argued that these explanations were disingenuous,
that surely animals themselves were the direct beneficiaries of this
duty. We can owe a duty *to* animals, according to Feinberg, because
animals have *interests* that can be promoted or harmed by our actions. For something to be said to have rights, this thing must have
interests, or a "sake" or a "good" of its own to be protected by
rights. A mere thing, even a very precious thing like the Taj Mahal or
a "beautiful natural wilderness," cannot be said to have rights because they cannot be said to have any interests of their own.
   Feinberg's view is focused on the question of rights, rather than
on the more general question of moral standing. But the point is
significant. In order to meaningfully say that we have an obligation
to some object, rather than merely an obligation *regarding* that object, the object of our obligations must have some welfare or good of
its own. If I have a duty to something, it must be the case that it
would be good for this thing that I fulfill my duty. But to say that
something has a "good" (or a "bad") is to say that it has *interests*.
For example, it is in a dog's interest not to be tortured. I can have a
duty not to torture animals if it can be said that it is good *for the dog*
not to be tortured. But what things can have interests? In Feinberg's
view, only things with a "conative" life, with "conscious wishes,
desires, hopes; or urges or impulses; or unconscious drives, aims, or
goals; or latent tendencies, direction of growth, and natural fulfill-
ments" can be said to have interests.[21]
   Feinberg then applies this criterion to various objects of environmental concern. Individual animals, at least those "higher animals"
can be said to have rights, although those of "lower orders" can be
treated as mere pests. Plants cannot be said to have rights because

they lack the "rudimentary cognitive equipment" necessary to possess interests. Neither can we say that species have rights, despite the fact that we might attribute rights to individual members of that species.

Thus, for example, we might say that an individual dolphin has an interest in not being drowned in fishing nets and therefore might be said to have a right not to be so killed. But the species dolphin has no corresponding right to survive. We might have a duty not to kill an individual animal, but we have no duty to a species to protect it from extinction. Our duties can only be to individual beings that possess the appropriate "cognitive equipment."

Finally, since we can say that future generations will have interests with as much certainty as we can say that they' will exist, it makes sense for us to talk about their rights as well.

Feinberg's essay broke new ground in many ways. Read narrowly, it offered merely a conceptual, or "metaethical," analysis of what can and cannot meaningfully be said about rights. Yet this essay also symbolizes a liberation of sorts for philosophical ethics. Environmental concerns encouraged philosophers to expand greatly the realm of moral considerability. Essentially for the first time philosophers considered the possibility that beings other than humans deserve moral consideration for their own sake, not merely because humans happen to be interested in them.

5.6 DO TREES HAVE STANDING?

Before turning to more systematic attempts to extend ethical consideration to animals, we should consider another early attempt at moral extensionism. Christopher Stone argued to extend legal, if not moral, rights to "forests, oceans, rivers and other so-called 'natural objects' in the environment—indeed, to the natural environment as a whole."[22] Unlike many defenders of animals' rights, Stone based his claim for standing less on the characteristics of humans and more on the nature of legal rights.

The occasion for Stone's defense of the rights of natural objects was the legal dispute concerning Mineral King Valley. The Sierra Club had filed suit to prevent Walt Disney Enterprises from building a large ski resort in the Sierra Mountains. This suit was rejected in California courts because the Sierra Club lacked "standing." That is, it could not show that members of the Club would suffer any legally recognized harm by the development of Mineral King Valley. As this case made its way on appeal to the U.S. Supreme Court, Stone wrote an essay titled "Should Trees have Standing?" Stone hoped to support the Sierra Club's case by arguing that the natural objects like trees and mountainsides that would be destroyed in this development should be given legal standing. The Sierra Club could then be seen as legal guardians of these rights.[23]

Stone's analysis began with an examination of the nature of legal rights. Implicitly rejecting the view that rights are somehow "out there" in nature to be discovered, Stone emphasized the evolutionary development of rights. Rights exist when they are recognized by "some public authoritative body [that] is prepared to give some amount of review" to violations of that right. Citing Darwin's observation that "the history of man's moral development has been a continual extension in the objects of his 'social instinctions and sympathies,'" Stone shows how the recognition of legal rights is witness to a parallel development. Rights function to protect rights-holders from injury and the list of rights-holders has been continually expanded. He reminds us that at one time only landowning white adult males enjoyed full legal rights. Legal standing now includes nonlandowners, women, blacks, Native Americans, and such "things" as corporations, trusts, cities, and nations. It is time to extend this protection to natural objects.

More is needed to establish the existence of rights than merely the recognition by some authoritative body.

> As I shall use the term "holder of legal rights," each of three additional criteria must be satisfied. All three, one will observe, go towards making a thing *count* jurally—to have a legally recognized worth and dignity of its own right, and not merely to serve as a means to benefit "us." . . . They are, first, that the thing can institute legal actions *at its behest*; second, that in determining the granting of legal relief, the court must take *injury to it* into account; and, third, that relief must run to the *benefit of it*.[24]

All three criteria can be satisfied by the proposal that trees and other natural objects be given legal rights.

How can natural objects "institute legal actions" on its own behalf? Keeping in mind the legal standing of corporations and mentally incompetent humans, Stone argues that a guardian or "conservator" or "trustee" could be appointed to represent the interests of natural objects. Just as a comatose person has a legal guardian, for example, or a corporation a board of trustees, so also forests, streams, and mountains could be legally represented by humans who are legally charged with representing their interests.

But do natural objects have interests that (1) we can agree on, and (2) that can be harmed in a legally recognizable way? Stone thinks they do. Again keeping in mind the parallel with corporations, Stone believes we can "know" the interests of and acknowledge the injuries to natural objects with at least as much certainty as we do in corporate cases: "The guardian-attorney for a smog-endangered stand of pine could venture with more confidence that his client wants the smog stopped, than the directors of a corporation can assert that 'the corporation' wants dividends declared."[25]

Similarly, Stone believes that we can give meaning to the concept of a legal "remedy" that can provide relief to the injured natural object. As a guiding principle, we could adopt a common legal standard and aim to make the environment "whole." Just as when a person is injured in an automobile accident and is compensated for medical costs to return that person to health, so we could require the responsible party to compensate the natural object by returning it to health. In this sense, environmental "health" would be the state in which it existed before the injury.

Let us consider how this proposal might work. During the summer of 1991, a train derailment dumped 20,000 gallons of pesticide into the Sacramento River in California. This resulted in the death of virtually all living things along a 40-mile stretch of the river. Unlike the lingering effects of an oil spill, however, the river flushed itself clean and was soon capable of supporting life once again.

Under present legal guidelines, the door is open for injured humans to file for damages against the Southern Pacific Railroad. Landowners downriver, businesses who depend on tourism and fishing, for example, might argue that they deserve to be compensated for certain losses. Under Stone's proposal, representatives of the river itself and the fish killed by the pesticide could also sue for damages. Thus not only would humans be compensated for their injuries, but the river itself should be "made whole"; that is, returned to its prederailment state.

There are, of course, challenges for this proposal to overcome. First, despite Stone's suggestions, it is not at all clear that we can agree on the interests of natural objects. For example, some believe that the Sacramento River should immediately be restocked with fish from hatcheries. Others argue that the river should be allowed to restock itself with wild fish swimming in from tributaries. Good reasons can be given to support either option. Which is in the best interests of the river?

A second challenge follows from this. Perhaps Stone's response would allow the river's guardians to make that decision in the same way that a legal guardian might decide what is best for an orphan child. But who should this guardian be? The Wilderness Society would have one view of the river's interests, a local fishing club another. Choosing the guardian will also be to choose the theory of "interests" that one ascribes to natural objects. Should the Sierra Club represent the interests of Mineral King Valley? Should a lumber company? Perhaps, as Mark Sagoff suggests, the mountain is tired of being undeveloped and would prefer to be represented by Walt Disney Enterprises.

None of this suggests that Stone's approach cannot work. But it does suggest that more work needs to be done to articulate and defend a view of nature's interests. Stone's proposal essentially relies on society reaching a consensus about the extension of legal standing to natural objects. It is, after all, something that needs to be "recognized" by a public body. But it would seem that this consensus can only be reached after the public has already reached a consensus about the nature and value of natural objects. This consensus, regrettably, is still to be achieved.

5.7 SUMMARY AND CONCLUSION

This chapter has examined a number of early attempts to extend ethical consideration to nonhumans. Many of these attempts challenged the mainstream approach to ethics, but they remained more suggestive than completely developed principles. By far the most sophisticated treatment of this question can be found in the works of those philosophers who turned their attention to the ethical status of animals. We turn now to those debates.

Notes

1. These estimates are given in Miller, *Environmental Science*, p. 354.
2. Edward O. Wilson, "Threats to Biodiversity." See also E. O. Wilson and Frances M. Peter, eds., *Biodiversity* (Washington, DC: National Academy Press, 1988).
3. Miller, p. 356.
4. These estimates are from Miller, chap. 15.
5. Genesis 1:26–29.
6. "The Historical Roots of our Ecological Crisis," by Lynn White, Jr., *Science*, 155 (March 1967): 1203–1207.
7. John Passmore, *Man's Responsibility for Nature* (New York: Scribner's, 1974).
8. Ibid., pp. 186–187.
9. Ibid., p. 189.
10. William Blackstone, "Ethics and Ecology," in William Blackstone, ed., *Philosophy and Environmental Crisis* (Athens: University of Georgia Press, 1974).
11. Ibid., p. 31.

12. Ibid., p. 32.

13. Alasdair MacIntyre, *After Virtue* (South Bend, IN: University of Notre Dame Press, 1981), p. 67.

14. For a more adequate treatment of how rights function as "trumps" over utilitarian benefits, see Ronald Dworkin, *Taking Rights Seriously* (Cambridge, MA: Harvard University Press, 1977).

15. Aristotle, *The Politics*, Bk. I, ch. 8, 1256b.

16. Thomas Aquinas, *Summa Contra Gentiles*, Bk. III, pt. II. See Genesis 9:2–3 for the command to Noah. See also Passmore, p. 6, for a brief discussion of Aquinas's views on this passage from Genesis. Passmore remains an excellent source for understanding the philosophical roots of the "man as despot" view.

17. See Passmore, chap. 4, for a discussion of Kant's concern for future generations and Annette Baier, "For the Sake of Future Generations," for further discussion of this issue.

18. Bentham, *Introduction to the Principles of Morals and Legislation*, Chap. XVII, sec. 1, footnote to paragraph 4. (Italics in the original.)

19. Joel Feinberg, "The Rights of Animals and Unborn Generations" in William Blackstone, ed., *Philosophy and Environmental Crisis* (Athens, GA: University of Georgia Press, 1974), pp. 43–68.

20. Ibid., p. 44.

21. Ibid., p. 49.

22. Christopher Stone, *Should Trees Have Standing? Towards Legal Rights for Natural Objects* (Los Altos, CA: Kaufmann, 1974), p. 9.

23. For a brief account of this history, see Roderick Nash, *The Rights of Nature* (Madison: University of Wisconsin Press, 1989), pp. 128–131.

24. Stone, p. 11.

25. Stone, p. 24.

Discussion Questions

1. The biblical story of creation speaks of a God who grants humans "dominion" over all other living things. Some have interpreted this to mean that humans rightfully may "dominate" or control other living things. Other biblical interpreters see in this passage a command to act as "stewards" or caretakers for other living things. What reasons can you see for either view?

2. There are many ways to explain legal prohibitions against abuse and torture of animals. List as many reasons for these prohibitions as you can. Do any of your reasons commit you to holding that animals have a moral standing in their own right?

3. Can nonliving natural objects have interests? What are the interests of Mineral King Valley? of the Sacramento River? Can certain things be said to be "good" for rivers, mountains, and forests?

4. Christopher Stone argues that trees should be granted legal standing. He suggests that trees and other natural objects should be awarded compensation when they are negligently harmed by humans. But how could a tree that is maliciously destroyed be compensated? At best, other trees,

perhaps of the same species, could be planted. But does this benefit the tree that was harmed? What deserves compensation, individual trees or species?

5. Try the following thought experiment concerning what objects have moral standing. Assume that competent adult human beings are placed at one end of a continuum and a rock at the other. Where along that continuum would you place the following: a child, a brain-dead adult, a fetus, a dolphin, a dog, an insect, an alien like *Star Trek*'s Mr. Spock, a species, a tree? Is there a single criterion that you have used either implicitly or explicitly?

For Further Reading

Roderick Nash, *The Rights of Nature* (Madison: University of Wisconsin Press, 1989), offers a historically informed argument for attributing rights to natural objects.

Eugene Hargrove, *Foundations of Environmental Ethics* (New York: Prentice-Hall, 1989), presents an aesthetic account of environmental values. See also Eugene Hargrove, ed., *Religion and Environmental Crisis* (Athens, GA: University of Georgia Press, 1986), for discussions of environmental theology.

Jay McDaniel, *Of God and Pelicans: A Theology of Reverence for Life* (Louisville, KY: Westminster Press, 1989), and Jay McDaniel, *Earth, Sky, Gods and Mortals: Developing an Ecological Spirituality* (Mystic, CN: Twenty-Third Publications, 1990) are solid contributions to a theological understanding of environmental issues.

Christopher Stone, *Earth and Other Ethics* (New York: Harper & Row, 1987) presents Stone's more recent environmental views.

6

Duties to Animals

CASE SIX

Animal Research and Factory Farming

The U.S. Environmental Protection Agency is charged with regulating such things as smokestack emission and the use of pesticides and many other potentially toxic chemicals. Likewise, the Food and Drug Administration must regulate consumer products to ensure that they will not harm the people who use them. To set standards and to determine whether or not some chemical is toxic, the EPA and the FDA must rely on the research conducted by scientists. Perhaps the most infamous procedure used in conducting toxicity research is the LD50 test—"lethal dose 50 percent." In a 1987 report, the director of the EPA's Toxicology Branch said that there were records of over 16,000 LD50 tests in the EPA's files.[1]

In LD50 tests, the substance being examined is administered to research animals in increasing doses to discover the level at which 50 percent of the animals will die from exposure to the substance. In most cases, before 50 percent die, all will be seriously poisoned and all will suffer. In the case of particularly toxic chemicals, the 50 percent level is reached with relatively low doses. Of course, this increases the poisoning of the remaining 50 percent. In the case of less toxic chemicals, like food additives and cosmetics, enormous quantities of the substance must be used before 50 percent of the animals die. These animals are force-fed and injected via feeding tubes or needles. Since the scientific validity of the tests requires that death be caused solely by the substance being tested, dying and suffering animals cannot be "humanely" put to death.

Due in large part to the protests of animal rights activists, the LD50 test is legally prohibited in some countries. Many companies involved in such research have suspended use of LD50 tests until alternative research methods can be developed. Nevertheless, we do not have to look far to discover many other cases in which animals are systematically mistreated and abused. To discover more suffering, we need only look at how food animals such as calves, pigs, and chickens are raised. In the words of Peter Singer, "It is here, on our dinner table and in our neighborhood super-market or butcher's shop, that we are brought into direct touch with the most extensive exploitation of other species that has ever existed."[2]

Singer's book, *Animal Liberation*, has done much to publicize the nature of modern "factory farming." We examine Singer's ethical analysis of these practices in some detail later. For now, let us just review briefly one well-known example, veal production.

Veal is the flesh of young calves. It tends to be an expensive cut of meat and therefore more likely found in restaurants and gour-met cooking than on the dinner tables of middle-class families. Veal is especially prized when it is very tender to chew and when it has a pink color. How does one produce animal flesh that is tender and pink?

First, the calves are taken from their mothers when they are just a few days old. To prevent exercise, which would develop mus-cles and therefore make the flesh less tender, these young calves are confined in small wooden stalls. The stalls are so small that the calf typically is unable either to turn around or even sit. The calf spends its entire life, perhaps sixteen weeks, confined to this stall.

Normal flesh is red because of the iron content of the blood that it contains. A cow gets iron from the grass and hay that it might otherwise eat. To prevent this, veal calves are systematically de-prived of a diet containing iron. They are, in other words, inten-tionally made anemic. Of course, if they become too anemic they would die, so a dietary balance is maintained. Just enough iron to keep them alive, but not enough so that their flesh and blood are red. All this is done despite the fact that the pink color adds nothing to the taste of veal.

To speed up the growth process and control the diet at the same time, veal calves are typically fed a liquid diet of powdered milk, vitamins, and growth-producing drugs. This may be all they eat in their entire lives. To ensure that the calves take in as much of this formula as possible, calves are denied water and are kept in warm buildings. Their only alternative is to turn to the formula to quench their thirst. As Singer concludes his description of this process,

> If the reader will recall that this whole laborious, wasteful, and painful process of veal raising exists for the sole purpose of pandering to people who insist on pale, soft veal, no further comment should be needed.[3]

6.1 INTRODUCTION

We could discuss many different arguments for why it is wrong to torture and kill animals for cosmetic research or for reasons of gourmet tastes. We can find many anthropocentric reasons to defend the position that we do have ethical duties *regarding* animals. After all, many people own animals and thus have property rights over them. Many people *care* about animals and thus would be affected by the mistreatment of them. Further, mistreating animals can have an adverse effect on the person doing the mistreatment. Such actions can make us callous and insensitive to suffering.

In short, animals are valued by people for a variety of reasons. Mistreating animals can deny or disrespect these values. But can we say that we owe any moral consideration directly to the animals themselves? Do they have moral standing? This question is one of the first ethical issues raised in connection with environmental concerns that received close and developed philosophical attention. We trace these discussions in what follows.

6.2 PETER SINGER AND THE ANIMAL LIBERATION MOVEMENT

Perhaps the person most associated with the extension of philosophical ethics to include animals is Peter Singer. For the past two decades, Singer has argued that our exclusion of animals from moral considerability is on a par with the earlier exclusions of blacks and women. Singer popularized the phrase "speciesism" to draw a parallel with racism and sexism.[4] Just as it is morally wrong to deny equal moral standing on the basis of race or sex, Singer argues that it is wrong to deny equal moral standing on the basis of species membership.

Singer begins his argument with a "fundamental presupposition" of moral theory, the "basic moral principle," that all interests are to be given equal consideration. Essentially this is the formal principle that any being that qualifies for moral standing "counts for one and none for more than one." Even racists and sexists can accept this principle; they would, however, deny that blacks or women have equal moral standing. Singer must therefore explain the criterion for inclusion. What characteristic qualifies a being for equal moral standing? Here Singer cites the passage from Bentham that we quoted earlier: "The question is not, Can they *reason*? nor Can they *talk*? but, Can they *suffer*?":

> The capacity for suffering and enjoyment is a *prerequisite for having interests at all*, a condition that must be satisfied before we can speak of interests in a meaningful way. It would be nonsense to say that it was not in the interests of a stone to be kicked along the road by a schoolboy. A stone does not have interests because it cannot suffer. Nothing that we can do to it could possibly make any difference to its welfare. The capacity for suffering and enjoyment is, however, not only necessary, but also sufficient for us to say that a being has interests—at an absolute minimum, an interest in not suffering. A mouse, for example, does have an interest in not being kicked along the road because it will suffer if it is.[5]

Like Joel Feinberg and Stone, discussed in the last chapter, Singer focuses on the concept of "interests" to explain moral standing. Unlike Feinberg and Stone, Singer is not concerned with using interests as a basis for attributing rights to animals. He is sympathetic to Bentham's dismissal of rights as "nonsense" or at least as only a shorthand way of speaking about moral protections. Nor does he turn to "cognitive" elements as the essential aspect of interests. In Singer's view, the capacity for suffering (and enjoyment) is all that is needed to establish that a being has interests.

Singer uses the term "sentience" to refer to the capacity to suffer and/or experience enjoyment. Sentience is *necessary* for having interests, in that an object without sentience—a rock, for example—cannot be said to have interests. But Singer also believes that sentience is *sufficient* for having interests. A being that is sentient has at least a minimal interest; that is, the interest in not suffering.

Because any and only sentient beings have interests, any and only sentient beings have moral standing. We are required to treat all sentient beings with equal moral consideration. This does not mean we are required to make no distinctions between humans and other animals. Humans are different from other animals. They have different interests. A "hard slap across the rump" of a horse causes relatively little pain and therefore is not particularly unethical. But this does not mean that the principle of equal consideration justifies an equally hard slap across the face of a child. Certain human mental capacities might cause humans to suffer more from certain actions and in other ways than would other animals. But the essential point is that the capacity to suffer and the amount of suffering is what determines specific moral requirements.

What are the implications of these views? Singer acknowledges that making comparisons between sufferings can be difficult, especially when these comparisons are made between species. Nevertheless, if we restricted ourselves to only those cases in which severe animal suffering was condoned for the sake of mere human convenience,

> we would be forced to make radical changes in our treatment of animals that would involve our diet, the farming methods we use, experimental procedures in many fields of science, our approach to wildlife and to hunting, trapping and the wearing of furs, and areas of entertainment like circuses, rodeos, and zoos. As a result, a vast amount of suffering would be avoided.[6]

As the references to Bentham and the emphasis on minimizing suffering suggest, Singer's approach is basically utilitarian. There is an account of intrinsic good (enjoyment and the absence of suffering), and our ethical duty is to minimize the overall amount of suffering. Before we examine the implications of Singer's views, let us turn to an alternative, nonutilitarian defense of animals' rights.

6.3 TOM REGAN AND ANIMAL RIGHTS

As Peter Singer has defended the moral standing of animals on utilitarian grounds, Tom Regan has developed a rights-based defense of animals. Regan explicitly argues that some animals have rights and that these rights imply strong moral obligations on our part. Like Singer, Regan condemns on ethical grounds a wide variety of human activities that affect animals. These activities include the use of animals in scientific and commercial research, the use of animals as food, and recreational uses of animals that include sport hunting, zoos, and pets. Regan believes that these practices are unethical, not because of the pain and suffering they cause, but in principle. They violate animals' rights by denying the intrinsic ethical value possessed by some animals. To understand this view, let us return to the example of veal production.

Imagine that veal producers are convinced by Singer's criticisms and change their methods to minimize suffering. The calves get some exercise, fresh air, a balanced diet, and perhaps are even regularly groomed. Like the cows in the old advertisements, these are contented calves. Imagine also that human taste for veal has increased so that for many consumers there is a real felt desire for veal. Consumers suffer, not much but many do, when they are denied veal.

In such a situation, it could be argued that Singer's utilitarian position allows the continuation of the veal industry. With these imagined changes in the farming practices of the veal industry, the calves suffer minimally, while human enjoyment increases notably.

A defender of Singer's position could dispute this example, of course. However, the dispute would likely involve specific calculations of relative suffering, pain, and enjoyments. That is, we would need to measure and dispute the consequences of the alternative practices. In this view, raising, slaughtering, and eating the calf for food is not wrong in principle, it is only wrong when the suffering it causes outweighs the resultant enjoyment. Regan's view picks up at this point:

> The forlornness of the veal calf is pathetic—heart wrenching. . . . But the fundamental wrong isn't the pain, isn't the suffering, isn't the deprivation. These compound what's wrong. Sometimes—often—they make it much worse. But they are not the fundamental wrong. The fundamental wrong is the system that allows us to view animals as *our resources*, here for us—to be eaten, or surgically manipulated, or put in our cross hairs for sport or money.[7]

How does Regan explain the principle that underlies this view? To understand this, we should consider why it would be wrong to subject humans to similar treatment. Suppose someone were to follow Jonathan Swift's "Modest Proposal" and treat disadvantaged young children as food. These children would be raised in a manner that kept them content and relatively free from suffering. However, at a certain point in their lives (Swift proposed a well-nursed one-year-old) these humans would be slaughtered, albeit painlessly, and "stewed, roasted, baked, or boiled." Presumably we would all acknowledge the moral evil of these activities even if the overall balance of enjoyment over suffering were increased. Why?

Regan argues that the answer to this lies in the fact that we believe humans possess a certain type of value, what he calls "inherent value." We have seen this concept before in the discussion of ethical theories. Essentially, to have inherent value is to have value independently of the interests, needs, or uses of anyone else. Inherent value is to have value in and of oneself. It is to be contrasted with instrumental value, in which a thing's value is a function of how it might be used by, or what it might mean to, others. Objects with inherent value are ends in themselves, goals, not merely means to some other end. It is wrong to treat humans (and, as it will turn out, some animals) as mere means to other ends—even if this includes the end of maximizing the net amount of enjoyment over suffering—because to do so denies to these humans the inherent value that they possess.

So far, this approach sounds very similar to the Kantian tradition in ethics, and clearly it is greatly influenced by that tradition. But Regan denies that the basis for inherent value lies in the capacity for autonomous action. To see why, we need to introduce a distinction between *moral agents* and *moral patients*.[8]

In our discussion so far concerning moral standing, we have taken competent adult human beings as the clearest example of things with standing. As we have seen, philosophers have disagreed over the criterion used to establish standing, but they all agree that competent adult humans have it. These adults are full *moral agents* because they are free and rational. As such, they can understand their duties, they can choose whether or not to act on them, and they can be held responsible for those choices.

This characterization raises familiar problems with noncompetent or nonadult humans however. Infants and mentally incapacitated or comatose individuals lack the ability to understand and choose. Therefore, they cannot be said to be *moral agents*; they have no duties and cannot be held responsible for what they do or fail to do. Indeed, they are *moral patients*. This means that they have moral standing—we cannot do just anything to or with them—even though they are not full moral agents. They cannot *act* morally or not, but they can be *acted on* morally or immorally.

When we understand this distinction and recognize that many things that are not full moral agents nonetheless have moral standing, we can discover what is missing from many of the standard discussions of moral standing. Too many philosophers have focused exclusively on moral agents in establishing the criterion of moral standing. The class of all things with moral standing includes *both* agents and patients. We need to ask what is it about moral agents *and* moral patients that explains their inherent value. Why is it wrong, in principle, to treat either agents or patients as food, targets, entertainment, or slaves?

Regan's answer is that they are *"subjects-of-a-life."* Having a life, as opposed to merely being alive, involves a fairly complex set of characteristics:

> To be the subject-of-a-life . . . involves more than merely being alive and more than merely being conscious. To be the subject-of-a-life is to . . . have beliefs and desires; perception, memory, and a sense of the future, including their own future; an emotional life together with feelings of pleasure and pain; preference and welfare-interests; the ability to initiate action in pursuit of their desires and goals; a psychophysical identity over time; and an individual welfare in the sense that their experiential life fares well or ill for them, independently of their utility for others.[9]

Regan argues that justice demands that we treat all individuals with inherent value in ways that respect that value. This "respect principle" identifies Regan's views as an *egalitarian* theory of justice. Justice demands that we treat individuals with respect. Since inherent value is not reducible to any other type of value, we fail to treat individuals who have inherent value with the respect deserved when we treat them as if they are valuable only as a means to some other end. Individuals with inherent value thus have the *right* to be treated with the same respect due to all individuals with inherent value.

It remains for Regan to conclude that animals can be subjects of a life. At least some mammals possess the characteristics required for "having a life." These animals therefore have inherent value, and justice demands that we treat them with respect. Minimally, this means that we have a strong *prima facie* obligation not to harm them. (Regan admits that this obligation can sometimes be overridden. But it can be overridden only in the same sorts of cases in which we would override the rights of an innocent human being.)

6.4 ETHICAL IMPLICATIONS OF ANIMAL WELFARE

Both Singer and Regan have written extensively on the ethical implications of their views. Although each has written on a variety of specific issues, I limit discussion here to four topics.[10] First, both would argue that we have an obligation, as a society, to dissolve commercial animal farming. None of the considerations that might be used to defend animal farming—taste, nutrition, convenience, efficiency, and property rights—can justify treating animals as food.

Similar arguments would not suffice to justify eating humans, and they cannot suffice to defend eating animals. Individually, we have an ethical duty to be vegetarians. As citizens, we should outlaw these practices.

Likewise, sport hunting and trapping is unjust. Killing and often torturing animals for sport and entertainment is more than cruel, it is a serious injustice. Likewise, abusing and mistreating animals for any form of human entertainment is wrong. Just as it was cruel and vicious for Romans to use Christians for a particularly brutal form of entertainment, it is wrong for us to use animals in zoos, rodeos, and the like.

A third issue concerns the use of animals in science and research. As we saw in the case of the LD50 case, experimentation on animal subjects can be especially harsh. We ordinarily would conclude that experimenting on human subjects who have not given their consent is unjust at best and barbarous at worst. People have been convicted as war criminals for such behavior. So, too, should we judge experimentation on animals.

Finally, like Feinberg, Regan and Singer do not support moral standing for species. Regan's view protects individual animals from harm but does not recognize species as having rights. An individual animal can be a subject-of-a-life, but a species cannot. Likewise, for Singer, although individual animals can suffer pain, a species itself cannot. Thus, although these views support efforts to save endangered species, they do so only because the remaining members of that species, as individuals, have a moral standing that we must respect. In this context, Regan raises an issue that becomes the focus of important discussions later in this text. Let me introduce this issue within the context of a general review of philosophical challenges to the views of Singer and Regan.

6.5 CRITICISMS

Before moving on to even further proposed extensions of the scope of moral considerability, let's step back at this point and consider some of the criticisms raised against the animal liberation and animal rights view. The work of Singer and Regan generated a significant response among philosophers, much of it critical. Many of these criticisms followed familiar lines.

For example, some philosophers, including Regan, challenged the utilitarian basis of Singer's program. Singer, after all, made no *in-principle* case against causing animals to suffer. Other philosophers developed the debate about attributing rights to nonhumans. Some argued that the concept of "interests" was so vague that it would allow tractors and buildings to have moral standing.[11] Although a complete review of these debates would take us too far afield, several challenges will help make the transition into the following chapters.

One type of criticism directed against Singer calls to mind the measurement problems discussed earlier, in the introduction to utilitarianism. On one level, the "equal consideration of interests" principle defended by Singer does suggest a helpful decision procedure. It directs us to take all suffering into consideration when deciding between alternative policies. However, it is not long before this directive confronts enormous complexity in application. As Singer himself admits, humans are different from animals and therefore equal consideration does not entail equal (or identical) treatment. Further, interests and suffering admit of degrees. Not all interests deserve to be treated equally, and not all suffering is created equal. For example, some philosophers distinguish between *basic* and *peripheral* interests.[12] Life, food, water, clothing, and freedom from intense pain might be thought of as basic interests; indoor plumbing, automobiles, fur coats, air-conditioning, and gourmet cooking might be considered peripheral interests.

But how are we to sift through these diverse and competing interests? Would a human's interest in fencing off prairie land for agricultural purposes (something that might be necessary if we follow Singer's and Regan's advice and become vegetarians) override a wild animal's interest in unobstructed habitat? How does the spotted owl's interest in old-growth forests in the Pacific Northwest compare with human interest in lumber? Would the lumber's use make a difference? As moral agents, do we have an obligation to interfere with the life of animals in the wild? Should we protect predators, or prey? Are the interests of a starving wolf equal to the interests of a single member of a large herd of caribou? Are the interests of pets equal to the interests of farm animals? of wild animals? Do we really want to give the interests of a rat *any* consideration when they conflict with the interests of a poor child who might be bitten by it?[13]

These questions suggest deep problems for any view that gives the interests of individual animals serious moral weight. The relationships between humans and animals, between animals of different species, between animals and their habitat, and among humans, animals, and the land, are many and diverse. Setting individual animals up with equal moral standing is really only the beginning of the debate. Indeed, it frames the debate as a conflict, as fundamentally adversarial. Without a clear and determinate decision procedure, the question that began this entire debate—"What is the proper relation between humans and other animals?"—remains unanswered, if not unanswerable.

Other challenges, more often aimed at Regan, suggest that the boundary of moral considerability is too restrictive. (Similar criticisms of Singer, who has suggested that the boundary of considerability be drawn somewhere "between shrimp and oysters," charge that his line is too inclusive!) While Regan most often speaks in general terms of "animals," the "subject-of-a-life" criterion most clearly applies to "mentally normal mammals of a year or more."[14] According to many environmentalists, this neglects important members of the ecological community.

The influence of ecology underlies other important criticisms of the animal welfare movement. For example, Regan acknowledges that his rights-based ethics, like most of traditional ethical theories, is *individualistic*. That is, ethics is concerned with protecting and promoting the well-being of individuals, not communities or societies or some one "common" good. This puts him at odds with much environmental and ecological thinking that is *holistic*. As we will see, many environmentalists emphasize "biotic communities" or "ecosystems" rather than individual members (including humans) of those communities. Alluding to a parallel issue in political philosophy, Regan warns us of "environmental fascism" in which individual rights are willingly sacrificed to the greater good of the whole. "Environmental fascism and the rights view are like oil and water: they don't mix."[15]

Further, as mentioned earlier, Regan is unwilling to attribute rights to species. His view is admittedly individualistic. Only individual animals can be said to have moral standing, or more specifically, can be said to have rights. This is a controversial claim even within the ethical tradition of which Regan is part. Corporations and nations are but two examples of collections of individuals taken to have rights that are not reducible to the rights of individual members. But beyond this issue, the individualistic bias of both Regan and Singer seems to imply other consequences that many environmentalists find unacceptable.

In Regan's view, the fact that an animal is a member of an endangered species gives it no special moral status. The last remaining pair of bald eagles or spotted owls have less moral claim on us than does a single whitetail deer. Deer, apparently, are more "subjects-of-a-life" than birds and thus have a direct moral standing that birds do not. Preservation of the endangered blue whales is ethically no more important than preserving cows. We have no greater duty to mountain gorillas and black rhinos than to a stray cat.

Similarly, Singer's views would also suggest counterintuitive conclusions to many environmentalists. Given the amount of suffering that can take place with intensive farming techniques, any one of literally millions of chickens might have a stronger moral claim against us (to relieve its suffering), than would the last remaining pair of elephants (assuming that they are left alone to die of old age).

The emphasis on individuals also leads to controversial suggestions for wildlife management. Singer, for example, recognizes that it is "conceivable" that human interference could improve the conditions of wild animals. Nevertheless, partly considering past failures, he recommends a policy of leaving wild animals alone as much as possible. We do enough, he tells us, "if we eliminate our own unnecessary killing and cruelty toward other animals."[16] Regan apparently endorses a similar laissez-faire attitude. As long as we protect the rights of animals (or, again, at least mammals), other ecological concerns will take care of themselves. In his rights view,

> assuming this could be successfully extended to inanimate natural objects [which he thinks is unlikely at best], our general policy regarding wilderness would be precisely what the preservationists want—namely, let it be! . . . Were we to show proper respect for the rights of the individuals who make up the biotic community, would not the *community* be preserved?[17]

But there are problems with this laissez-faire approach. First, there is a long history of destruction and habitat loss that would need to be reversed before biotic communities could be preserved. Next, full noninterference with the environment is impossible. The idea that there can be some "untamed, wilderness" untouched by human activity is a mirage. There is no place on earth, no animal on earth, and no period on earth for quite some time that escapes human influence. If only through the pollutants that we dump into the air and water (and our influence is much greater than that!), humans affect every corner of the earth. The question is not *should* we actively influence the wilderness, it is *how* should we?

Second, the answer to Regan's question would seem, in many cases, to be no. Showing proper respect for the rights of whitetail deer, for example, has disastrous consequences for its ecological community.[18] In many areas, the population of these deer often overwhelms the carrying capacity of their habitat. With abundant food, protective hunting laws, and loss of natural predators, deer populations wreak havoc on their own habitat and on the many species of plants that make up that habitat. The result is destruction of many other life-forms in that ecological community.

Similar consequences face wildlife managers in parts of Africa. In some protected East African refuges, the elephant population grew so large that it threatened to outpace its own food supply. Left alone, many elephants would die a slow death of starvation—but not before destroying much of the surrounding vegetation. One alternative seems to be selective killing ("thinning" or "culling" the herd, in less blunt terms).[19]

The point of these examples is that animals, like humans, are a part of a complex ecological community. Although constantly changing, this community seems to involve a delicate balance of interdependencies. For many environmentalists, the equilibrium of natural ecosystems should be the goal of an environmental ethics. Giving special ethical protection to individual animals threatens to upset that balance and cause damage elsewhere within that system. A laissez-faire attitude in conjunction with animal rights may well lead to serious ecological harms. There simply is no guarantee that a species, or more generally an ecological community, would be preserved if only we "show proper respect for the rights of the individuals who make up the biotic community."[20]

Most of these challenges arise from the *individualistic* approach characteristic of Regan and Singer. Defending individual animals may not be the most appropriate environmental strategy. Other criticisms suggest that, in a peculiar way, the extension of moral standing to animals has remained, despite its intentions, *anthropocentric*. Developing this challenge will help provide a transition to a discussion of more holistic environmental ethics.

How could moral standing for animals remain anthropocentric? Consider the philosophical method employed by Feinberg, Singer, and Regan. They all begin by taking human beings as the paradigm case of beings with moral standing. They then all ask, "What about humans gives them moral standing?" Feinberg answers with "having interests," Singer with the "capacity to suffer," and Regan with "being a subject-of-a-life." But each of these criteria is essentially a *human* characteristic. In effect, Feinberg, Singer, and Regan all say that if only animals are enough like us, they have (or, we can "give them") moral standing. Moral standing seems a benefit that a living being can receive only if it is enough like humans. If it is too different from humans, then it does not qualify for standing.

Roderick Nash likens this approach to the attitude of many whites toward African-Americans. Many white liberals abhorred racism and fought for equal rights and equal consideration for people of color. What this meant in practice, of course, was that African-Americans should become more like white Americans. They should be middle class, desire the same things, take part in the same cultural practices—they should, in other words, become "white." Many liberals little understood or accepted the desire of many African-Americans to retain their own cultural heritage and their own "Black Pride."[21] Arguing against the extensionism of the animal liberation movement, John Rodman claimed that the presumption that *"we* can liberate *them"* is "patronizing and perverse."[22] It is to treat animals as human beings, albeit somewhat inferior or incompetent humans.

Thus, many critics have come to believe that the animal welfare movement is not an environmentally sound approach at all. In their view, an adequate environmental ethics must reject both the individualism and the anthropocentrism of such philosophers as Singer and Regan.

6.6 SUMMARY AND CONCLUSION

Whether or not Singer or Regan fall victim to these challenges, an important point has been established. Environmental ethics requires more than simply a concern for animals. At a minimum, we need to consider questions about the moral status of ecological communities and about our role in those communities. A shift to holistic and truly nonanthropocentric ethics requires a fairly radical break from tradition.

Toward the end of *Animal Liberation*, Peter Singer tells us,

> Philosophy ought to question the basic assumptions of the age. Thinking through, critically and carefully, what most of us take for granted is, I believe, the chief task of philosophy, and the task that makes philosophy worthwhile. Regrettably, philosophy does not always live up to its historic role.[23]

In the view of many environmentalists, Singer himself, along with Tom Regan, is guilty of exactly this failure. All of what follows in this text implicitly takes up this challenge to "question the basic assumptions of the age."

Notes

1. As quoted in Peter Singer, *Animal Liberation*, 2d ed. (New York: New York Review of Books, 1990), p. 60. Much of this discussion of LD50 is taken from Singer.

2. Ibid., p. 95.

3. Ibid., p. 136.

4. Singer attributes the term "speciesism" to Richard Ryder's essay, "Victims of Science," in Stanley and Roslind Godlovitch and John Harris, eds., *Animals, Men, and Morals* (New York: Grove Press, 1974). This book was the subject of Singer's book review, "Animal Liberation," *New York Review of Books* (April 1973), pp. 17–21.

5. Singer, *Animal Liberation*, pp. 7–8.

6. Ibid., pp. 16–17.

7. Tom Regan, "The Case for Animal Rights," in Peter Singer, ed., *In Defense of Animals* (Oxford: Blackwell, 1985), p. 13.

8. See Gary Varner, "The Schopenhauerian Challenge in Environmental Ethics," *Environmental Ethics* 7, no. 3 (Fall 1985): 209–230 for a more detailed analysis of the distinction between moral agents and moral patients. Varner argues that Regan's account of agents and patients is flawed because he fails to distinguish moral patients, which have a good of their own, from those objects that are merely intrinsically valuable but are not patients. Varner admits that this second class nonetheless is morally considerable.

9. Tom Regan, *The Case for Animal Rights* (Berkeley: University of California Press, 1983), p. 243.

10. These are the four that Regan considers in *The Case for Animal Rights* (1983). For other discussions, see especially Tom Regan, *All That Dwell Therein* (Berkeley: University of California Press, 1982). Singer's *Animal Liberation* remains the best single source for his views.

11. See, for example, R. G. Frey, "Rights, Interests, Desires, and Beliefs," *American Philosophical Quarterly* 16, no. 3 (July 1979): 233–239.

12. See Donald VanDeVeer, "Interspecific Justice," *Inquiry* 22, nos. 1–2 (Summer 1979): 55–70.

13. This example is from Singer's *New York Review of Books* essay, p. 21.

14. Regan, *The Case for Animal Rights* (1983), see especially pp. 77–78. Regan later expands this a bit, suggesting that while it is always difficult to draw such lines, it would not be unreasonable to give the benefit of the doubt to any animal that shares the "relevant anatomical and physiological properties" with mammals. His example of such a relevant property is the central nervous system.

15. Ibid., pp. 361–362.

16. Singer, *Animal Liberation*, p. 226.

17. Regan, *The Case for Animal Rights* (1983), p. 363.

18. For a review of these and similar challenges, see J. Baird Callicott's "Review of Tom Regan's *The Case for Animal Rights*," *Environmental Ethics* 7 (1985): 365–372. Callicott also cites Mark Sagoff, "Animal Liberation and Environmental Ethics: Bad Marriage, Quick Divorce," *Osgoode Hall Law Journal* 22 (1984): 306, as a reference for this particular point.
19. For a good discussion of the Tsavo National Park dispute, see Botkin, *Discordant Harmonies*, chap. 2.
20. To see this claim developed, see Sagoff, "Animal Liberation and Environmental Ethics," p. 26; Callicott, pp. 365–372, and J. Baird Callicott, "Animal Liberation: A Triangular Affair," *Environmental Ethics* 2 (1980): 311–328.
21. This suggestion is found in Nash, *The Rights of Nature*, p. 152.
22. John Rodman, "The Liberation of Nature?" *Inquiry* 20 (Spring 1977): 94–101, as quoted in Nash.
23. Singer, *Animal Liberation*, p. 236.

Discussion Questions

1. How exactly would you distinguish between Jonathan Swift's "Modest Proposal" and modern veal production? What are the relevant similarities, if any? relevant differences?
2. Do you see any morally relevant differences between domesticated and wild animals? Would Singer? Regan? Do you see any morally relevant differences between animals threatened with extinction and those that are not?
3. What kinds of arguments might be given for vegetarianism? Which are moral arguments? Are you convinced by any of these arguments? Why or why not?
4. Regan argues that only "mentally normal mammals of a year or more" have moral rights. Singer draws a line somewhere "between shrimp and oysters." Are you willing to draw a line between animals that have moral standing and those that do not? On what grounds do you defend your answer?
5. Whitetail deer are overpopulating many local habitats across the United States. Do you favor selective hunting to thin these overpopulated herds? Do you favor human interference in any form? Why or why not?
6. Hunting and fishing are among the most popular sporting activities in the world. Does either raise a moral issue in your view? Why or why not? If not for food, why hunt?

For Further Reading

The already classic positions of Singer and Regan can be found in Peter Singer, *Animal Liberation*, 2d ed. (New York: New York Review of Books Press, 1990), and Tom Regan, *The Case for Animal Rights* (Berkeley: University of California Press, 1983).

Interesting discussions of the intellectual and linguistic lives of chimpanzees can be found in Eugene Linden, *Apes, Men, and Language* (New York:

Penguin, 1976), and Jane Goodall, *In the Shadow of Man* (Boston: Houghton Mifflin, 1971).

Bernard Rollin, *The Unheeded Cry: Animal Consciousness, Animal Pain, and Science* (Oxford, England: Oxford University Press, 1989), provides ample evidence about the sentient life of animals.

Mary Midgely, *Animals and Why They Matter* (Athens, GA: University of Georgia Press, 1983), offers a perceptive account of the social and communal relations that exist between humans and animals.

PART

THEORIES OF ENVIRONMENTAL ETHICS

7

Biocentric Ethics

CASE SEVEN

Biodiversity

Most of us have a very limited knowledge of animal and plant species. If asked, only some of us would be able to name more than a few dozen different species of animals. Still fewer would likely be able to name as many plant species. However, biological science has been categorizing animal and plant species since before Aristotle began his taxonomy of living organisms over two thousand years ago. Present estimates suggest that over 1.4 million different species have been scientifically categorized.[1] If these species could all be displayed in a museum and you could view each of them for just one minute, it would take nearly three years simply to look at them all.

But the categorized species represent only a small percentage of the actual number of species that presently exist. Conservative estimates suggest the number to be over 4 million total species. Based on research conducted in tropical forests in Brazil and Peru, other estimates place the number at more than 30 or 40 million species. That means 30–40 million different life-forms exist on earth.

Each of these species contains from a few members (for example, the California condor) to many billions of members (for example, bacteria). To sustain its life and propagate its species, each individual organism must take in nutrition from its environment. Each species exists in an ecological niche where its members interact with their environment to maintain life. The ability to do this has evolved through millions of years of mutations and natural selection. This ability is stored in the genetic code of each individual organism. Each organism contains from one million to 10 billion bits of information in its genetic code. This code represents an enormous genetic library of information developed over billions of years.

Life on earth is tremendously diverse and complex. It has inspired scientists, philosophers, and poets for millennia. Many instrumental justifications can be given to support the preservation of this biodiversity. Tremendous medicinal, agricultural, economic, aesthetic, recreational, and scientific potential exists in the variety and diversity of life. Indeed, we depend on other life-forms for our very existence. But does the simple fact that they are alive imply that we have any ethical relationship to them? Is it reasonable to speak of a life-centered, or *biocentric*, ethics?

7.1 INTRODUCTION

The past four chapters have shown how standard ethical principles and concepts can be applied to environmental issues. Sometimes traditional ethical analysis can be applied to these issues directly; at other times, standard principles and concepts must be modified to cover a wider range of pressing issues. But, as some criticisms of the animal welfare movement suggest, even these modifications are not fully satisfying to many environmentalists.

Applying even the modified version of standard ethics seems, at best, incomplete. A number of important environmental concerns seem ignored by these applications. At worst, some applications, such as the defense of animal rights, appear inconsistent with sound environmental policy. Up to this point, we have focused on philosophers who happened to be interested in some environmental issues, rather than on environmentalists who were developing an ethical philosophy. Beginning with this chapter, the focus changes as we consider more systematic attempts at developing comprehensive environmental philosophies. These approaches all question the wisdom of simply *extending* traditional ethics, or what can be called *ethical extensionism*, in favor of more dramatic and radical shifts in ethical perspective.

The problems with ethical extensionism center around three issues. First, despite the explicit claim of such philosophers as Singer and Regan, the principles and concepts employed in their ethics often remain fundamentally anthropocentric. The criteria for moral considerability defended by many philosophers were most clearly found in adult human beings. Therefore only those animals that most closely resembled humans were "given" moral standing. As a result, these extensions remained fundamentally hierarchical. For example, both Singer and Regan attribute moral standing only to "higher" animals. Other living things remained outside the range of moral consideration. This hierarchical ordering strikes many environmentalists as a mistake.

Second, these extensions remained thoroughly individualistic. Individual animals had standing, but plants, species, habitat, and relations had no standing in their own right. Yet much of the science of ecology stresses the interconnectedness of nature. Ecology emphasizes such "wholes" as species, biotic diversity, ecological communities, ecosystems, and biological, chemical, and geological cycles. Relations, communities, systems, and processes play a major role in the science of ecology. Unfortunately, there is little room in standard ethical theories for such concerns. Indeed, we need only remember Regan's dismissal of the ethical focus on communities as "environmental fascism" to see how unreceptive these standard ethical views can be. To some environmentalists, this is the perfect example of a perspective caught in the grasp of a philosophical theory and ignoring the facts of science.

Finally, these extensions were not, nor were they intended as, comprehensive environmental ethics. Philosophers applied ethics to specific problems as they arose and as they were perceived, with little or no attempt at building a coherent and comprehensive "theory" of environmental ethics. This focus had two unhappy results. First, the extension of ethics to cover, for example, the rights of animals, could provide no guidance for many other environmental issues, such as global warming or pollution. Second, extensionism tends to remain critical and negative: we often are told what is wrong with various policies and actions, but seldom find much about what the alternative "good life" should be.

The following chapters begin a survey of attempts at developing a more systematic environmental ethics. Much recent philosophical work on the environment makes a radical break with standard ethical theory and strives to rethink the human–nature relationship. Indeed, it might be more appropriate to describe some of these emerging schools of thought as environmental "philosophies" rather than as "ethics." As philosophers seek a comprehensive account of the place of human beings in their natural environment, they are forced to address more than merely ethical questions.

Topics in metaphysics ("nature" and the "natural," the ontological status of systems, relations, species, and so forth), epistemology (the logical relation between descriptive and normative claims), aesthetics (beauty and intrinsic value), and political philosophy (civil disobedience and ecoterrorism) become important issues when we begin to rethink ethics in this way.

7.2 WHAT IS AN ENVIRONMENTAL PHILOSOPHY?

With this chapter, then, let's step back from the debates so far reviewed. For now, put aside the role of the philosopher who addresses environmental problems. Instead, adopt the viewpoint of an environmentalist (or more simply, a concerned citizen) seeking to articulate, develop, and defend a coherent and comprehensive environmental philosophy.

To understand what is involved with such an ethic, you need only review the opening paragraph of the introduction to Chapter 1 in this book. It might be helpful to repeat it here:

> As we approach the twenty-first century, it is fair to say that human beings face environmental challenges unprecedented in the history of this planet. Largely through human activity, life on earth faces the greatest mass extinctions since the end of the dinosaur age 65 million years ago. Some estimates suggest over a hundred species each day are becoming extinct and that this rate could double or triple within the next few decades. The natural resources that sustain life on this planet—air, water, and soil—are being polluted or depleted at alarming rates. Human population growth is increasing exponentially. The 1990 world population of 5.5 billion people will increase by a billion people (nearly a 20 percent increase) within ten years. The prospects for continued degradation and depletion of natural resources multiply with this population growth. Toxic wastes that will plague future generations continue to accumulate around the world. The world's wilderness areas, its forests, wetlands, mountains, and grasslands are being developed, paved, drained, burned, and overgrazed out of existence. With the destruction of the ozone layer and the potential for a "greenhouse" effect, human activity threatens the very atmosphere and climate of the planet itself.

No rational person can reflect on these developments without some concern and distress. But to understand the goals of an environmental philosophy, we need to go beyond the stage of merely reacting to these sins. We need to examine the source of this concern. Why, exactly, are we troubled by these facts? Why *should* we be troubled by these facts?

Clearly there is no single answer to these questions. In some cases, our reasoning lies in the fact that environmental destruction poses a clear danger to us. In other cases, the way we treat the environment offends spiritual, aesthetic, or cultural values. In still other cases, we seem to be causing real harm to natural objects themselves. To help in sorting through these issues, let us return to some concepts that we saw earlier and distinguish between *instrumental value*, *intrinsic value*, and *inherent worth*.[2]

7.3 INSTRUMENTAL VALUE, INTRINSIC VALUE, AND INHERENT WORTH

Instrumental value is a function of usefulness. An object with instrumental value possesses that value because it can be used to attain something else of value. A pencil is valuable because I can write with it. A dollar bill is valuable because I can use it to buy something. Thus the instrumental value of some object lies not in the object itself but depends on what it can be used for. When such an object no longer has any use, or when it can be replaced by something of more effective or greater use, it can be ignored or discarded.

Gifford Pinchot's conservation movement emphasized the instrumental value of forests and wilderness areas. We should protect and conserve the wilderness because it is the home of vast resources that humans can use. Very many other environmental concerns rest on the instrumental value of the environment. Clean air and water are valued because without them human health and well-being are jeopardized. The preservation of plant and animal species is valued because of the vast potential for medical and agricultural uses. Virtually any utilitarian or economic proposal is based on the instrumental value of nature.

Appealing to the instrumental value of the environment can be an effective strategy in the political realm. Public opinion is often most responsive to claims of lost opportunities, wasted resources, and so on. Yet an environmental ethics based solely on the instrumental value of the environment is unstable. As human interests and needs change, so too would human uses for the environment. The instrumental value of the Colorado River as a water and hydroelectric power source for southern California will quickly override its instrumental value as a wilderness or recreation area. Emphasizing only the instrumental value of nature effectively means that the environment is held hostage by the interests and needs of humans.

An object has *intrinsic* value when it is valued for itself and not simply valued for its uses. Not all things we value are valued instrumentally. Some things we value because we recognize their symbolic, aesthetic, or cultural importance. We value them for themselves, for what they mean, for what they stand for, for what they are.

Some examples can help explain this distinction. Typically we value a dollar bill only for its instrumental value. We can use the bill to buy something. But consider the small business owner who keeps and displays the first dollar bill ever spent in this business. That particular dollar bill not only has instrumental value (it still can be used to buy something), but because of what it symbolizes it also has an intrinsic value to this owner. Now imagine offering this person four quarters in exchange for that dollar bill. Although the four quarters possess exactly the same instrumental value as the bill, they simply lack the intrinsic value of that bill.

Think also of friendships. If you value your friends only for their usefulness, you have seriously misunderstood friendship. Consider historical monuments or cultural and aesthetic objects. The Liberty Bell, the Taj Mahal, or Michelangelo's *David* possess an intrinsic value far beyond their usefulness.

It would seem that both instrumental and intrinsic value are dependent on humans who value. Although all value depends on people who value, people value things for very different types of reasons. Without humans around to appreciate their value, neither friendship, the Liberty Bell, the Taj Mahal, nor *David* would be valuable. But this does not mean that they are valued only for their usefulness to humans. This does not mean that all human valuing is instrumental.

Clearly, many of our environmental concerns rest on the intrinsic value that we recognize in nature. Wilderness areas, scenic landscapes, national parks are valued by many people because, like the Liberty Bell, they are a part of our national heritage and history. (This essentially is the argument Mark Sagoff makes; see Chapter 3.) The grizzly bear may have little instrumental value, but knowing that they still exist in Yellowstone National Park is important to many people. The symbolic value of the bald eagle transcends any instrumental value that it might have. Undeveloped and unexplored wilderness areas are highly valued, even by people who will never visit, explore, or use these areas.

When we say that the environment is degraded by human activity what we are often expressing is the loss of intrinsic value. When sections of the Grand Canyon are eroded by flooding caused by water released from hydroelectric dams upriver, when acid rain eats away at ancient architecture in Greece and Rome, when shorelines are replaced by boardwalks and casinos, human activity destroys some of the intrinsic value we find in nature.

Unfortunately, appeals to intrinsic value are often met with skepticism. We seem to lack the language for expressing intrinsic value. Many people think that such value is merely subjective, a matter of personal opinion: "Beauty is in the eye of the beholder." Thus when a measurable instrumental value (such as profit) conflicts with intangible and elusive intrinsic value (such as the beauty of a wilderness), the instrumental value too often wins by default.

For a number of philosophers working in environmental ethics, the biggest challenge is to develop an account of intrinsic value that can counter arguments based on instrumental values. As we saw in Chapter 4, John Passmore called for an emphasis on the "sensuous" to offset the materialism and greed dominant in modern culture. After criticizing the dominant economic model (which sees all value as instrumental), Mark Sagoff summons philosophers to articulate the cultural, aesthetic, historical, and ethical values that underlie our environmental commitments. These values, Sagoff tells us, determine not just what we *want* as a people, but what we *are*.

But both instrumental and intrinsic value depend on humans who value them. Some philosophers seek to defend an account of value that does not depend on humans. These philosophers defend what I call *inherent worth*. An object has inherent *worth* if it is good (or has a good) in itself, independently of any human valuing.

Significant controversy, and not just in environmental matters, surrounds claims of inherent worth. Some critics claim that it makes little sense to speak of "worth" that is fully independent of human valuing. To these critics, all judgments of value and worthiness depend on human judges. Thus, according to these critics, there is no distinction between intrinsic value and inherent worth. Nevertheless, a reasonable case can be made for attributing inherent worth to at least some objects.

In a variety of ethical traditions, human beings themselves are thought to possess inherent worth. Such concepts as human dignity and respect seem to get at this notion of inherent worth. Humans are said to possess a certain dignity that gives them a moral standing independent of value judgments made by other humans. Likewise, religious traditions often claim that as creatures of a benevolent God, humans have a worth that transcends human valuing. The biblical notion of beings created "in the image and likeness of God" conveys some of this idea. The claim is that humans possess not only a noninstrumental *value*, but also a special kind of worth or dignity in and of themselves.

So the concept of inherent worth seems to make sense, but serious questions arise about whether or not anything beside humans can or should have it. Some environmentalists claim that all living things have an inherent worth that is violated by environmental destruction and degradation. Defenders of animal welfare claim that at least some animals have a worth that is independent of human values.[3] In this way, some of our environmental concerns reflect the belief that human activity is violating the dignity (perhaps "sacredness" would be a better word) of nature.

Something like inherent worth is necessary to account for environmental concerns not explained by either instrumental or intrinsic value. Malicious or random destruction of plant life or a natural rock formation, for example, might destroy nothing that humans value, yet we might want to judge such acts as unethical. The fear is that even with an account of intrinsic value, we leave the moral status of natural objects dependent on the existence of humans. While human beliefs and judgments of intrinsic value may not be as fickle and variable as the desires that underlie instrumental value, nevertheless they can and do change over time. After a while, and in a different culture perhaps, the Liberty Bell, the Taj Mahal, and Michelangelo's *David* all could lose their intrinsic value if no one cared.

Developing the concept of inherent worth thus is another major challenge facing philosophers who seek to develop a comprehensive environmental ethics. Does it make sense to say that natural objects or ecological systems possess inherent worth? On what grounds would something have inherent worth? What practical implications would follow from the attribution of inherent worth? In the remainder of this chapter, we rely on the categories of instrumental value, intrinsic value, and inherent worth to examine the next step in the development of environmental ethics.

7.4 BIOCENTRIC ETHICS AND THE REVERENCE FOR LIFE

The term "biocentric ethics" refers to any theory that views all life as possessing inherent worth. (The word *biocentric* means "life centered.") Thus, although someone like Tom Regan is willing to attribute an inherent worth to some animals, his view is not "biocentric," because it is not extended to include all living things.

An early version of a biocentric ethics is Albert Schweitzer's "reverence for life" principle. Schweitzer (1875–1965) wrote extensively about religion, music, ethics, history, and philosophy. He also, of course, devoted much of his life to bringing medical care to remote and isolated communities in Africa. His ethics, captured in the phrase "reverence for life," is an extremely interesting precursor of contemporary biocentric ethics.

Schweitzer's was an active and full life committed to caring and concern for others. Yet he was also a prolific writer, devoting many volumes diagnosing the ethical ills of modern society and seeking a cure for them. "Reverence for life" was the attitude he believed offered hope to a world beset with conflict. It is worth our while to examine briefly Schweitzer's diagnosis and cure.[4]

Modern industrial society had moved away from a worldview that connected the goodness of life with the goodness of nature. This belief, what Schweitzer called "world and life affirmation," is reminiscent of the natural law tradition in ethics. The rise of science and technology, and the industrialized society that accompanies them, splits the connection between ethics and nature by viewing nature as an indifferent, value-free, mechanical force. Modern science views nature as a machine, governed by physical and mechanical laws. There is no good (nor for that matter evil) inherent in nature itself. Set adrift in such a world, human ethics was left without foundation. Ethical value became no more than personal opinion or sentiment. Modern industrial society, with its wars, impersonal bureaucracies, meaningless work, and cultural decay, is the result of this separation.

Schweitzer's ethical thinking sought to re-establish the bond between nature and ethics. Yet, having spent time traveling in the most remote sections of Africa, Schweitzer did not deceive himself into thinking of nature as benign and gentle. He had been made more than aware of the destructive and arbitrary force of nature. He was convinced nonetheless that there was good in nature, an inherent worth, which could help provide a basis for human ethics. The idea that Schweitzer developed to solve this issue is captured by his phrase "reverence for life."

Schweitzer himself describes in almost mystical terms the moment when this idea came to him. It is perhaps not surprising that it came to him in a natural setting. While riding on a barge traveling upriver in Africa, "at the very moment when, at sunset, we were making our way through a herd of hippopotamuses, there flashed upon my mind, unforseen and unsought, the phrase "Reverence for Life."[5]

What does "reverence for life" mean? Schweitzer's original German phrase is *Ehrfurcht vor dem Leben*. "Ehrfurcht" implies an attitude of awe and wonder. Although "reverence" perhaps connotes a religious tone that is missing in *"Ehrfurcht,"* it seems clear that

Schweitzer had something like this in mind. The etymological roots of *"Ehrfurcht"* suggest a combined attitude of honor and fear. It would not be misleading to think of the attitude often inspired by majestic vistas seen from atop high mountains, or the attitude inspired by violent storms.

Schweitzer held that the most fundamental fact of human consciousness is the realization that "I am life which wills to live, in the midst of life which wills to live."[6] Ethics begins when we become fully aware, and fully in awe, of that fact:

> The man who has become a thinking being feels a compulsion to give to every will-to-live the same reverence for life that he gives to his own. He experiences that other life in his own. He accepts as being good: to preserve life, to promote life, to raise to its highest value life which is capable of development; and as being evil: to destroy life, to injure life, to repress life which is capable of development. This is the absolute, fundamental principle of the moral.[7]

In our terms, Schweitzer is claiming that all living things have an inherent worth, a worth that commands our awe and reverence. Life is not a neutral, value-free "fact" of the universe. Life is good in itself, it is inspiring and deserving of respect.

Unfortunately, it is easy to caricature the "reverence for life" ethic. Is Schweitzer suggesting that the life of a virus or of bacteria is as worthy as human life? Does he suggest that we treat the life of an ant with as much respect as we treat human life? If not, does he offer any formula for resolving conflicts between human life and the life of, for example, the HIV virus?

Schweitzer himself lived his life in a manner that many people would find overly demanding. He would go to great lengths to avoid killing even mosquitoes, going so far as to carry them out of the room rather than killing them. Even when fighting disease-carrying mosquitoes, he was reluctant to kill. He resisted using DDT, for example, because he mistrusted the way it killed indiscriminately. Nevertheless, Schweitzer was not naive about the necessity of sometimes taking lives, especially out of reverence for other lives. To maintain life, other life must be sacrificed as food. He was also willing to take an animal's life to end its suffering.[8]

But this does not mean that Schweitzer defended some formula or rule to be applied in cases of conflict to establish priorities. Such a hierarchy would undermine the foundation of the reverence-for-life ethic by suggesting that there is some rule or criterion more fundamental than reverence itself. It would also downplay the serious dilemma that we often face when we must take life. A principle or rule that unequivocally resolves conflict would suggest that any ethical conflict is only apparent and not real.

Schweitzer did not envision reverence for life merely as some rule that we could apply to specific situations and, as it were, simply read off the recommended decision. Reverence for life is more an attitude that determines who we are rather than a rule for determining what we should do. It describes a character trait, or a moral virtue, rather than a rule of action. A morally good person stands in awe of the inherent worth of each life.

But what does this say about those circumstances in which the good person must choose to kill? What about the doctor who kills a virus? the butcher who kills a pig? the farmer who cuts down a tree? Schweitzer denies that we can escape responsibility for these decisions. They must be made, but they should be made responsibly and consciously. Reverence for life is that character trait that sensitizes us to the responsibility of these decisions. It is an attitude that makes us aware of the full implications of these decisions. It makes us reluctant to take a life randomly, or callously, or without remorse. In doing this, it helps us live an authentic and moral life.

Schweitzer's ethical views are richly textured and firmly based in the experiences of many years in the African wilderness. Yet these views never attained wide popularity, among either the public or philosophers. Perhaps the tendency to see such a perspective as overly romantic or naive is too common and too strong an obstacle. Schweitzer also never developed the type of scholarly defense of this position that professional philosophers demand. However, recent biocentric theories, some strongly reminiscent of Schweitzer, may be more persuasive.

7.5 ETHICS AND CHARACTER

Before moving to more recent biocentric views, it will be helpful to reflect for a moment on a philosophical issue that is in the background of this discussion. In the opening section of this chapter, I suggested that recent environmental philosophies represent a break with many traditional theories. We have seen hints in recent pages of what this might involve, and it will help to develop these hints at this point.

For many defenders of traditional ethical theories such as utilitarianism, deontology, and natural law, the fundamental question for ethics is "What should I do?" The goal of ethics is to articulate and defend rules or principles that can guide our behavior. The philosopher's job then is to justify that rule by demonstrating why all rational people should act in accord with it. For most philosophers in these traditions, this task ultimately requires showing that obeying the rule is in a person's rational self-interest.[9]

Given this approach to ethics, it is understandable why many people would have difficulty accepting Schweitzer's views on the reverence for life. If we do treat it as a rule for guiding our actions, reverence for life might well commit us to the type of counterintuitive positions just mentioned.

But as already suggested, Schweitzer did not offer reverence for life as an ethical *rule*. Reverence for life would be a fundamental *attitude* that we would take toward the world. In this sense, Schweitzer's ethics focused not on the question "What should I do?" but on "What type of person should I be?" His was not an ethics solely of rules as much as it was an ethics of *character*, seeking first to describe morally good people in terms of their character and dispositions rather than in terms of their actions.

This shift represents a return to a tradition of philosophical ethics that goes back to Plato and Aristotle. An *ethics of virtue* emphasizes moral character, or virtues, rather than rules or principles. Such ethical systems as utilitarianism, deontology, and natural law focus on human *actions* and seek to defend some rule or principle in terms of which those actions are judged right or wrong. Virtue-based ethics construct a philosophical account of the morally good person, describing and defending certain character traits of that good person. As for Aristotle, most virtue-based theories are teleological. Virtues are distinguished from vices (the opposite of a virtue), by their connection with attainment of some human *telos*, or goal. For Aristotle, the virtues were those character traits and dispositions that enable people to live a meaningful and fulfilling human life.

It will be helpful to keep this distinction in mind as we examine more recent environmental philosophies. Many of these emerging philosophies are not simply proposing alternative rules or principles to utilitarianism or deontology. Instead, they require us to make a shift in our philosophical perspective, a shift away from a concern with rules of behavior and on to a concern with moral character. These shifts require not only a different view of the environment, but at least as importantly, a different view of our selves.

Recollect an earlier discussion by Mark Sagoff. Sagoff says that a satisfactory environmental ethics must address not only those values that determine what you *want*, but also those values that determine what you *are*. Implicit in this distinction is the recognition that your own identity as a person is constituted in part by your values and attitudes. Your *character*, those dispositions, relationships, attitudes, values, and beliefs that popularly might be called a "personality," is not some feature that remains independent of your own identity. Your character is not like a suit of clothes that your "self" steps into and out of at will. Rather, the self is identical with your most fundamental and enduring dispositions, attitudes, values, and beliefs. Thus, when an environmental philosophy requires that you change your fundamental attitude toward nature, it is requiring quite literally that you change yourself.

Note how this shift changes the nature of justification in ethics. If, as seems true in many traditional ethical theories, justification of some rule requires that it be tied to self-interest, then we should not be surprised to find that this justification often fails. Ethical controversies very often involve a conflict between self-interest and ethical values. Consider how you would "justify" the reverence for life. For a self that does not already include a disposition to treat life with reverence, the only avenue open for justification involves showing how the disposition serves some other interest of the self. "Why should *I*, who do not already treat life with reverence, do so now?" It would appear that the only way to answer this question is to show how it is in your self-interest to adopt this attitude. But this means connecting the attitude to, in Sagoff's terms, those values that determine what you *want* instead of those that determine what you *are*. But this is to say that reverence for life must be reducible to some instrumental value: you should adopt the attitude of reverence because it in some way serves your purposes or satisfies your wants. Of course, this is exactly what the reverence-for-life ethic denies. Life has *inherent worth*, it is much more than merely *instrumentally* valuable.

On the other hand, for the person already characterized by a reverence for life, the question of justification is irrelevant. If one of your fundamental attitudes is a reverence for life, the question "Why should I revere life?" ordinarily would not arise.[10] Thus, "justification" for an ethics that requires a fundamental shift in moral attitude involves something other than an appeal to self-interest.

7.6 TAYLOR'S BIOCENTRIC ETHICS

Paul Taylor's book *Respect for Nature* (1986) is one of the most fully developed and philosophically sophisticated contemporary defenses of a biocentric ethics. Although Schweitzer tried to explain what reverence for life meant and what practical implications follow from this attitude, he never provided an adequate justification for adopting that attitude. Part of the strength of Taylor's view lies in his careful defense of why it is reasonable to adopt the attitude of respect for nature. For this reason, I concentrate on his view as an example of biocentric ethics.

As a biocentric theorist, Taylor seeks a systematic and comprehensive account of the moral relations that exist between humans and other living things. Taylor sees this relationship as being based on the inherent worth of all life:

> The central tenet of the theory of environmental ethics that I am defending is that actions are right and character traits are morally good in virtue of their expressing or embodying a certain ultimate moral attitude, which I call respect for nature.[11]

Taylor's explanation and defense of this theory proceeds through a number of steps. He first argues that it is meaningful to say that all living things have a good of their own. We can say this, in part, because all living things are, in Taylor's phrase, "teleological-centers-of-life." Having a good of itself is necessary, but not sufficient, for attributing inherent worth to that entity. To say that an entity has inherent worth is to make the normative claim that this entity deserves moral consideration and that moral agents have duties toward it. We move from the descriptive claim that a being has a good of its own to the normative claim that it possesses inherent worth when we come to understand and accept what Taylor calls "the biocentric outlook on nature." Accepting this outlook and recognizing the inherent worth of all living things is to adopt respect for nature as your "ultimate moral attitude." In turn, adopting this attitude means that you will act in morally responsible ways toward the natural environment. It is worth reviewing each of these steps in turn.

We first need to distinguish things that have a good of their own from things that do not. Taylor cites as his examples a child as a being with a good of its own, and a pile of sand as something of which it makes no sense to talk of its having a good. Parental decisions aim to promote the child's own good; the child is benefited when that good is furthered and harmed when that good is frustrated. Yet it is meaningless to talk of the sand's own good, as if the sand itself could be harmed or benefited in any way.

Taylor next relies on a traditional philosophical distinction between *real* and *apparent* good, or between what he calls *objective* and *subjective* value concepts. A thing's good is not always identical with what that being *believes* is its good. What *appears* to me to be good for me (subjectively), may not *really* (objectively) be good for me. This distinction allows Taylor to include in his biocentric ethics any being that has an objective good of its own. By ignoring the concept of apparent or subjective goods, he is not limited to including only those beings that possess the beliefs, interests, or desires presupposed in any account of subjective good.

What entities have an objective good of their own? Taylor's answer is to be found in the concept of a "teleological-center-of-a-life." To understand this, it is helpful to draw some parallels with Schweitzer's reverence-for-life ethics and the natural law tradition of Aristotle. It is also informative to contrast what Taylor says here with the concept of a "subject of a life" as used in Regan's animal rights ethics.

Let us begin with an example from Taylor:

> Concerning a butterfly, for example, we may hesitate to speak of its interests or preferences, and we would probably deny outright that it values anything in the sense of considering it good or desirable. But once we come to understand its life cycle and know the environmental conditions it needs to survive in a healthy state, we have no difficulty in speaking about what is beneficial to it and what might be harmful to it. . . . Even when we consider such simple animal organisms as one-celled protozoa, it makes perfectly good sense to a biologically informed person to speak of what benefits or harms them, what environmental changes are to their advantage or disadvantage, and what physical circumstances are favorable or unfavorable to them. The more knowledge we gain concerning these organisms, the better are we able to make sound judgments about what is in their interest or contrary to their interest.[12]

This is something that most of us, at least when we are not caught in the grips of a philosophical theory, would accept. It makes perfect sense to talk about the "good" of any living thing. This good is objective in the sense that it does not depend on anyone's beliefs or opinions. It is a claim that can be supported with biological evidence. It is something we can come to *know*. When we know an entity's good, we know what would be in that entity's interests, even if the being itself, like a plant, has no conscious interests of its own. Thus, even the weekend gardener can meaningfully talk about compost being good for tomatoes, pruning being good for an apple tree, drought being bad for vegetables, aphids being bad for beans, and ladybugs being bad for aphids.

All living things have a good because living beings are "teleological-centers-of-life." Remember from the discussion of natural law ethics in Chapter 2 that the Greek word *telos* is translated as "purpose," or "goal," or "end." Aristotle was led by his biological observations to claim that all living things act toward some distinctive goal or "telos." Like Aristotle, Taylor claims that each species has a distinctive nature that determines the specific good for that species. Unlike Aristotle, this nature need not be identified with the organism's essence or soul. For Taylor, this nature is more like the ecological niche or function fulfilled by that species.

As the aphid and ladybug example suggests, however, the good of one species may not be good for another species. Each species has its own specific end, but all living things do have ends. In general, that end is growth, development, sustenance, and propagation. Life itself is directional in the sense that it tends toward this end. Each living thing is the center of this purposive activity; each living thing is the "teleological-center-of-a-life."

Schweitzer's phrase in this context was "I am life which wills to live in the midst of life which wills to live." As long as we do not assume that all things that "will to live" must do so consciously, Schweitzer's thinking is very similar to Taylor on this point. Each living thing has its own good because, as a living thing, each life has direction, has a goal, has a *telos*. This is true whether or not the being itself is consciously aware of that fact. The "will to live" is manifested in the biological processes of growth, development, propagation, and sustaining life.

This view can be contrasted with Tom Regan's defense of animal rights. Chapter 6 discussed Regan's argument that all beings which are "subjects-of-a-life" have the inherent value that qualifies that being for moral standing. (Regan's use of "inherent value" functions for him as "inherent worth" does in this chapter.) To be a *subject* of a life involves a complex set of characteristics that go beyond merely being alive and merely being conscious. In this way, Regan defends moral standing only for "mentally normal mammals of a year or more." Taylor's concept of "teleological-center-of-a-life" is more inclusive than Regan's "subject-of-a-life."

> To say it is a teleological center of a life is to say that its internal functioning as well as its external activities are all goal-oriented, having the constant tendency to maintain the organism's existence through time and to enable it successfully to perform those biological operations whereby it reproduces its kind and continually adapts to changing environmental events and conditions. It is the coherence and unity of these functions of an organism, all directed toward the realization of its good, that make it one teleological center of activity.[13]

Like Regan, and unlike Aristotle and Schweitzer perhaps, Taylor is especially careful in moving from the *descriptive* claim that some being has a good of its own, to the *normative* claim that we have ethical duties toward that being.[14] According to Taylor, it is a matter of biological fact that living things have a good of their own. But this is not an ethical good in the sense that this fact alone does not commit us to any particular ethical stance toward living things. Having a good of its own does not, by itself, confer moral standing on a being.

Taylor explains the normative claims that all living things have moral standing and that we have duties toward them by reference to the concept of inherent worth. As he uses this phrase, inherent worth commits us to making two further normative judgments: entities with inherent worth deserve moral consideration, and all moral agents have duties to respect that entity's own good.[15]

What is the connection between a thing's having a good of its own and its possessing inherent worth? Having a good of its own makes it possible for a living thing to be the object of human duties. That is, we can have duties to promote or preserve a being's good only if it does, in fact, have a good of its own to be promoted. Having a good of its own is therefore necessary for a being to possess inherent worth. But it is not sufficient. The *normative* claim that living things have an inherent worth is to be explained and justified by reference to what Taylor calls the "biocentric outlook."

The biocentric outlook is a system of beliefs that conceptualizes our relationship to other living things. It is a system of beliefs that provides a fundamental worldview of the natural world and our relationship to it. Once we adopt this worldview, we see that treating all living things as possessing inherent worth is the only way of treating them that makes sense. Only this way of understanding them is coherent with the biocentric outlook.

The biocentric outlook on nature centers around four central beliefs. First, humans are seen as members of earth's community of life in the same sense and on the same terms as all other living things. Second, all species including humans are part of a system of interdependence. Third, all living things pursue their own good in their own ways (the teleological center of life belief). Finally, humans are understood as not inherently superior to other living things.[16]

Taylor goes on to explain that the biocentric outlook is a way of conceiving nature that all rational and factually informed people should adopt. It is an outlook that is firmly based on reasonable scientific evidence. Rejecting this outlook would require us to give up or significantly revise a good deal of what has been learned by the science of ecology. Once it is adopted, such a person would see that recognizing the inherent worth of all living things is the only perspective on life that is coherent with this outlook.

To regard living things as possessing inherent worth is to adopt the attitude of "respect for nature." It is to adopt a fundamental attitude toward nature that establishes certain basic motivations and dispositions. To adopt this attitude is to be disposed to promoting and protecting the good of other living things simply *because* it is their own good. It is to accept the good of other beings as a reason for one's own action.

Taylor's biocentric ethics addresses a number of philosophical issues that were missing in Schweitzer's reverence-for-life ethics. His account of how the biocentric outlook makes the attribution of inherent worth to all living things reasonable offers a rational basis for this belief that is missing in Schweitzer. Likewise, his description of inherent worth and a good of one's own adds much to the philosophical debate. It then remains for Taylor to turn to issues of normative ethics and offer more practical advice.

7.7 PRACTICAL IMPLICATIONS

Taylor's normative ethics focuses on two basic issues: the general rules or duties that follow from the attitude of respect for nature, and priority rules for resolving conflicts between the ethical claims of humans and other living things. I'll briefly review these normative implications as an example of how more recent ethical thinking might be applied to environmental practice.

Taylor develops four general duties that follow from the attitude of respect for nature. They are the rules of *nonmaleficence, noninterference, fidelity,* and *restitutive justice.*[17] As the name suggests, the duty of nonmaleficence requires that we do no harm to any organism. Taylor understands this as a negative duty. That is, we have the duty to refrain from any act that would harm an organism with a good of its own. We do not, however, have the positive duty to prevent any harms that we are not causing. Nor do we have the duty to reduce suffering or aid the organism in attaining its own good. Finally, like all duties, this requirement applies only to moral agents. Predatory animals, for example, cannot be required to refrain from harming their prey.

The rule of noninterference also establishes negative duties. By this rule we are required not to interfere with the freedom of individual organisms nor, in general, with ecosystems or biotic communities. Because humans can interfere with individual organisms in a variety of ways, there are a variety of specific duties that follow from this general rule. We should neither actively prevent organisms from freely pursuing their good, nor should we act so as to deny them the necessities required to attain that goal. Thus, we should not trap or enslave organisms, nor should we do anything that would deny them health or nutrition. The duty of noninterference requires that we "not try to manipulate, control, modify, or 'manage' natural ecosystems or otherwise intervene in their normal functioning."[18] Finally, because this is a negative duty, we have no positive obligation to help such organisms fulfill their *telos*, except where our own actions are the cause of the harm.

Taylor applies the rule of fidelity only to animals that live in the wild. Respect for nature requires that we not deceive or betray wild animals. Most hunting, fishing, and trapping—and much of the enjoyment and challenge of these activities—involve the attempt to deceive and then betray wild animals. As in any case of deception, the deceiver assumes a superiority over the deceived. The deceived, whether an animal or another human, is taken to have a lower worth than the deceiver. While hunting, fishing, and trapping also typically involve violating the duties of nonmaleficence and noninterference, breaking the rule of fidelity is yet another means of showing disrespect for nature.

The fourth rule, the duty of restitutive justice, requires that humans who harm other living organisms make restitution to those organisms. Justice demands that when a moral subject has been harmed, the agent responsible for that harm must make reparations for the harm. In general, the previous three duties establish the basic moral relationship between humans and other living organisms. When any of these rules are violated, the rule of restitutive justice requires that the moral balance between the two be restored. Thus, if we destroy an animal's habitat, justice demands that we restore it. If we capture or trap an animal or a plant, justice demands that we return it to its natural environment.

Finally, Taylor argues for a priority relation between these four rules. He believes that the duty of nonmaleficence is our "most fundamental duty to nature." He also believes that with careful attention, conflicts between the other three can be minimized. However, when conflicts cannot be avoided and when significant good can result without permanent harm, restitutive justice outweighs fidelity, which outweighs noninterference.

Perhaps the biggest challenge to any biocentric ethics arises when human interests conflict with the interests of nonhumans. In many ways, this is the primary test of any environmental philosophy and it is typically the major motivation behind any attempt to develop an environmental philosophy. What to do when important human interests come into conflict with the welfare of nonhuman organisms?

We need to recognize that in order to remain consistent with the fundamental principle of biocentric ethics, any resolution of such conflicts must not privilege human interests. That is, we cannot accept as a solution any decision that grants an in-principle advantage to humans. Any solution to conflict must respect the inherent moral worth of nonhumans.

We thus recognize that many of these moral conflicts and dilemmas would not arise within an anthropocentric framework. It is only after we acknowledge the inherent worth of other living things that a wide variety of conflicts can arise. Taylor mentions several as examples: filling in a wetland to build a marina, bulldozing a meadow of wildflowers to build a shopping mall, plowing a prairie to plant wheat or corn, strip-mining a mountainside. These activities raise moral problems only when we acknowledge that they create significant harm to other living organisms. But how do we resolve these conflicts without automatically favoring humans?

Following a long tradition in liberal political philosophy, Taylor argues for several formal or procedural rules to provide fair and impartial resolution of these conflicts. These rules are (1) self-defense, (2) proportionality, (3) minimum wrong, (4) distributive justice, and (5) restitutive justice.

The self-defense rule justifies favoring human interests when the conflicting interests of nonhuman organisms threaten or endanger human health or life. Thus, one would be justified in killing an attacking grizzly bear or exterminating an infectious organism or insect. As in the case of human self-defense, this principle holds only as a last resort.

The other four principles come into play when no serious harm to humans is threatened. They all rely on a distinction between *basic* and *nonbasic* interests. The principles of proportionality and minimum wrong govern those cases where the basic interests of nonhumans conflict with the nonbasic interests of humans. In this case, if the nonbasic human interest is incompatible with the basic interests of nonhumans, the principle of proportionality prohibits us from satisfying the human interests at the expense of the [basic] nonhuman interests. Thus, for example, human interest in killing reptiles to make fashionable shoes and handbags is prohibited, via the principle of proportionality, by the respect for nature.

When nonbasic human interest can be made compatible with the basic interests of nonhumans, even though they threaten or endanger the nonhumans, the principle of minimum wrong sets the conditions on satisfying human interests. Thus, the respect for nature might allow damming a river for a hydroelectric power plant even when this will adversely affect other living things.

The principle of distributive justice sets the conditions for resolving conflicts between the basic interests of humans and nonhumans. In general, fairness demands that burdens be shared equally and that the distribution of benefits and burdens be accomplished impartially.

Finally, restitutive justice demands that restitution be made any time a resolution of conflict fails to meet the conditions established by the principles of minimum wrong or distributive justice.

7.8 SUMMARY AND CONCLUSION

Even Taylor's careful defense of biocentric ethics faces serious challenges. I'll review several that have implications for the environmental philosophies discussed in the following chapters.

First, the emphasis on "noninterference" as a major normative principle suggests a view of humans and nature that is questionable at best. To say that we ought not "interfere with" nature, implies that humans are somehow outside of, or distinct from, nature. Humans are separate from nature, and thus we should leave natural processes alone. Thus, the claim is that environmental change—or even environmental destruction—is allowable (good?) if it results from "natural" processes. Change or destruction is wrong if it results from human interference.

But surely humans are as much a part of natural processes as any other organism. Thus, the fact that change is brought about by humans should not, in itself, have any ethical implications.

More importantly, a number of challenges center on Taylor's emphasis on individual organisms. He says inherent worth resides only in individual organisms; people have no *direct* duty to ecosystems, nonliving objects, or species, for example. Thus, although Taylor's biocentrism is nonanthropocentric, it remains individualistic. Several problems follow from this.

First, Taylor's ethics tends to assume an *adversarial* relationship between individuals. By focusing on individuals, each pursuing their own *telos*, Taylor assumes that conflict and competition is the natural state of life. The challenge for biocentric ethics, in this model, is to discover a procedure for resolving these conflicts impartially. Other philosophers (discussed later) suggest that a more holistic philosophy would emphasize cooperation and mutual dependencies rather than conflict between individuals.

Further, the focus on individuals seems to place Taylor in a serious dilemma. Consider the following example: I am planning to dig up a small section of my front yard and replace the lawn with a concrete and brick patio. In the process, I will be destroying countless living things, from the individual blades of grass to millions of microbiotic organisms. Does this action raise a serious moral conflict?

As we have seen, Taylor cannot simply grant the human interest a priority without abandoning his biocentric egalitarianism. Thus, to resolve this conflict he relies on the distinction between basic and nonbasic interests and the principles of proportionality, minimum wrong, and restitutive justice. Ultimately, I will either be allowed to build the patio, or I will not.

If I am not allowed to build the patio, Taylor's ethics may require too much of us. This is more than simply saying that it is "counterintuitive." (Taylor argues that the fact that a conclusion is counterintuitive provides no reason for rejecting it.) Rather, Taylor's standard would require a level of attention and care far beyond the abilities of most people. (Should I refrain from walking across my lawn too often for fear of creating a path and thereby destroying countless blades of grass? Do I really need to provide an ethical justification for eating vegetables?) It is difficult to see how we could ever be justified in doing much of anything if we did treat all nonhuman life-forms as deserving moral consideration.

Yet if I am allowed to build the patio Taylor must show exactly why such a nonbasic interest as this can override the basic interests of the grass and micro-organisms. Clearly, we could never allow the mass killing of humans for the sake of a patio. So, in order to maintain the nonanthropocentrism we need strong justification for why it is allowed in the case of plants. Taylor seems to suggest that, finally, the principle of restitutive justice comes into play. I can build the patio as long as I "restore the balance of justice between us and them."

Unfortunately, because I cannot "restore the balance" with those organisms that I have destroyed, this option seems to imply that my duty is to the organism's species. Perhaps I ought to replant some grass elsewhere in my yard. But of course, this requires us to abandon the individualism on which Taylor's ethics rests.

Surely there is room for a response, and this debate could continue to be developed. My point is not to suggest that Taylor's views are easily refuted. Rather, I focused on Taylor as the best representative of biocentric ethics to help us recognize how difficult a challenge lies ahead for biocentrism. For many other philosophers, a more attractive alternative lies with a more *holistic* approach. The remaining chapters explore in detail a variety of theories that place greater emphasis on ecosystems and ecological wholes.

Notes

1. See, for example, E. O. Wilson, "Threats to Biodiversity"; E. O. Wilson, "The Current State of Biological Diversity," in E. O. Wilson and Frances Peter, eds., *Biodiversity* (Washington, DC: National Academy Press, 1988); and John C. Ryan, "Conserving Biological Diversity," *State of the World 1992* (New York: Worldwatch Institute, 1992).
2. No consensus exists among philosophers on a consistent meaning for these terms. Perhaps it is too much to want one. The most developed and relevant discussion of these concepts can be found in Paul Taylor's *Respect for Nature* (Princeton, NJ: Princeton University, 1986), especially Chapter 2. See also the review of Taylor by Bryan Norton in *Environmental Ethics* 9, no. 3 (Fall 1987): 261–267, for a helpful discussion of Taylor and Callicott. Although my discussion owes much to Taylor, it differs slightly from his.
3. Tom Regan's notion of "inherent value" is perhaps the best example of this. Following Taylor (see *Respect for Nature*, p. 75), I treat Regan's "inherent value" as identical with Taylor's "inherent worth."
4. The most complete statement of Schweitzer's ethical views are found in his *Civilization and Ethics* (London: A. & C. Black, 1946). His autobiographical *Out of My Life and Thought*, trans. A. B. Lemke (New York: Holt, 1990) is also quite helpful. James Brabazon's *Albert Schweitzer: A Biography* (New York: Putnam, 1975) is a good secondary source.
5. Schweitzer, *Out of My Life and Thought*, p. 130.
6. Ibid., p. 130.
7. Ibid., p. 131.
8. Brabazon's biography, p. 257, reports the story that Schweitzer was willing to kill his own pelican when he recognized that its injuries were untreatable. The other anecdotes reported in this paragraph are also from Brabazon.
9. See K. Goodpaster's "From Egoism to Environmentalism," in K. Goodpaster and K. Sayre, eds., *Ethics and Problems of the 21st Century* (Notre Dame, IN: University of Notre Dame Press, 1979).
10. Of course, people do have moments in which their fundamental attitudes are questioned. Such moments of existential crisis, however, tend to reinforce rather than counter the view that no further justification can be given.
11. Taylor, p. 80.
12. Ibid., pp. 66–67.
13. Ibid., pp. 121–122.
14. For Regan's views on this "naturalistic fallacy," see *The Case for Animal Rights* (1983), pp. 247–248.
15. Taylor, p. 75.
16. Ibid., especially Chapter 3, fully develops the biocentric outlook.

17. Taylor, chap. 4, for the full presentation of these duties.
18. Ibid., p. 175.

Discussion Questions

1. Compose a list of things you value. Distinguish those things you value only instrumentally from those you value intrinsically. How many different types of things do you value for their own sake?

2. Do you value your education for its own sake, or only as a means to some other end, such as a career? Do you value art, music, and literature for their own sake, or for some other goods that they produce, or both?

3. Can morally good people freely and intentionally do morally bad things and remain good? What does it mean to say that someone "acts out of character"?

4. Like Aristotle, Taylor suggests that each species has a distinctive nature that can be identified by a characteristic activity. How else might you distinguish between species?

5. Taylor uses a distinction between *basic* and *nonbasic* interests to mediate conflicting interests. Do you find this distinction helpful? What might some basic human interests be? some nonbasic interests? How do these compare with basic and nonbasic interests of other living things?

6. On Taylor's account, would it make sense to attribute interests or goods to a wilderness area, or river, or other ecosystem? Are such things "teleological-centers-of-life"?

For Further Reading

Besides the works by E. O. Wilson mentioned in note 1 of this chapter, other helpful resources on biodiversity can be found in John Ryan, *Life Support: Conserving Biological Diversity*, No. 108 (Washington, DC: Worldwatch Institute, 1992).

James Brabazon, *Albert Schweitzer: A Biography* (New York: Putnam, 1975), is an excellent source on Schweitzer's life.

Environmental Ethics has published numerous discussions on intrinsic value and nature over the past fifteen years. As always, this journal is the first place to turn to for relevant philosophical discussions.

8

Ecology and Ethics

CASE EIGHT

The Yellowstone Fires

The Greater Yellowstone Area (GYA) encompasses nearly 5 million hectares (approximately 12 million acres) of mostly public land surrounding Yellowstone National Park and Grand Teton National Park. Besides the two national parks, GYA includes two national wildlife refuges and six national forests in Idaho, Wyoming, and Montana. The summer of 1988 was the driest summer in Yellowstone's recorded history, with virtually no rain during June, July, and August.

Each year dozens of fires burn within the GYA. Many result from lightning, and most are naturally extinguished after burning little more than an acre or two. But the summer of 1988 was different. Through May and June, numerous small fires were routinely allowed to burn and most were naturally extinguished after a short burn. But by mid-July high winds and continued drought conditions led to a growing intensity of the fires. By late July the National Park Service declared all the fires "wildfires" and began a major effort to suppress them. Despite the efforts of nearly 25,000 fire fighters, hundreds of fire-fighting vehicles and airplanes, personnel from the National Guard and the U.S. Army, Air Force, and Marines, and expenditures of over $120 million, the fires continued to burn out of control throughout August and into September. For nearly two months, Americans watched and read news accounts of the fire as it burned through Yellowstone Park. Only a snowstorm in September finally brought the fires under control. By that time nearly one million acres inside of Yellowstone Park and an additional half-million acres outside of the park had burned. Wild landscapes that had appeared as lush green forest in the spring had become devastated black terrain by early fall.

For a hundred years after the creation of Yellowstone National Park in 1872, fire suppression was the guiding policy of wilderness management, both in national parks and national forests. Smokey the Bear was the well-known symbol of the effort to fight fires wherever possible. This policy was almost universally supported. Timber interests saw it as a means for preserving valuable resources. Recreationists saw it as protecting their varied uses of the land. Preservationists saw it as a means for preserving the natural beauty of the wilderness.

As early as the 1940s the Forest Service had begun to use fire as a tool for managing some forests. Through the 1950s and 1960s the National Park Service experimented at times with controlled burns in certain areas. During that period, people charged with the management of national forests and parks began to recognize the natural and beneficial function that fires can play within an ecosystem. Fires contribute to biotic diversity and natural plant succession. Seeds of some species—the giant sequoia and the jack pine, for example—can germinate only after exposure to the intense heat of fires. Some animal species, like the Kirtland's warbler, in turn depend on such "fire species" of trees for habitat.[1] Fire can help decomposition of forest litter and aid in recycling soil nutrients. Fires also help maintain habitat for larger species and allow access to food sources that sprout after a burn.

By the early 1970s, many parks, including Yellowstone, adopted a fire policy that would allow certain naturally occurring fires to burn unchecked, as long as lives and property were not threatened. Between 1972 and 1988, hundreds of these so-called prescribed fires were allowed to burn within Yellowstone Park. (When a fire does not meet these prescriptions, it is designated as a "wildfire" and efforts are made to suppress it.) Most prescribed fires extinguished naturally after burning small areas. This "prescribed natural burn" policy was considered a success by most observers. Then came the summer of 1988.

In response to public pressure, the Bush administration declared a moratorium on the prescribed burn policy and ordered federal agencies to aggressively fight all fires. This moratorium stayed in effect until these agencies could develop a fire management plan that would better control forest fires.

8.1 INTRODUCTION

As described in the last chapter, biocentric ethics represents a significant departure from recent ethical thinking in at least two ways. By making life itself, and not any particular characteristic of living things, the criterion of moral standing, biocentric ethics seeks to avoid the moral hierarchy implicit in traditional theories. Life-centered ethics is nonanthropocentric in a way that even the animal welfare ethics of Singer and Regan are not. The criterion for moral considerability is not some human attribute that only some animals happen to possess.

Further, there is a shift of emphasis among some biocentric approaches away from ethical actions and on to ethical character and attitudes. We are asked to focus on biocentrism as an attitude with which we experience the world, rather than simply a rule according to which we should act. Thus, biocentrism goes beyond the ethical extensionism characteristic of much environmental ethics.

But for some people biocentric ethics has not gone far enough in breaking with tradition. According to a variety of approaches that we can call *ecocentric ethics*, an adequate environmental ethics must also give moral consideration to nonliving natural objects and ecological systems, relationships, and processes. Ecological ethics thus should be "holistic" in the sense that ecological "wholes" such as species and ecosystems, as well as the relationships that exist among natural objects, are seen as having direct moral standing.

Ecocentric ethics owes much to ecology, the science that studies the interactions of living organisms with each other and with their nonliving environments. *Ecosystems—forests, wetlands, lakes, grasslands, deserts—are areas in which a variety of living organisms interact in mutually beneficial ways with their living and nonliving environments. Ecologists seek to understand and explain these systematic interactions and dependencies. They focus more on the interdependencies than on individual organisms.*

Ecocentric ethics likewise will focus more on the ecological communities formed by these interdependencies than on individual organisms. It is thus a "holistic" rather than an "individualistic" ethics. One of the major challenges to any ethics that takes ecosystems seriously is to provide a philosophically adequate defense of *holism*. As we shall see, different thinkers adopt different models of the ecological "whole" and draw different ethical implications from it.

Ecology plays a major role in each of the ecocentric philosophies examined in the following chapters. This chapter, therefore, offers a general introduction to some important ecological concepts. A help-

ful start can be provided by a brief introduction to various understandings of the "wilderness." Wilderness areas are prominent examples of natural ecosystems, and the preservation of wilderness
areas is at the forefront of many environmental disputes. How we
understand the wilderness, how and why we value it, and how we
relate to and manage wilderness areas therefore are central questions of ecocentric ethics.

8.2 THE VALUE OF THE WILDERNESS

The **Wilderness Act of 1964** defines wilderness as those areas
"where the earth and its community of life are untrammeled by
man, where man himself is a visitor who does not remain." The
wilderness denotes an area unspoiled and undisturbed by human
activity. The Wilderness Act allowed the federal government to set
aside large tracts of public land to protect them from development.
Wilderness areas are set aside "for the use and enjoyment of the
American people in such a manner as will leave them unimpaired
for future use and enjoyment as wilderness." Typically this means
that activities such as hiking, camping, nonmotorized boating, and
some hunting and fishing are allowed. Commercial activities such
as mining and timber harvesting, and permanent buildings or road
construction are prohibited.

Taken literally, there are no wilderness areas left on earth. Humans inhabit much of the globe, and human activity affects the
entire earth. The climatic and atmospheric affects of pollution are
just one example of human activity that reaches every area of earth.
Most wilderness areas themselves are human constructs, in that
human activity is necessary to preserve and manage them. Thus,
even the decision to set aside and preserve a wilderness area involves the active management of the wilderness. This decision
therefore involves ethical questions of how we *should* manage wilderness ecosystems.

Many areas in the United States, and especially in Alaska, are still
relatively undisturbed by human activity and relatively uninhabited
by permanent human settlements. A significant portion of environmental activism is aimed at protecting and preserving these areas.
Indeed, an environmental ethics that does not address the question
of wilderness preservation would seem, at best, incomplete. But
what principles should guide human interaction with the wilderness? Should we actively *manage* the wilderness (if so, how?), or
should we be more passive and merely seek to *preserve* or *protect* it?
Do we have a responsibility to *restore* wilderness areas that have

been developed? If so, what exactly would count as restoration? The Yellowstone fires of 1988 and the resultant controversies of fire suppression policy provide a prime example of such questioning.

It appears that for many ethical traditions our responsibility to the wilderness is derived from other responsibilities. Tom Regan, for example, argued that the ecological community would be protected if only we were "to show the proper respect for the rights of the individuals who make up the biotic community."[2] Our responsibility concerning habitat, for example, derives from our responsibilities to individual animals (mammals, in Regan's view) that inhabit that area. But, in this view, we have no direct responsibility to habitat or wilderness areas themselves.

As mentioned at the end of Chapter 6, this approach makes the standing of an ecosystem dependent on factors that may or may not turn out for the good of the ecosystem. For example, showing "proper respect" for the rights of whitetail deer might well have disastrous ecological effects on an area where deer population is beyond the carrying capacity of the land. The population of various plant species, for example, could well be devastated by an overpopulation of deer. So, too, therefore could all other living things that interact with, and depend on, that species.

So how should we make decisions about wilderness management? One answer that has had a significant impact on contemporary environmentalism was offered by Aldo Leopold. In an often-quoted passage, Leopold tells us that "A thing is right when it tends to preserve the integrity, stability, and beauty of the biotic community. It is wrong when it tends otherwise."[3] More than any other person, Leopold's thinking has guided the philosophy of ecocentric ethics, and his emphasis on the "biotic community" becomes the focus of ecocentric ethics. Before examining his view in the next chapter, however, it is helpful to look at some traditional understandings of the wilderness.

8.3 THE IDEA OF THE WILDERNESS

Policy decisions about wilderness management depend greatly on how we conceive of the wilderness. As suggested earlier, a primary role of descriptive ethics is to make explicit the models and metaphors that shape our understanding of the world. In this section, I describe several traditional ways in which recent generations, especially Americans, have conceived of the wilderness.

As the word sometimes suggests, the wilderness is often taken to refer to a "wild" or untamed area. In this model, the wilderness is a threat to human survival; it is cruel, harsh, and perilous. This is an ancient view, common to many Judeo-Christian traditions that trace it to biblical discussions of the wilderness.

Both the Old and the New Testaments describe the wilderness as a barren and desolate place. In truth, the arid desert surrounding the ancient settlements of the Middle East was an exceptionally inhospitable place. Humans truly were only visitors here, because prospects for long-term survival outside of the settlement were bleak. But besides this practical understanding, the wilderness had a deeper symbolic meaning as well.

The Bible states that Adam and Eve were banished from the Garden of Eden into an "accursed" wilderness that "will grow thorns and thistles for you and none but wild plants for you to eat."[4] Moses later leads his people out of slavery and wanders in the wilderness for forty years before entering the "promised land." In the New Testament, Christ enters the wilderness to fast for forty days only then to be tempted by Satan.[5] The symbolism is clear. The wilderness not only is dangerous, it is home to the devil. It is the very antithesis of Eden and the "promised" land.

An interesting contrast to this can be found in the views of other cultures. Nomadic cultures, for example, rely too heavily on the wilderness to consider it an enemy. Chief Luther Standing Bear, an Oglala Sioux, illustrates this point in the following:

> We do not think of the great open plains, the beautiful rolling hills, and the winding streams with tangled growth as "wild." Only to the white man was nature a "wilderness" and only to him was the land "infested" with "wild" animals and "savage" people. To us it was tame. . . . Not until the hairy man from the East came and with brutal frenzy heaped injustices upon us and the families we loved was it "wild" for us.[6]

To a large degree, the "hairy man from the East," the European settlers and pioneers, shared the biblical view of the wilderness.

When the *Mayflower* arrived at Plymouth in 1620, these new settlers confronted a "hideous and desolate wilderness," according to William Bradford.[7] Two years later, Michael Wigglesworth described it as

A waste and howling wilderness
Where none inhabited
But hellish fiends and brutish men
That devils worshiped.[8]

Time and again, Puritan writing and preaching noted the biblical parallels to their own experiences. Like the Israelites, they too had escaped persecution, only to be led into the wilderness where God would test their faith. The wilderness was indeed the "Devil's den," home to "savages" trapped in "the snare of the Devil," "men transformed into beasts" serving as "slaves of Satan."[9]

The *Puritan model* gave rise to an ambiguous attitude toward the wilderness. On the one hand, the wilderness was an area to be avoided and feared. It was the area forsaken by God and home of the devil. Cities and towns were where humans could flourish, Bradford's "hideous and desolate wilderness" was where they suffered and died.

On the other hand, the wilderness represented an escape from oppression and, if not exactly the promised land itself, at least a temporary haven from which the promised land could be built. The Puritans believed that their own faith was being tested in the New England wilderness. The wilderness, after all, was the location where their God entered into a covenant with the Israelites. Proof that the Puritans were indeed the new "chosen people" would come from how well they fared in this wilderness. In this way, the wilderness also represented a challenge to be overcome, an enemy to be dominated, a threat to be conquered.

The Puritan model thus encouraged an aggressive and antagonistic attitude toward the wilderness. The wilderness must be tamed. New land must be conquered. Humankind is called to subdue and master the wilderness. The land is "improved" and its value enhanced when woodlands are cleared, wetlands drained, soil tilled, and permanent settlements established. Like some of the native inhabitants, the Puritans relied on fire as a tool for controlling and conquering the wilderness.

As these European settlers succeeded in this mission, the early Puritan model gave way to a different understanding of the wilderness. The wilderness could now be seen as supplying the resources for building the good life. Once conquered, nature gets identified with natural resources. Once human mastery is assured, the wilderness is less of a threat and more of a promise. Here we are reminded of Locke's image (Chapter 2) of a great, unowned frontier being transformed by human labor into productive and valuable property. This *Lockean model* sees the wilderness as given by God to all people in common, waiting for an individual with initiative and ambition to go out and work it and in the process convert it into private, personal property.

Thus the Lockean model sees the wilderness as real estate, as a commodity to be owned and used. Its value is a function of the human labor with which it is "mixed." No longer something to be feared, the wilderness represents great potential for serving human ends. The wilderness itself is relatively passive; it is "just there" serving no purposes other than those of its owners. Unowned and therefore unused land literally is a "wasteland." Unless and until put to human use, it is wasted potential.

It is fair to say that much of the early conservation movement shared this Lockean model of the wilderness. For Gifford Pinchot and other conservationists, the wilderness was identified with resources and valued primarily for the commodities that it produced. Of course, the Lockean model also was shared by those who opposed the conservation movement. Those who sought to control and exploit the wilderness in pursuit of personal fortune shared the Lockean assumption that the value of the wilderness is a function of human use. They agreed with the conservationists that the wilderness should be controlled and managed for human use; they disagreed over the range of beneficiaries of these resources.

Unlike the Puritan model, the Lockean model tends to support a fire suppression policy. Although fires could be used to clear land for some uses, forest fires represent a loss of resources and potential. The early conservationists guided the fire suppression policy in National Forests and National Parks. Smokey the Bear is a product of the conservation movement.

A third model of the wilderness, very influential among many people in the environmental movement, can also be traced to early American roots. The *Romantic model* views the wilderness as a symbol of innocence and purity. In this model, the wilderness is the last remaining area of unspoiled and uncorrupted nature. In contrast to the Puritan model, the wilderness is identified with paradise, the Garden of Eden. This is the place to which humans can turn to escape the corrupting influences of civilization. Where the Puritans saw threats and satanic temptations, the romantic sees a sacred purity. Where the Puritans saw the city as home to human flourishing, the romantics see the city as the genuine wasteland.

The philosophical roots of this view can be found in Jean-Jacques Rousseau and in the Americans Ralph Waldo Emerson and Henry David Thoreau. Like Locke, Rousseau spoke in general terms about a "state of nature" that contrasted with the present state of life within a society. For Rousseau, nature represented what was genuine, authentic, and virtuous about human existence. Society imposes artificial desires, selfishness, and inequality on human life. While not proposing a return to nature, Rousseau did believe that education and politics should be guided by principles derived from an understanding of the natural and intrinsic goodness of human beings. He held out as a model a life lived in harmony with nature, characterized by self-sufficiency, simplicity of desires, independence from culture and technology, and tranquility. In this view, the innate goodness of human nature was inseparable from the innate goodness of nature itself, a nature Rousseau often identified with the unspoiled wilderness of the Swiss Alps.

But it was the writings of Emerson, and especially of Thoreau, that had the earliest philosophical impact on the romantic view of the wilderness. Emerson was influenced by the European romantic movement of the eighteenth and nineteenth centuries. This outlook rejected scientific empiricism and rational analysis as the primary mode of understanding nature. The world of our ordinary experience, the world observed and analyzed by science, is largely a product of human creation and cultural conventions. We see and experience what we are taught to see and experience by our culture. That world only mirrors a deeper reality, a reality unconditioned by human beliefs and values. True understanding comes only when this deeper, or "transcendent" reality is grasped.

The American philosophical movement associated with European romanticism is called New England Transcendentalism. Transcendentalists, of whom Emerson and Thoreau are the best known, held that this deeper reality is grasped, not by scientific and technological analysis, but through intuition and imagination, through poetry and literature. Unspoiled by human activity, the wilderness was the most authentic instance of this transcendent reality. It is the purest example of God's creation. Thus the wilderness represented a retreat from the corrupting influences of civilization. The wilderness was the environment in which humans could attain their closest contact with the highest truths and with spiritual excellence.

Thus Thoreau retreats to his cabin on Walden Pond. Walking in the wilderness had a "tonic" effect on his spirit, where "my nerves are steadied, my senses and my mind do their office." The wilderness provides the opportunity to "settle ourselves, and work and wedge our feet downward through the mud and slush of opinion, and prejudice, and tradition, and delusion . . . till we come to a hard bottom and rocks in place, which we call *reality*."[10]

Perhaps nowhere is this romantic vision more fully observed than in James Fenimore Cooper's Leatherstocking Tales. In a series of novels beginning with *The Deerslayer, The Last of the Mohicans, The*

Pathfinder, The Pioneers, and *The Prairie,* Cooper traces the life of Natty Bumpo. Natty—known variously as the Deerslayer, Hawkeye, and Leatherstocking—is the ideal romantic hero. He was raised among the natives of upstate New York and from them he learns the ways of the wilderness. He is a simple man, innocent yet wise, honorable, forthright, and virtuous. He is totally without pretense or any of the other vices conditioned by social life. He is at home in the wilderness, living in harmony with it.

As Natty's life unfolds through these novels, he is continuously being pushed further westward by advancing civilization. He lives always on the border between civilization and the wilderness, a border located in central New York early in his life and on the Great Plains by the end of his life. From this perspective, we can see how the demands and expectations of society turn natural innocence and virtue into greed, destructiveness, and vice. With Natty, we lament the loss of wilderness, and with it the loss of a simpler life of authenticity and integrity.

8.4 ENVIRONMENTALISM AND THE ROMANTIC WILDERNESS MYTH

These various models for understanding the wilderness have had a significant impact on contemporary environmentalism. Obviously, Pinchot's conservationism and its view of the wilderness as a vast warehouse of natural resources has greatly influenced much of twentieth-century environmental policy. But the romantic model has had, in all likelihood, a more pervasive and pivotal influence on contemporary environmentalism. As mentioned in Chapter 1, part of the role of a descriptive approach to ethics is to uncover and examine the implicit models that guide our thinking and shape our values. In this section, we examine the influential romantic model of the wilderness.

As early as the mid-1800s, the romantic appreciation of the wilderness and the corollary regret over its destruction led to calls for the preservation of wilderness areas. Thus the lines between conservationists and preservationists described in Chapter 3 were drawn six decades before the public debates over Hetch Hetchy. During the first decades of the nineteenth century, John James Audubon, for whom the Audubon Society is named, mourned "the destruction of the forest." He witnessed "the woods fast disappearing under the axe" and concluded that "the greedy mills told the sad tale, that in a century the noble forests should exist no more."[11] In an 1858 essay, Thoreau explicitly called for the creation of wilderness preserves: "Why should not we have . . . our national preserves . . . in which the bear and the panther, and some even of the hunter race, may still exist and not be 'civilized off the face of the earth'—our forests . . . not for idle sport or food, but for inspiration and for our own true recreation?"[12]

This transcendentalist conviction that wilderness areas could be the source of inspiration if not divine revelation was shared by perhaps the most influential preservationist, John Muir. Muir's writing and organizing contributed significantly to the creation of national and state parks and wilderness preserves. Although it is far from clear that the earliest parks, such as Yellowstone, were established solely for preservationist reasons, it is clear that Muir's defense of the wilderness underlies much of the contemporary understanding of parks and preserves. To a large extent, this defense is based on the romantic wilderness model as described by Emerson and Thoreau.

The influence that the romantic model has had on the environmental movement can hardly be overestimated. But remember, it is only a model. It is a way of understanding that sheds light on the wilderness and helps us to see wilderness in new and important ways. But it can also be misleading. More recent perspectives, including contributions from ecology, stress several important shortcomings of the romantic model.

First, there can be a tendency to identify the "wilderness" with an idealized image of North America as it existed at the time of the first European settlers. These "virgin forests" "untrammeled by man" were of course much "trammeled" by the native inhabitants. There was a large human population already living in these forests when the first Europeans arrived. There is more than a small amount of cultural bias if not racism in a view that systematically ignores that fact.[13]

There can also be a tendency to view the "unspoiled wilderness" as a relatively benign and temperate place. Many romantic landscape portraits suggest a lush, green forest, with open meadows, clear of underbrush, spectacular sunsets, plentiful sources of food and shelter, docile animals, and temperate climate. In reality, of course, the wilderness can be a "wild" and harsh place. Deserts, arctic tundras, and rain forests are not at all like the romanticized image of nature that one forms while walking around Walden Pond. Even the relatively favorable areas within national parks and forests are quite inhospitable places with modern conveniences. And even when the sublime wilderness is appreciated, typically this is done from a perspective distant and apart from nature.

More importantly, the romantic model tends to encourage thinking that might be called "pre-Darwinian." Humans are seen as separate from nature, drawing inspiration from it perhaps, but nevertheless radically different from it. The human spirit is "transcendent" and, while unspoiled nature is our closest contact with transcendent reality, it remains part of a lower physical reality. Ecocentric ethics stresses the Darwinian understanding that humans are very much a part of nature, neither transcendent to nor radically different from it. From this perspective, acceptance of a dualism ("man and nature") only encourages moral hierarchies ("man above nature") and conflict ("man against nature").

Finally, the romantic model is inclined to see the wilderness as a static, unchanging place. The suggestion is that if we simply leave it alone, the wilderness will be "preserved" in its natural, unspoiled state. This view is expressed by George Perkins Marsh, a nineteenth-century environmentalist whose writings influenced both conservationists and preservationists. In his book *Man and Nature*, Marsh claimed,

> In countries untrodden by man, the proportions and relative positions of land and water, the atmospheric precipitation and evaporation, the thermometric mean, and the distribution of vegetable and animal life, are subject to change only from geologic influences so slow in their operation that the geographical conditions may be regarded as constant and immutable.[14]

But there are problems with this assumption. First, of course, it is not true. As suggested earlier, no area on earth is unaffected by human activity. Even the decision to protect an area as a wilderness preserve makes the wilderness dependent on human actions. But more to the point, as the controversies over the Yellowstone fires imply, the image of an unspoiled "constant and immutable" wilderness is incompatible with the ecological reality of natural processes. Does the commitment to preserving Yellowstone as a wilderness area require that we allow it to be devastated by a fire started by natural events? Lightning-caused fires occurred by the dozens every year in Yellowstone. Yet, a charred, blackened, treeless landscape is not the romantic wilderness image typically envisioned by Thoreau or Muir. But to prevent this from happening and therefore to "preserve" the wilderness, would require substantial human interference with nature. On the other hand, allowing natural processes to unfold will result in a wilderness unlikely to inspire the sort of unity with a transcendent reality suggested by the romantic images of Yosemite and Yellowstone.

Imagine, for example, that you sought to preserve the Boundary Waters Wilderness Area of northern Minnesota in its natural state. What would that look like? Are snowmobiles and canoes part of this natural state? Are Native Americans? Would hunting, fishing, and rice harvesting by native peoples be consistent with an "unspoiled" wilderness? Would Native Americans be allowed to pursue these traditional activities only in the traditional manner, or would they be allowed to use motorized boats? Is the ideal an image of what this area was like before Europeans arrived? Should we seek to reinstate the tundra environment that characterized this area many centuries ago? Perhaps its natural state is as it was during the last ice age. Such questions challenge the view of nature as "constant and immutable."

Contemporary ecologists reject the view of an unspoiled and unchanging nature. The wilderness must be understood as dynamic rather than static. Change and evolution is the norm, uniformity and constancy the exception. Ecologist Daniel Botkin makes this point in *Discordant Harmonies*:

> George Perkins Marsh's idea of nature as undisturbed by human influence is the one generally advocated; this point of view is dominant in textbooks on ecology and in the popular environmental literature. Perhaps even more significant, this idea of nature forms the foundation of twentieth-century scientific theory about populations and ecosystems. . . . Until the past few years, the predominant theories in ecology either presumed or had as a necessary consequence a very strict concept of a highly structured, ordered, and regulated, steady-state ecological system. Scientists know now that this view is wrong at local and regional levels—whether for the condor and whooping crane, or for the farm and the forest woodlot—that is, at the levels of populations and ecosystems. Change now appears to be intrinsic and natural at many scales of time and space in the biosphere . . . in at least some cases these changes are necessary for the persistence of life, because life is adapted to them and depends on them.[15]

The challenge for an ecocentric approach is to develop a coherent philosophical ethics that is consistent with ecology's emphasis on biotic wholes, and with ecology's recognition that change rather than constancy is the normal course of things. Thus we need an explanation of the relationship between parts-to-whole and an explanation of the dynamics of change that govern this whole. Again, any ethics that takes ecology seriously must provide a philosophically adequate account of these topics. As background to these challenges, let's now review some of the principal models of nature that guided the development of ecology.

8.5 ECOLOGICAL MODELS OF NATURE

As a distinct science, ecology is little more than a hundred years old. The first use of the term *ecology* is usually attributed to the German biologist Ernst Haeckel in the 1860s. Haeckel combined two Greek words—*oikos*, meaning "household" or "home," and *logos*, meaning "study of"—to coin *ecology*, the science that studies living organisms in their home or environment. ("Economics" has similar Greek roots, *oikos* and *nomos* meaning the "rules of the household.")

As some of the earlier discussions of science in this book have suggested, scientists are guided in their study by various theories, or frameworks, or models. The development of ecology usefully can be reviewed in terms of several basic models that guided the work of ecologists. These models shaped and directed the thinking of ecologists as they studied biological "households." They have also, therefore, shaped the thinking of those whose ethical thinking has ecological roots.

One of the earliest models to guide ecological science was the *organic* model. In this view, individual species were related to their environment as organs were related to the body. Just as an organism grows through developmental stages toward a mature level, so too do ecological "households" grow, develop, mature. Ecological environments can therefore be described as "healthy," "diseased," "young," "mature," and so on according to a normal developmental standard. Thus, this model explains the part-to-whole relationship in terms of an organism and the nature of change in terms of development or maturity.

This organic model can be found in the pioneering work of two late-nineteenth-century U.S. ecologists, Henry Cowles and Frederick Clements. These scientists focused their research on the process of plant succession within a particular geographical area. Working out of the University of Chicago, Cowles studied the plant succession along the sand dunes of Lake Michigan. He discovered that as one moves away from the lakeshore, plants are replaced by other species in a determinate and well-defined progression. Thus, the ecologist could describe the normal or natural sequence of plant succession at any given location along the lakeshore.

At the University of Nebraska, Frederick Clements was pursuing similar research on the prairies and grasslands of the western plains. Clements was also taken with the dynamic process of biological change that occurs within a particular habitat. He recognized that, through time, various species will be introduced into an area, will become more and more prevalent before eventually declining and disappearing. But Clements denied that this plant succession was random or arbitrary. He believed that for any given location and climate, plant succession develops toward a stable and relatively permanent population, what he termed the "climax vegetation." Thus, for any particular location or habitat, ecologists could determine the specific climax community that would be most at home in this area.

In the organic model, the ecologist is like a physician. Just as the physician studies anatomy and physiology to determine the normal and proper function of the body, the ecologist studies a habitat—temperature range, rainfall, soil conditions, and so on—to determine the normal and proper functioning of that area. The ecologist can then diagnose problems and prescribe treatment to ensure a healthy and balanced organism.

For Clements, this climax community can be understood as itself a "complex organism." It is

> of a higher order than an individual geranium, robin or chimpanzee. . . . Like them it is a unified mechanism in which the whole is greater than a sum of its parts and hence it constitutes a new kind of organic being with novel properties.

Later in the same page Clements claims that

> The unit of vegetation, the climax formation, is an organic entity. As an organism, the formation arises, grows, matures, and dies. . . . The climax formation is an adult organism, the fully developed community, of which all initial and medial stages are but stages of development. Succession is the process of the reproduction of a formation.[16]

By the early twentieth century, the organic model began to give way to a *community model*. In this view, ecologists began to view nature more as a community or society than as an organism. Thus, parts are related to the whole as citizens are related to a community or as individuals are related to their family. Change is viewed less as development or growth, and more in terms of interactions and mutual dependencies. Members of a community fill different roles or "professions" that contribute to the overall functioning of the community. In the community model, ecology truly does study nature's "household."

Some defenders of the community model were motivated by a desire to refute the Darwinian (and, to them, the irreligious) emphasis on competition and conflict between species.[17] Nature is designed as a household, where each member cooperates and contributes to the whole. Many of these defenders were more comfortable identifying their project with a phrase older than "ecology." Studying nature's household is to study "nature's economy."

Perhaps the most influential and respected scientist associated with the community model is the English zoologist Charles Elton. Elton described his own subject as "the sociology and economics of animals." His goal was to present a description of nature as an integrated and mutually dependent economy.

Elton's community model therefore was a *functional* model: individual members are identified by the function that they perform in the system. The system itself is seen in economic terms. Some members function as producers, some as consumers. The commodity is food, and ecological communities can be described as "food chains" in which individual members fill various "occupations." The laws of nature thus describe the processes of producing, distributing, and consuming food. Accordingly, an individual species's function or role within a food chain—its ecological "niche," in Elton's terms—is determined by what it eats and by what eats it.

The idea of a "food chain" is perhaps the most familiar concept of the community model. Some organisms, called "producers," manufacture their own food by producing organic compounds (sugars, starches, cellulose) from inorganic molecules (carbon dioxide and water) and energy. Photosynthesis is the primary process through which producers manufacture food.

Other organisms, "consumers," depend on producers, directly or indirectly, for their food source. Herbivores, or primary consumers, feed directly and exclusively on plants (producers). Carnivores feed either on plant-eating animals (and are therefore called secondary consumers) or on other animal-eating animals (in which case they are called tertiary consumers). Omnivores, such as pigs, rats, and humans, eat both plants and animals.

On the other end of the food chain, decomposers (mostly fungi and bacteria) feed on dead organic material, breaking it down into simpler inorganic molecules. The inorganic molecules can, again, be used by producers while the decomposers are, in turn, eaten by worms, insects, and other organisms.

Although this community model continues to influence both ecologists and others, it has been replaced by a less metaphorical and anthropomorphic version. In a 1935 essay, the English biologist Arthur Tansley proposed that the language of superorganisms and communities be replaced by the less metaphorical language of physics.[18] Tansley sought to eliminate such qualitative terms as "food," "producers," "consumers," "communities," "occupations," and replace them with the more objective language of "ecosystems" and "energy."

On the *energy* model, the ecological whole is to be understood as an energy system or circuit. Just as the physicist studies the flow of energy through a physical system, the ecologist studies the flow of energy through an ecosystem. The language of a food chain is replaced with the mathematically more precise language of chemistry and physics. The ecosystem appears as just another physical, mechanical system.

Further, the distinction between living (biotic) and nonliving (abiotic) components of the system is broken down. The abiotic components, such as solar energy, temperature, water, chemical molecules, and so on, are equally important elements in the system.

We can trace the flow of energy through an ecosystem in a way that parallels the flow of food through the food chain but without using economic or household metaphors. Photosynthesis is the process through which solar energy breaks the chemical bonds of carbon dioxide and water molecules forming new molecules of carbohydrates and oxygen. Respiration transforms carbohydrates and oxygen back into carbon dioxide, water, and energy. The energy released in this process powers the chemical and physical processes of life, growth, reproduction, and so on. Photosynthesis and respiration are the processes of the carbon and oxygen cycles in ecosystems.

Living organisms also need nitrogen, which provides the chemical basis of proteins, DNA, and other essential molecules. Nitrogen can also be traced through an ecological cycle. Atmospheric nitrogen, which makes up 78 percent of the atmosphere, is converted into water-soluble nitrate ions by various biological and physical processes. Bacteria living in the soil and in the roots of various plants, algae living in water, and even lightning contribute to this conversion. Plants in turn convert nitrates obtained from the soil to the more complex nitrogen-based molecules such as proteins and DNA. Animals obtain the nitrogen-based molecules that they need by eating plants or other animals. Finally, when plants and animals die, decomposers eventually break these nitrogen molecules back down into nitrogen gas and nitrate ions. Thus, the cycle begins again.

Since the carbon, oxygen, and nitrogen cycles—as well as a similar cycle for phosphorus and the more familiar water cycle—are all ultimately driven by solar energy, ecologists can account for ecosystems solely in terms of the energy that flows through various chemical, biological, and climatic cycles.[19]

Although the energy model appears to be the predominant model among contemporary ecologists, all three models continue to influence our understanding of ecosystems. As shown in what follows, each also has important philosophical implications about nature and ethics.

8.6 SUMMARY AND CONCLUSION

Ecocentric approaches to environmental ethics develop from the conviction that ecology must play a primary role in our understanding and valuing of nature. However, as shown in this brief survey, the science of ecology itself is evolving. Thus, we need to recognize that with ecocentric approaches we are dealing with environmental philosophies that are not yet fully formed.

At the beginning of this chapter, I suggested that "holism" is the unifying idea common to ecocentric theories. But this concept, like so many philosophical abstractions, is very elusive. At one level, it can be grasped easily enough. The common expression that "the whole is more than the sum of its parts" seems to get at the essence of holism. Yet just below the surface of this ordinary insight lies deep philosophical complexity. As a transition into the next chapter, let me just suggest some of the complexity that lies ahead for ecocentric philosophies.

What does it mean to say that "the whole is more than the sum of its parts"? In one sense, what might be called *metaphysical holism*, this claim can mean that "wholes" *exist* apart from or are as real as their parts. Metaphysical holism claims that wholes are real, and perhaps more real than their constituent parts. For our purposes, this would involve the claim that ecosystems have an independent existence beyond the existence of their individual elements. If this were so, the door would be open for arguing that they qualify for moral standing in their own right.

We have seen hints of this before. The organic model, for example, seems to suggest a metaphysical holism. We noted that Frederick Clements refers to the "climax community" as itself a "complex organism" that "constitutes a new kind of organic being." A similar point is made by J. Baird Callicott, the leading philosophical interpreter of Leopold's land ethic:

> Ecology is the study of relationships of organisms to one another and to the elemental environment. . . . The ontological primacy of objects and the ontological subordination of relationships characteristic of classical western science is, in fact, reversed in ecology. Ecological relationships determine the nature of organisms rather than the other way around. A species is what it is because it has adapted to a niche in the ecosystem. The whole, the system itself, thus, literally and quite straightforwardly shapes and forms its component parts.[20]

And further:

> From the perspective of modern biology, species adapt to a niche in the ecosystem. Their actual relationships to other organisms (to predators, to prey, to parasites and disease organisms) and to the physical and chemical conditions (to temperature, radiation, salinity, wind, soil and water pH) literally sculpt their outward forms, their metabolic, physiological, and reproductive processes, and even their psychological and mental capacities.[21]

This seems to suggest that individual organisms do not comprise their ecosystems; instead, ecosystems create individuals. Callicott's "ontological primacy" would seem equivalent to metaphysical holism.

A second sense of holism might be called *methodological* or *epistemological* holism. Unlike metaphysical holism, this version is not concerned with claims about what exists or what is real. Methodological holism focuses, instead, on how best to understand or come to know various phenomena. In this view, we would have an inadequate and incomplete understanding of an ecosystem even if we knew everything about its constituent parts, if that is *all* we knew.

In some ways, the community model may suggest methodological holism. In offering *functional* explanations for individual organisms, the community model implies that an adequate understanding comes only in viewing the system of interdependencies as a whole. The food chain, for example, identifies individuals in terms of the role that they play in the chain.

Finally, what we can call *ethical* holism would suggest that moral considerability should be extended to wholes. Just as we recognize that corporations, for example, have a legal standing independent of the legal standing of their individual members, the ethical holist argues that ethical standing can also be extended to relevant kinds of nonindividuals.

There is perhaps no better example of such a view than Leopold's statement, quoted earlier, that "A thing is right when it tends to preserve the integrity, stability, and beauty of the biotic community. It is wrong when it tends otherwise." Right and wrong is a function of what is good or bad for the whole community, not for its constituent members.

This is not the place to review the philosophical debates concerning holism. Serious philosophical challenges can be raised against each of these types of holism. Indeed, we will see specific versions of these criticisms raised in what follows. But this should indicate the challenges that lie ahead for ecocentric environmental philosophies.

Notes

1. For a discussion of the Kirtland's warbler and its dependence on the jack pine, see Daniel Botkin, *Discordant Harmonies*, pp. 68–71.
2. Regan, *The Case for Animal Rights* (1983), p. 363.
3. Leopold, *Sand County Almanac*, pp. 224–225.
4. Genesis 3:17–19.
5. Matthew 4:1.
6. Luther Standing Bear, *Land of the Spotted Eagle* (Boston: Houghton Mifflin, 1933) as quoted in T. C. McLuhan, ed., *Touch the Earth: A Self-Portrait of Indian Existence* (New York: Promontory Press, 1971), p. 45.
7. William Bradford, *Of Plymouth Plantation, 1620–47* (Boston: Wright and Potter, 1899), p. 62, as quoted in Roderick Nash, *Wilderness and the American Mind* (New Haven, CN: Yale University Press, 1967), p. 24. Much of this section relies on Nash's superb history of the wilderness idea.
8. *Proceedings of the Massachusetts Historical Society* 83 (1871–73) as quoted in Sagoff, *Economy of the Earth*, p. 125.
9. John White, *The Planter's Plea* (1630), quoted in Peter Carroll, *Puritanism and the Wilderness* (New York: Columbia University Press, 1969), p. 11.
10. Henry David Thoreau, *Walden* (New York: Library of America, 1985), p. 400.
11. John James Audubon, *Delineations of American Scenery and Character*, ed. Francis Hobart Herrick (New York: Baker, 1926), pp. 9–10, as quoted in Roderick Nash, *Wilderness and the American Mind* (New Haven, CN: Yale University Press, 1967), p. 97.
12. Henry David Thoreau, *Maine Woods*, in *The Writings of Henry David Thoreau* (Boston: Houghton Mifflin, 1894–95), vol. 3, pp. 212–213.
13. Cooper's Leatherstocking Tales are a perfect example of the connection between the romantic wilderness myth and culturally biased and racist attitudes toward Native Americans.
14. G. P. Marsh, *Man and Nature*, ed. D. Lowenthal (Cambridge, MA., Harvard University Press, [1864]1967), pp. 29–30. As quoted in Botkin, p. 8.
15. Botkin, p. 9.
16. Frederick Clements, *Research Methods in Ecology* (Lincoln: University of Nebraska Press, 1905). As quoted by Donald Worster in *Nature's Economy* (Cambridge, England: Cambridge University Press, 1985), p. 211.

17. See Worster, chap. 14.

18. Arthur G. Tansley, "The Use and Abuse of Vegetational Concepts and Terms," *Ecology* 16 (1935): 284–307.

19. A very readable summary of these topics can be found in David Gates, "The Flow of Energy in the Biosphere," *Scientific American* 224 (1971): 89–100.

20. J. Baird Callicott, "The Conceptual Foundations of the Land Ethic," in *In Defense of the Land Ethic* (Albany, NY: SUNY Press, 1989), p. 87.

21. J. Baird Callicott, "The Metaphysical Implications of Ecology," in *In Defense of the Land Ethic* (Albany, NY: SUNY Press, 1989), p. 110.

Discussion Questions

1. If you were responsible for a national park such as Yellowstone, would you support or oppose road building plans to provide access to the back-country for more people? How would you defend your views to citizens who disagreed? Would you seek to make the park more accessible for RVs, and trailers? for handicapped visitors?

2. What images come to mind when you think of the "wilderness"? What is the origin of these images? What adjectives would you use to describe a wilderness?

3. What model should guide public policy when seeking to restore a wilderness area? Should it be restored to the point at which it was found by the first white settlers? Should it simply be left alone, even if this means that nonnative species will populate the area?

4. Can inspiration or aesthetic appreciation be taught? Could you persuade someone that a mountain vista is beautiful if that person doesn't already appreciate it? If you believed that a scenic mountain valley was beautiful or inspirational and some developers disagreed, could anything be done to change their perception?

5. Is "man" in a struggle for survival against "nature"? What kind of evidence could you marshall for or against this view?

6. Should Native Americans be allowed to hunt, fish, and trap on their traditional lands if these lands are now a part of wilderness preserves? If so, should they be allowed to use only traditional methods for hunting and fishing, or should modern techniques and vehicles be allowed? Should Eskimo peoples be permitted to hunt otherwise protected animals such as whales and seals for food? Should they be permitted to engage in commercial hunting and trapping?

7. Is the good for some collective such as a team or a country identical with or reducible to the good of its individual members? Can the good for an individual become identical with the good of some group?

For Further Reading

Beside Roderick Nash's excellent history of the wilderness idea in America, see also Max Oelschlaeger, *The Idea of Wilderness from Prehistory to the Present* (New Haven, CN: Yale University Press, 1990), for a more general discussion of these topics.

Michael Cohen, *The Pathless Way* (Madison: University of Wisconsin Press, 1984), provides an excellent intellectual biography of John Muir.

Holmes Rolston, III, *Philosophy Gone Wild: Essays in Environmental Ethics* (Buffalo: Prometheus Books, 1986), is an original philosophical defense of an ecocentric ethics.

9

The Land Ethic

Predator–Prey Relationship

In its most direct meaning, the "predator–prey relationship" simply refers to the fact that some species feed on members of other species. When the member of the feeding species lives in or on its food, it is called a *parasite* and its food a *host*. When the feeding species does not live in or on its food, it is called a *predator* and its food is the *prey*. Thus most nonmicroscopic life-forms, including all the familiar herbivores and carnivores, are predators. Further, as suggested by the image of a "food chain," most predators themselves turn out to be prey for another species.

Beyond this neutral description of predators and prey, however, lies a more value-laden and provocative connotation. "Predator" suggests malevolence and cruelty. A predator is a menacing presence, secretly stalking its prey. Thus, we never think to call a songbird, a deer, or a squirrel "predator." We usually reserve this name for the larger carnivores, those animals with sharp claws or teeth that just might have humans as their prey. Bears, wolves, coyotes, mountain lions, and sharks are the classic predators. It is not surprising then, perhaps, that all these animals have been hunted and poisoned to near extinction at the hand of humans.

But something other than fear of being attacked must account for the vengeance with which humans have hunted down these animals. In fact, even before these populations were devastated, very few humans actually became prey to large carnivores. Certainly the Puritan tradition of viewing the wilderness as evil and threatening reinforced the fear of wild animals. Perhaps the biggest factor is that large carnivores compete with humans for food. Ranchers, farmers, and hunters, and government-sponsored programs working on their behalf, are the single greatest factor in the near extinction of wolves, grizzly bears, and mountain lions in North America. These animals threatened livestock and game—our food—and thus had to be eliminated.

Government policy regarding predators parallels, in many ways, policy toward forest fires. By the first decades of the twentieth century, federal policy was guided by the progressive-conservation movement associated with people such as Gifford Pinchot. The conservation movement aimed to guarantee a steady supply of natural resources, whether these were trees, livestock, or crops. By later in the century, the growing influence of ecology had introduced a more tempered approach to apparent threats to these resources, be it from fire or predators.

The conservationists of the early twentieth century fought the greed and exploitation that characterized almost all previous attitudes toward natural resources. They fought to conserve these resources and manage them in the public interest. Scientific forestry and, later, scientific game management pursued the most efficient use of natural resources. They also involved the commitment to protect these resources from predators.

By and large, the conservation movement adopted a Lockean view of the wilderness and wild animals. They were understood as property, private or public, that should serve as a resource for human use. The conservation movement could also be seen as consistent with the climax community model emerging from the early science of ecology. This model suggested that in each specific locale populations normally develop toward a single stable "climax" community. Thus, guided by ecological science, experts could manage wildlife so as to ensure the natural stability of a local ecosystem. They would be managing wildlife the way Pinchot's foresters managed the forests, in a way that guaranteed a long-term, stable supply of resources.

Unfortunately, within such a model, predators could be viewed as a threat to the stability and health of natural resources. Like a cancer growing within an organic body, predators eat away at resources, jeopardizing the continued health and well-being of the supply—and thereby jeopardizing the efficient management of natural resources. Large carnivores were on a par with locusts and other pests that threatened crops; they should be eradicated to protect human interests.

Through the first half of the twentieth century, various government agencies aggressively pursued policies aimed at exterminating predators. In the beginning, these policies carried on the centuries-old bounty system in which private individuals were rewarded for killing predators. By 1920 the bounty system was supplemented by government-trained and -paid hunters, trappers, and poisoners. For decades, millions of dollars a year were spent to kill bears, wolves, coyotes, and mountain lions. By the 1970s, all but the coyote were nearly extinct in the lower forty-eight states.

A minority perspective began to emerge among scientists and wildlife managers during the 1920s and 1930s. Influenced in part by ecology's growing focus on interdependent communities, this perspective pointed out the functional role that predators play in the "economy of nature." Paralleling foresters who saw a beneficial role for fire in forest management, these people believed that predators acted as a natural check on the populations of other wild animals. Like all other members of the ecological community, predators filled a role and contributed to the overall balance of nature.

Specifically, predators were seen as nature's way of maintaining stable and healthy populations. Unchecked, populations would increase exponentially. In reality, various factors work together to keep populations in check. This idea can be expressed mathematically in terms of an S-shaped curve called a *logistic*. A population increases until it reaches a point at which it exceeds the capacity of its habitat to support that number of organisms (the habitat's "carrying capacity"). The population then decreases—through starvation, for example—below the level that could be supported by its habitat. Once a population falls below the habitat's carrying capacity, the population level is then free to resume its growth. This growth rate oscillates back and forth across the line that represents a population's equilibrium with its habitat's carrying capacity.

Predators serve as one of the ecological factors that keep a population in check. When a prey's population increases, plentiful food is available to predators. Not only is food abundant, but predators tend to eat the least fit organisms within a population. This helps maintain the genetic strength and fitness of a population. The abundance of prey leads to an increase in the predator population, which in turn leads to a decrease in the prey population. Over time, this decrease in prey leads to a decrease in predators, which once again leads to an increase in prey. Thus, the population size of predators and prey can be pictured as a set of symmetrical S-curves, mathematically known as the Lotka-Volterra equations.[1]

By the middle of the twentieth century, the model held sway among most ecologists. This has resulted in a reversal of earlier environmental sentiment against predators. Recent attempts to restore large carnivores to some of their original habitats within the lower forty-eight states are the direct results of this reversal. It should be mentioned that more recent scholarship casts doubt on this precise, mathematical model of the relation of predator and prey. The facts seldom exactly match the theory.

9.1 INTRODUCTION

Aldo Leopold (1887–1948) is the single most influential figure in the development of an ecocentric environmental ethics. The science of ecology developed during his lifetime, and he was the first person to call for a radical rethinking of ethics in light of this new science. His life's work sought to integrate ecology and ethics. Leopold was an eloquent and prolific writer, and the collection of his essays published posthumously as *A Sand County Almanac* is one of the classic texts of the environmental movement. The definitive essay of this book, titled "The Land Ethic," is the first systematic presentation of an ecocentric ethics. This chapter focuses on Leopold's "Land Ethic" as the best example of an ecocentric ethics.

The development of Leopold's thinking parallels the change in thinking about predators. In many ways, Leopold is the person most responsible for this change. In his early research, Leopold was to game management what Pinchot was to forestry. He introduced scientific techniques and principles to the management of natural resources, in this case to the management of game. Leopold was trained at the Yale Forest School, and his book, *Game Management*, published in 1933 became the classic text in this field. It was a classic conservationist text: game species such as deer and quail were "resources" or "crops" that should be managed to increase their harvest: "Like all other agricultural arts, game management produces a crop by controlling the environmental factors which hold down natural increase, or productivity, of the seed stock."[2] One of the "environmental factors which hold down" game resources, of course, was the existence of predators.

In an early essay published in 1915, Leopold set out the conservationist position regarding predators, or as they were labeled, "varmints." Regretting the antagonism that seemed to exist between ranchers and hunters, Leopold advised that stockmen and game protectionists are "mutually and vitally interested in a common problem. This is the reduction of predatory animals." In a passage that, today, would outrage most ecologists and environmentalists, Leopold explains,

> It is well known that predatory animals are continuing to eat the cream off the grower's profits, and it hardly needs to be argued that, with our game supply as low as it is, a reduction in the predatory animal population is bound to help the situation. If the wolves, lions, coyotes, bob-cats, foxes, skunks, and other varmints were only decreasing at the same rate as our game is decreasing, it might at least be said that there was no serious occasion for worry. . . . Whatever may have been the value of the work accomplished by bounty systems, poisoning, and trapping, individual or governmental, the fact remains that varmints continue to thrive and their reduction can be accomplished only by means of a practical, vigorous, and comprehensive plan of action.[3]

But as his own ecological understanding developed as a result of his field experiences and research, Leopold began to see problems with this conservationist approach to nature.

Specifically, the conservationist approach tended to view nature mechanically, as a mere object that could be manipulated for human ends without repercussions. Leopold recognized that this conflicted with a more ecological perspective in at least two ways. First, it seriously underestimates the interconnectedness of nature. Manipulating one part of nature—by exterminating predators, for example—surely will have significant implications elsewhere as, for example, the overpopulation of deer herds. Further, unlike a mechanistic model, ecology teaches us that we never know with any kind of certainty what consequences will follow from these manipulations. Second, the mechanistic approach treats the earth as "dead" when, in fact, ecology recognizes that even a handful of "dirt" contains an abundance of living organisms. Less than ten years after writing his essay "The Varmint Question," Leopold discusses conservation as a "moral issue" that transcends the utilitarian-economic calculations of earlier conservationism:

> Many of the world's most penetrating minds have regarded our so-called "inanimate nature" as a living thing, and many of us . . . have felt intuitively that there existed between man and the earth a closer and deeper relation than would necessarily follow the mechanistic conception of the earth.

> Philosophy, then, suggests one reason why we cannot destroy the earth with moral impunity; namely that the "dead" earth is an organism possessing a certain kind of degree of life, which we intuitively respect as such.[4]

This new perspective, what we might call an "ecological conscience," developed over decades and gets presented most fully in the late 1940s in "The Land Ethic." This ecological conscience represents a shift from a view of nature as having only instrumental value, to one which recognizes an inherent worth in natural systems.

9.2 THE LAND ETHIC

Leopold opens "The Land Ethic" by repeating the story of Odysseus who, on returning from the Trojan War, hangs a dozen of his women slaves for misbehavior. Since slaves were understood as property, Odysseus' action was not seen as unethical or inappropriate. Since that time, ethics has evolved so that moral standing now is extended to all human beings. "The Land Ethic" is Leopold's call to continue this extension of ethics to include land, plants, and animals. At the present time, land, like Odysseus' slaves, is understood as mere property; we have privileges in respect to the land, but no obligations to it.

An ecological understanding of land rebuts the Lockean view of land as property. We can no longer treat the land as a mere object, as "dead" matter that can be used and shaped in just any way that humans desire. Land should be viewed as a living organism, that can be healthy or unhealthy, that can be injured or killed. "Land, then, is not merely soil; it is a fountain of energy flowing through a circuit of soils, plants, and animals."[5]

Thus, Leopold opens "The Land Ethic" by suggesting the sort of moral extensionism that we traced in earlier chapters. He speaks of the "extension of ethics," and tells us that "the land ethic simply enlarges the boundaries of the community to include soils, waters, plants, and animals, or collectively, the land." Although "we have no land ethic yet, we have at least drawn nearer the point of admitting that birds should continue as a matter of biotic right."[6] His suggestion seems to be that we should extend moral consideration, what he termed "biotic rights," to birds, soils, waters, plants, and animals.

However, Leopold never abandons his belief that these natural objects can and should be used as "resources" that can be managed for human benefit. As a result, it would be difficult to read Leopold as a defender of animal and plant rights, in the style of Singer, Regan, or Stone.[7] It is difficult to reconcile granting moral rights to animals while at the same time being willing to treat them as resources. Leopold's own long-standing practice of hunting also suggests that he cannot be placed in the animal rights camp.

This apparent inconsistency is resolved when we view the land ethic *holistically*. It is the "land community" that is granted moral standing; individual members of that community can still be treated as resources as long as the community itself is respected. The "ecological conscience" teaches us that humans are but members of the biotic community, "biotic citizens," rather than "conquerors" of nature. Ecology shifts the focus of moral consideration away from individuals and on to biotic wholes.

Accordingly, the moral extensionism that is at work in Leopold's writing does not ask that we simply make room in our moral deliberations for yet another type of individual moral subject. Leopold asks that we make a radical category shift away from individuals. We now ought to grant moral standing to communities, symbolically represented as the "land."

This aspect of the land ethic is concisely summarized in Leopold's most celebrated and controversial statement: "A thing is right when it tends to preserve the integrity, stability, and beauty of the biotic community. It is wrong when it tends otherwise."[8] When combined with some basic ecological observations, this principle can be used to generate specific normative conclusions.

Leopold uses the image of a "biotic pyramid" or "land pyramid" to help us understand the nature of the biotic community. This is an important image for it contains elements of Elton's functional community model, and Tansley's energy system model of ecological wholes. The land pyramid is a "highly organized structure" of biotic and abiotic elements through which solar energy flows. This structure can be represented as a pyramid, with soil on the bottom, followed in turn by a plant layer, an insect layer, a bird and rodent layer, "and so on up through the various animal groups to the apex layer, which consists of the larger carnivores."

Thus, species are arranged in layers according to the food they eat. Because there must exist numerically more members of a prey species than its predators (otherwise the predators would soon starve), "each successive layer decreases in numerical abundance" forming the pyramidal shape of the system. The "lines of dependency for food and other services are called food chains":

> Each species, including ourselves, is a link in many chains. The deer eats a hundred plants other than oak, and the cow a hundred plants other than corn. Both, then, are links in a hundred chains. The pyramid is a tangle of chains so complex as to seem disorderly, yet the stability of the system proves it to be a highly organized structure. Its functioning depends on the cooperation and competition of its diverse parts.[9]

With this, we can begin to reach some general normative prescriptions. Given the complexity of this "highly organized structure," only a "fool would discard seemingly useless parts." Preservation of life-forms in all their diversity is the first general rule that we ought to follow, since not even ecologists understand how this complex system operates.

Because this complex structure has developed through millions of years of evolution, human interference with it ought always to be humble and constrained. Any change in the system will require that many other elements adjust themselves to it. When this occurs slowly, as it does through evolution, the system is self-regulating. When change is introduced abruptly and violently, as it typically is through human intervention, the potential for disaster is genuine. Thus we should tread lightly on the ecosystem. It is also wise to assume that native plants and animals are best suited for a particular locale. Introducing nonnative species is courting disaster. So, too, one can speculate, would reliance on chemical pesticides, herbicides, and fertilizers.

More generally, while reading *A Sand County Almanac* one sees a portrait of a stable and harmonious ecological relationship. The many images one gets of Leopold himself living on his Sand County farm depict a healthy relationship with the land. One feels that if we could only generalize life on a small, self-sustaining farm we would be close to the ideal ecological and environmental lifestyle.

Just one of the many images that is particularly moving is the almanac entry for February:

> There are two spiritual dangers in not owning a farm. One is the danger of supposing that breakfast comes from the grocery, and the

other that heat comes from the furnace. To avoid the first danger, one should plant a garden, preferably where there is no grocer to confuse the issue. To avoid the second, he should lay a split of good oak on the andirons, preferably where there is no furnace, and let it warm his shins while a February blizzard tosses the trees outside. If one has cut, split, hauled, and piled his own good oak, and let his mind work the while, he will remember much of where the heat comes from, and with a wealth of detail denied to those who spend the weekend in town astride a radiator.[10]

Leopold then "lets his mind work" as he traces the life cycle of an oak tree.

The oak that is now used as firewood was killed by lightning during a July storm. The lightning "put an end to woodmaking by this particular oak" and "bequeathed to us three cords of prospective fuel wood." Leopold mourns the loss of the old tree, but is satisfied to know that a dozen of its progeny have already set down roots in the nearby woods. After a year of drying, the oak was cut by hand, each pull of the saw cutting through years of the oak's life as captured in its annual rings. Leopold traces the life of the oak with each pull, rehearsing the changes in the local environment back through the years to the time around the Civil War when the oak first sprouted from an acorn. At the other end of the cycle, the oak is reduced to ashes in the fireplace while providing heat for the farmhouse. Eventually, the ashes will be returned to the land as compost only to reappear, in time, as a red apple or a "fat squirrel bent on planting acorns."

Thus, the death of a single magnificent oak tree, while sad in itself, can be viewed from a broader perspective. All living things, including humans, must be viewed as members of the ecological community. The oak is honored as a member, even as it is used as firewood. One oak dies, and other species benefit by consuming it. Yet in a harmonious and stable relationship, each member of the community is a "resource" for the continuation of the lives of others. An oak dies, but oaks live on. Resources are used, but never without being "recycled" back into the system. The community is characterized by countless of these interdependencies; its health is characterized by its long-term integrity and stability.

At this point we can mention several elements of the land ethic that make it an attractive philosophical option. First, the land ethic offers a fairly *comprehensive* perspective. At first sight, it appears to offer a decision procedure for most, if not all, environmental and ecological issues. Unlike the animal welfare movement, it does offer a systematic approach to issues as diverse as pollution, conservation, energy, resource depletion, and so forth.

Second, it also can avoid many of the counterintuitive conclusions that burden the individualistic biocentric approach. We do not need to be overly concerned with such seemingly insignificant issues as killing a mosquito, cutting a tree, or tearing up one's lawn. The continued healthy functioning of the *system* is the primary concern.

Finally, the land ethic is thoroughly nonanthropocentric. Humans are said to have no privileged status in the ecological community. They are reduced from "conquerors" to mere members. Not only does this shift accord natural objects and systems moral standing, it also is more consistent with the teachings of ecology. For many environmentalists, this is the single most important prerequisite for a sound environmental perspective.

9.3 LEOPOLD'S HOLISM

Before we can assess the land ethic, it is important to have an understanding of the nature of Leopold's version of holism. The summary statement just quoted clearly suggests that Leopold is committed to a form of *ethical holism*. Right and wrong are a function of the well-being of the "community," not of its constituent members.

In this view, one could argue that it is ethically permissible to kill individual deer as long as the "integrity, stability, and beauty" of the deer population were preserved. In fact, in the many cases where an overpopulation itself threatens the stability of the herd or the integrity of an entire ecosystem within which the deer live, it might well be the case that we have an *obligation* to selectively kill individual deer.

But why is it reasonable to adopt ethical holism in regard to ecological communities? We can find traces of three answers in Leopold's writings. First, ethical holism is the most *practical* approach to take when making decisions concerning resource management. Second, ethical holism is implied by an *epistemological* holism implicit in ecology. Finally, ethical holism acknowledges the *metaphysical* reality of ecological wholes.

A practical reason for adopting ethical holism stems in part from the failure of more individualistic thinking. History supplies ample evidence that when we think only in terms of individual plants and animals we adopt misinformed and risky land management policies. There is more than ample evidence for the abuse and destruction that follows from ignoring the interdependencies within an ecosystem. As an example, Leopold cites the effects that the destruction of predators can have on the population of deer. There-fore treating ecosystems *as if* they themselves had moral standing—"thinking like a mountain" in Leopold's words—would be a significant corrective to these errors. When Leopold writes to ranch-ers, farmers, hunters, and policymakers, he tends to adopt this more pragmatic approach to ethical holism.

Epistemological holism follows from the claim that an adequate understanding of ecology can only come from holistic, or func-tional, explanations. A full understanding of a wolf, for example, must include an account of how that species functions within the ecosystem. As a member of the biotic community, the wolf plays a role in the overall stability and integrity of the system. This func-tional community model of the ecosystem in turn provides a basis for ethical holism. The value of an individual organism is derived, in part, by its function, role, operation, relationships, and so on. In short, this value that can be attributed with a holistic ethic. Ecologi-cal understanding thus gives reasons for adopting an ethical per-spective that grants moral consideration to factors other than individual organisms.

We have also seen Leopold, in passages quoted earlier, suggest that the land itself might be regarded as a living thing. The meta-physical holism implied by the organic model provides further rea-sons for accepting ethical holism. Quoting the Russian philosopher Ouspensky, Leopold tells us that it is possible "to regard the earth's parts—soil, mountains, rivers, atmosphere, etc.—as organs, or parts, of a coordinated whole." Our belief that the earth is dead matter arises in part from our inability to recognize the "enormously slow, intricate, and interrelated functions" of its life processes. And in a passage that makes the connection between metaphysical and ethi-cal holism explicit, Leopold says, "Philosophy, then, suggests one reason why we cannot destroy the earth with moral impunity; namely that the 'dead' earth is an organism possessing a certain kind and degree of life, which we intuitively respect as such."[11] If the earth itself is alive and if we can attribute to it such attributes as healthy, sick, growing, and dying, then we can argue along familiar lines that the earth itself deserves moral consideration.

But to say that there are various reasons for adopting ethical ho-lism is not yet to explain the nature of the biotic "wholes" in ques-tion. As we saw in the last chapter, ecologists have relied on several different models of ecological systems and each of these models can have different ethical implications. How, exactly, should the "biotic community" be understood? Which model best describes the activi-ties of ecosystems?

Since, as we have said, Leopold's own life spanned the early years of ecology, we should not be surprised to find all three models represented in his writing. We have already seen quotes in which Leopold refers to the earth itself as a living "organism." Throughout much of "The Land Ethic" essay, Leopold relies on the community model of ecology. The crucial image of the "food pyramid" has strong ties to Elton's functional community model. But even in the midst of this Eltonian model, we find Leopold using the later language of Tansley's energy model: "Plants absorb energy from the sun. This energy flows through a circuit called the biota which may be represented by a pyramid consisting of layers." It may make an ethical difference if we are concerned with "food" flowing through "food chains" of "producers and consumers" or "energy" flowing through "circuits."

Take for example the images of land "health" and "death." Leopold often emphasizes our duty to preserve the health of the land and often laments those cases where the land has died. But whereas health and death can straightforwardly be applied to organisms, they can be applied only metaphorically to communities and energy circuits. Most of us would be willing to defend the intrinsic value of health, but what is its value when used metaphorically? Again, the "integrity and stability" of an organism may mean one thing; the integrity and stability of a community or energy circuit quite another.

What, exactly, was Leopold's model for understanding ecological "wholes"? The honest answer likely is that he was not as finely attuned to the nuances of these various models, and perhaps especially to the ethical nuances, as we might like. It would seem that the organic model is mostly abandoned in Leopold's later writings.[12] But if we take "The Land Ethic" as his most mature work, we must conclude that he either did not see, or did not think it important to make, a clear and constant distinction between the community and the energy models. The significance of this fact is examined in the following critical section.

9.4 CRITICISMS OF THE LAND ETHIC: FACTS AND VALUES

I separate criticisms of Leopold's land ethic into two general sections: the move from the facts of ecology to the values of ethics, and the ethical implications of Leopold's holism. The first topic focuses on what philosophers have called the "naturalistic fallacy," and the second on the nature of ecological wholes.

A central challenge to any attempt to ground ethical values in natural facts is the claim that there exists a logical gap between statements of fact and judgments of value, between "is" and "ought." Identified in recent decades as the "naturalistic fallacy," many philosophers reject as fallacious the conclusion that something is good or right based solely on a description of what is natural. On first read, Leopold's identification of right and wrong with the natural facts of ecological integrity and stability seem a clear example of such reasoning.

The problem with such reasoning has been recognized by philosophers since at least the time of Plato. In Book I of the *Republic*, Plato shows many of the confusions that underlie the view identifying justice with the "advantage of the stronger." More recent discussions have focused on eighteenth-century philosopher David Hume's distinction between "is" and "ought."[13] The point of these challenges is that grounds for proving that "this is the way things *are*" are logically distinct from the grounds for proving that "this is the way things *ought* to be." Even after something has been established as natural, it always remains an open question to ask if it is also good.[14]

Chapter 2 showed how the *natural law* or *teleological* tradition in ethics makes much of the connection between natural activities and the good. From a description of the normal and natural activity of the heart, for example, we reason to an account of a good or healthy heart. From a description of a normal progression of growth from birth through maturity and eventually to death, we also can reason to an account of a good, healthy life. Living systems can be described in teleological terms, and they seem open to evaluations based on this naturalistic description.

If we adopt the organic ecological model and view an ecosystem as an organic whole, then this type of teleological reasoning would seem fitting. From a natural science description of the normal development of the system (its integrity and stability), we could reason about what is good or bad, right or wrong, healthy or unhealthy, for elements of that system. Predators are good and ought to be protected, for example, because they contribute to stable populations within the system.

But note that there always remains an open question: why *should* one value the overall health of the system itself? If the organism in question is an individual human, we would have fairly standard ways of explaining the value of a healthy heart. But why should we value the integrity and stability of a wetland, or a desert, or a prairie? The teleological model of value is attractive when we are concerned with the relation of parts to whole (the heart) or with the growth and development of a single organism. But can an ecosystem be understood and valued in either of these two ways?

One defense of the value of an ecosystem would appeal to human interests and preferences. Wetlands provide habitat for game, provide a source for water, act to filter pollutants, and so on. But, of course, this instrumental and anthropocentric approach is not open to the land ethic. This would open the gate to utilitarian tradeoffs between human interests and deny the intrinsic value of ecosystems that Leopold seems so committed to protecting.

Or one could appeal to the role that particular ecosystems play in the overall stability and integrity of some larger organic whole. Thus, like a heart, a wetland performs a function for some organic whole. Following this line, one would eventually argue, as Leopold sometimes does, that the earth itself should be considered an organic whole. But, this simply pushes the open question back a step. Why value the integrity and stability of this larger organic whole? Since instrumental and individualistic reasons (such as that the larger whole contributes to the well-being of its constituent parts) are not open to the land ethic, one would have to argue that there is some teleological goal for the entire system itself. And here the teleological model seems to break down. Neither ecology nor philosophy have produced a plausible account of what the earth's *telos* might be.

The third option for the land ethic is to argue that an ecosystem, like an individual organism, goes through developmental stages. The normal developmental progression would thereby provide a basis, as it does in human medicine, for evaluating the health and well-being of that system. Unfortunately, this would work only assuming the truth of the "climax community" model wherein every locale has a single "climax" stage toward which ecological succession aims. Given that individual ecosystems develop—*change* would be the better word—through various forms, the plausibility of this option is weakened. For example, the populations of a field might go through a series of ecological transformations from weeds to perennials and grasses to shrubs, to pine forests to oak forests. What would the "integrity and stability" of *this* system be? Should we seek to preserve the field as home to prairie grasses and shrubs? or as a pine forest? or stay out altogether and let whatever happens happen? The important point is that we can meaningfully *ask* these questions; hence, the leap from ecological fact to ethical value remains an open question.

It is still open for the land ethic to adopt the community or energy circuit model of ecosystems and attempt to argue from these facts to its ethical conclusions. But neither of these choices answer the open question.

Basically, neither the community nor the energy circuit model is as obviously teleological as the organic model. In the community model, individuals are related to each other functionally (as members of a food chain), but there is little reason to assume a function for the chain itself. We might be able to give a teleological evaluation of the roles of individual organisms and species in the food chain; for example, it is good for ladybugs that there are many aphids in my garden. But why any particular food chain, or more to the point, any particular arrangement of the food chain, should be valued in itself is yet to be answered. There is even less reason to assume a teleological account of energy circuits. Why is preserving the integrity and stability of a food chain or energy circuit good or right?

We should be careful to avoid overstating the force of these criticisms. The point is not that we cannot support ethical judgments by appeal to naturalistic facts. The point is that in defending something as right or wrong, we need to do more than simply say it is normal or natural. Ecological facts, in themselves, do not "prove" that ecological integrity and stability are ethical values.

We can find indications in "The Land Ethic" for how Leopold might respond to these challenges. Leopold suggests that the ethical revolution implicit in his extension of ethics to the land can come about only alongside a radical change in human psychology. This change in psychology, brought about through moral and ecological education, might bridge the gap between is and ought.

> It is inconceivable to me that an ethical relation to land can exist without love, respect, and admiration for land, and a high regard for its value. By value, I of course mean something far broader than mere economic value; I mean value in the philosophical sense.[15]

This passage suggests that ethical holism, extending direct ethical consideration (the "philosophical sense" of value) to ecological wholes, can come about only when humans change their attitudes toward the land. Only when humans come to love, respect, and admire the land will they have reasons to act in ways that benefit it. But how will humans come to love, respect, and admire the land? "One of the requisites" for an ecological valuing of land "is an understanding of ecology." Thus the natural facts of ecology lead, not directly to ethical conclusions, but instead to a change of attitude, which can in turn lead to a change in ethical evaluations. Accordingly, we value the preservation of an ecosystem not simply *because* it is natural or normal, but because, given what we have learned of it from ecology, we love it, respect it, admire it.[16] In this interpretation, the role of ecology is focused more on moral education than on normative ethics.

Unfortunately, if we take this approach then the "integrity and stability" principle loses some of its force. In this view, the principle is not a straightforward normative principle: "Act in ways that tend to preserve the integrity, stability, and beauty. . . ." Rather, it is an exhortation to get people to think in a certain way: "Stop thinking solely in economic and instrumental terms; try thinking this way: a thing is right when. . . ." The principle becomes, as Leopold suggests, a challenge to the log-jam preventing the "evolutionary process" from extending ethical consideration to land. It provides an alternative and a challenge to the economic way of thinking. But it provides no independent reason for acting on behalf of the land.

9.5 CRITICISMS OF THE LAND ETHIC: HOLISTIC ETHICS

A second group of challenges to the land ethic center on its holism. Two general concerns underlie these challenges: can a meaningful account of ecological "wholes" be defended, and are its ethical implications acceptable?

The most serious ethical criticism of the land ethic's holism is that it condones sacrificing the good of individuals to the good of the whole. If we do define right and wrong in terms of the "biotic community," then it would seem possible that for the good of the community individual members—for example, individual human beings—might be sacrificed. For example, Leopold seems willing to condone hunting individual animals to preserve the integrity and stability of the biotic community. But since he also describes humans as equal "members" of that community, he seems committed to the permissibility of hunting humans if doing so would preserve the integrity, stability, and beauty of that community.

Versions of this challenge have been offered in different ways by various critics. Marti Kheel has called ethical holism "totalitarian," and Eric Katz has claimed that it subverts respect for individuals.[17] Another criticism was voiced by Tom Regan, who labeled Leopold's approach "environmental fascism":

> The difficulties and implications of developing a rights-based environmental ethic . . . include reconciling the *individualistic* nature of moral rights with the more *holistic* view of nature. . . . Aldo Leopold is illustrative of this latter tendency. . . . The implications of this view include the clear prospect that the individual may be sacrificed for the greater biotic

good, in the name of "the integrity, stability and beauty of the biotic community." It is difficult to see how the notion of the rights of the individual could find a home within a view that . . . might be fairly dubbed "environmental fascism."[18]

These are serious charges, and if they cannot be answered by defenders of the land ethic we have good reason to look elsewhere for a satisfactory environmental ethic.

One approach might develop the suggestion discussed earlier concerning practical holism. Given the history of human destruction of natural environments, we are well advised to act as if ecosystems themselves had moral standing. The problem with this approach is that it merely postpones the question of fascism. What ought we to do when the good of an ecological community conflicts with the good of an individual human? Either we do act as if the community itself had standing and override the interests of the human, or we abandon the pretense and allow human interest to take precedence. With the first option, we face the fascism charge; with the second, we abandon holism.

A second response is suggested by Don Marietta.[19] Marietta points out that ethical holism can have a variety of implications. A statement such as Leopold's "integrity and stability" claim might imply that the *only* source of right and wrong is the good of the biotic community; or it might imply that the *most important* source lies with the good of the community; or it might imply simply that *one* source of right and wrong lies with the good of the community.

Marietta goes on to argue that treating the good of the biotic community as the only or necessarily the most important source of right and wrong cannot be justified. These extreme positions are reductionistic in that they treat human beings as if they were *only* biological entities. Humans are more than that, of course, and a satisfactory ethics must take into account the wide range of morally relevant factors about humans. This includes, but is not limited to, the fact that humans occupy a biological role in nature.

Thus, Marietta concludes that ethical holism should be seen as introducing one, perhaps new, source of right and wrong into ethics. Only if we assume that it introduces the only or the most important source does holism fall victim to the fascism charge. As it stands, we should recognize that we face very complex moral situations with few specific and overriding rules that determine exactly what we should do. Holism calls our attention to some complexity that we may have missed otherwise. It does not necessarily commit us to environmental fascism.

But can Leopold's holism be defended in this way? At first glance, it cannot. Leopold's principle that "A thing is right when. . . . It is wrong when it tends otherwise" would seem to suggest exactly the sort of overriding rule Marietta rejects. This principle suggests that something is either right or wrong and hence leaves no room for the type of moral pluralism that Marietta accepts. But perhaps there is a way to synthesize these two views.

First, we can follow Marietta's suggestion and recognize that in a morally complex world certain acts might be both right in one way and wrong in another. Thus, it might be both right and wrong for a farmer to fill in a wetland in order to increase the land available for agriculture. From the ecocentric point of view, it might be wrong. From the viewpoint of the farm family facing bankruptcy, it might be right. In this case, right or wrong would simply mean that good, plausible reasons can be given for both sides.

A second approach is suggested by Jon Moline.[20] Moline's interpretation focuses on the word "thing" in Leopold's account of right and wrong (a "thing" is right when . . .). If by "thing" we mean an individual *action*, then Leopold would be open to the fascism charge. But if we interpret "thing" to mean a *type* of action, or a rule, or attitude, then the fascism charge is less plausible. Moline calls the first option "direct holism," and the second "indirect holism" and suggests that Leopold ought to be read as an indirect holist:

> I argue that Leopold, by contrast, is an *indirect* holist, i.e., one who applies holistic criteria not directly to acts, but only indirectly to these through criticisms of practices, rules, predilections, and attitudes. He criticizes above all our manner of thinking and wishing, seeing that all our actions flow from this.[21]

Moline's suggestion can be integrated with the discussion of an ethics of character discussed in Chapter 7. Leopold's "integrity and stability" principle should be viewed as normative for human character: our attitudes, dispositions, "our manner of thinking and wishing." It proposes the type of person we should be, a trait of character, not the specific acts we should perform.

Moline acknowledges critics who charge that direct and indirect holism ultimately are indistinguishable.[22] In any particular instance, either the indirect principle has exactly the same prescription as the direct version, or it does not. If it does, then there is no practical difference between the two (if the direct holism is fascistic, so is the indirect version). If it does not, then the indirect version is not, after all, holistic (because, in tough cases, it abandons the holistic conclusion).

But this criticism works only if it is assumed that in any particular case there will always be one, unambiguous and knowable, prescription. But time and again Leopold points out that even the ecologist does not know exactly what will preserve the integrity and stability of the biotic community. "The ordinary citizen today assumes that science knows what makes the community clock tick; the scientist is equally sure that he does not. He knows that the biotic mechanism is so complex that its workings may never be fully understood."[23] Given the complexity of ecosystems, and given the realization that they undergo constant change, we should not presume that we ever know with certainty what will or will not preserve integrity or stability in any particular case. Thus, as a direct guide for action, Leopold's principle would be empty and irrelevant.

We now can see a way to integrate Leopold's appreciation of the ecological complexity of nature, Marietta's appreciation of the moral complexity of our world, and Moline's indirect holism. Ecology teaches that natural biotic systems are extremely complex. We need to abandon the mechanistic view of nature and be suspicious of any abrupt and man-made changes to it. Marietta cautions us to be sensitive to moral complexity as well. Combine these two perspectives, and one would conclude that ecological ethics is fundamentally indeterminate. That is, we just might never be able to know, in any particular case, what the ethically "correct" act is. We often do not know enough about an ecosystem to understand the consequences of our actions, and competing values might be pulling us in different directions. But it is exactly in such a situation that a second-order principle of the type Moline describes can help us.

In these situations, we should be guided by those attitudes, dispositions, and practices that have tended to preserve the integrity and stability of ecosystems. In general, these are attitudes of "love, respect, and admiration." In practice, this implies a relatively conservative approach to natural systems: presumptions in favor of natural, evolutionary changes rather than man-made changes, in favor of native plants and animals, in favor of slow rather than rapid change, in favor of biological rather than mechanical, artificial, and manufactured solutions to environmental problems.

In this view, Leopold's ethics is focused less on rules that guide action, and more on moral dispositions, or virtues. We may be unable to specify in any detail what the "correct" act or decision is, but we can determine if a person is acting responsibly. If the person acts out of a "loving and respectful" character, her decision will be a responsible one. Both the world of ecology and the world of morality make it unlikely that any specific moral rule will be able to offer us unambiguous, practical advice. In such a situation, the best we can do is to rely on the best judgment of a particular type of person. This would be a person who loves, respects, and admires the biotic community. Whatever this person decides will be the ethically responsible thing, even though we have no way of independently and antecedently specifying what that ought to be.

Before turning to a final consideration of Leopold's holism, we should discuss one further point. Philosophical critics may not find the foregoing line of reasoning persuasive. After all, they might charge, implicit in whatever act the virtuous person performs will be a rule (or "maxim") that could be made explicit. Either that maximum should be followed in relevantly similar situations, or it should not. If it should, then we do after all have a rule to guide our actions and we can get on with the philosophical examination of that rule. If it should not, then we have abandoned ethics completely in favor of an arbitrary decision procedure.

Perhaps. But perhaps an example arising in medical ethics will help illustrate the alternative. We have all become familiar with cases in which individuals who are suffering from major physiological damage are kept alive (or at least their bodies are kept functioning) only by complex technological devices. Many states have responded to these tragedies by passing legislation that recognizes the validity of "living wills." In such cases, people can specify while they are competent the conditions under which they would choose to have life support technology removed. We seem, as a society, to have accepted the principle of self-determination. Competent individuals can decline any medical procedures.

But the problem confronting living wills is not unlike that facing the ecologist. Science, in this case medicine, is often indeterminate. Given the complexity of the human organism, physicians simply never know with certainty a patient's prognosis. When writing a living will therefore, people face extreme uncertainty: about what their condition might be, about the prognosis, about technology that might become available in the future, and so on. But they are also faced with moral uncertainty; strong reasons can be given for and against the decision to discontinue life support.

In the face of this deep complexity, one might argue that a living will should be an *indirect*, not a *direct* guide. The will should specify *who* should be empowered to make the decision, not the conditions under which a specific decision should be made. Thus, we might decide that a loved one—a spouse, a parent, a child—should have the authority to decide for us. The view is that whatever such a person decides will be the correct decision. Our justification for this judgment lies in the character of this person. While writing the living will, one might reason as follows. Because this person loves me and is generally a reasonable, thoughtful, and sensitive person, he or she will make the best decision in a complex situation. I recognize that this is a decision that even I cannot make in the abstract, and I also recognize that good reasons can be given for and against whatever that decision turns out to be.

This interpretation makes Leopold sound like a modern-day Aristotelian. As with Aristotle's ethics, the land ethic would be focused on the formation of an ethical character rather than on the defense of some ultimate moral rule or principle. As for Aristotle, moral education and moral psychology have an important role to play in the development ("evolution"?) of ethics. Whether or not this is a plausible reading can be left for another time. At this point, we should acknowledge that the land ethic faces serious challenges but is not without resources for answering these challenges.

We can now turn to a final challenge to Leopold's holistic ethics. Can a meaningful account of ecological "wholes" be defended? We have seen that ecologists have defended different models of an ecosystem: organic, community, energy circuit. Which, if any, can be made compatible with the land ethic?

Leopold at times adopts an organic model of ecosystems; the land itself is seen as a living organism. In some ways, this is the model best suited for the land ethic. When we treat ecosystems as organic wholes, we seem most able to move between the facts of ecology and the values implicit in such concepts as "integrity and stability," "health," and "well-being."

Human and veterinary medicine provide a powerful example of how this reasoning could develop. Given a scientific understanding of the normal growth and development of an individual organism, medical science has proven itself very capable of diagnosing ills and promoting health. If it turns out that ecosystems are relevantly similar to these individual organisms, then the potential exists for a similar synthesis of science and values.

But we have already seen that ecologists have moved beyond this organic model. The very science Leopold relied on to present the holism of ecosystems has concluded that the organic model of ecological systems is inadequate. The classical refutation of the organic model is found in the writings of Arthur Tansley.[24]

Tansley argues that ecosystems can be viewed as organisms only in a metaphorical way. They are not literally organisms because individuals within an ecosystem, unlike the individual organs of a body, can exist outside the organism. Ecosystems do not have the "unity and definiteness" of real organisms and their constituent parts are quite capable of moving into other systems and becoming full members of them. This independence means that members of an ecosystem are quite unlike the organs of a body.

Perhaps then Leopold's holism should be understood on the community-functional model. Here, members of an ecosystem are not understood as parts to a whole or as organs to a body, but as functionally dependent on each other. An individual organism is identified as part of the biotic community, or the "food chain," by reference to what it eats and what eats it. The arrangement of individual organisms and their relations to one another are what constitute the *system*.

But can this account of an ecosystem provide what is required of it in Leopold's ethics? Leopold is clear that (at least one) object of our moral consideration (our "love, respect, and admiration") is the "community" itself, not its constituent members. The well-being of this community consists of its "integrity and stability." But what can integrity and stability mean if we are talking about food chains, not organisms?

Consider what is being asked. In the reading of Leopold offered so far, human beings are encouraged to act out of love, respect, and admiration for the biotic community. But this seems possible only in so far as this community has some good or some interests of its own. (Otherwise, we would be acting for the good of the community only as a means for attaining the good of its constituent members. And this would be to abandon the holistic perspective.) But is it reasonable to hold that we can love and respect a "biotic" community? Leopold's principle suggests it is. A community can be loved and respected because it has interests and its interests rest on its integrity and stability. But are biotic communities the kinds of things that possess integrity and stability?

At any given time, it might appear they do. A small pond, for example, can be said to possess integrity and stability if it is not drained, if its various biotic populations remain stationary, if the climate remains constant, if artificial or nonnative elements are not added, and so on—in short, if its functional relationships can be maintained. But as we have seen, ecosystems do not remain stable over time. Through natural biological, chemical, geological, and climatic forces, biotic communities themselves evolve into very different types of ecosystems. Thus we are faced with a choice: either interfere with these natural processes to preserve a particular integrity and stability, or allow these natural processes to continue and abandon the most obvious sense of integrity and stability.

But perhaps "biotic community" can be understood to refer not to the particular members of the community or to a particular arrangement of those members, but to the conditions under which the biological processes and relationships can be preserved. Thus an ecosystem, now meaning something more akin to a locale, has integrity and stability to the degree that it is capable of sustaining biological processes. Thus, a healthy community has topsoil that is rich in nutrients and not eroded, rain that is not acidified, is pesticide- and herbicide-free, does not suffer from an overpopulation of any species, and so on.

Unfortunately, there are several problems with this answer. First, it might allow too much into the concept of ecosystem health. Certain biological processes have shown themselves quite capable of surviving in the most ecologically blighted areas. For example, the HIV, smallpox, and polio agents seem to thrive in conditions of something less than the ecological ideal. One would need some further standard to decide which biological processes contribute to a system's health and which do not.

More importantly, this answer also seems to base the land ethic on instrumental and nonholistic values. In effect, this answer says that we ought to preserve the integrity and stability of a system or community, not because it has value in itself, but because it contributes to the well-being of other things that themselves have intrinsic value.

9.6 SUMMARY AND CONCLUSION

Thus, serious philosophical challenges remain for the land ethic. Nevertheless, Leopold's work holds great promise for philosophical reflection on the environment. Perhaps his greatest contribution lies in focusing attention on ecosystems and relationships—in short, to take ecological "wholes" as worthy of serious moral consideration. Whether this consideration turns out to be in the form of direct or indirect moral standing, after Aldo Leopold this issue can no longer be ignored.

Notes
1. For a helpful critical discussion of this model, see Daniel Botkin, *Discordant Harmonies*, chap. 3.
2. Aldo Leopold, *Game Management* (New York: Scribner, 1933).

3. Aldo Leopold, "The Varmint Question," reprinted in *The River of the Mother of God and Other Essays by Aldo Leopold*, ed. Susan Flader and J. Baird Callicott (Madison: University of Wisconsin Press, 1991), pp. 47–48.

4. Aldo Leopold, pp. 86–97.

5. Leopold, *Sand County Almanac*, p. 253.

6. Ibid., pp. 253, 239, 247.

7. This point is forcefully argued by J. Baird Callicott in "Animal Liberation: A Triangular Affair," *Environmental Ethics* 2 (1980): 311–338. Callicott tempers his claims a bit in later essays, but the essential point that Leopold's views are incompatible with the animal rights movement is not abandoned. See J. Baird Callicott, *In Defense of the Land Ethic*. Jon Moline makes a similar point in "Aldo Leopold and the Moral Community," *Environmental Ethics* 8 (1986): 99–120.

8. Leopold, *Sand County Almanac*, p. 262.

9. Ibid., pp. 252–253.

10. Ibid., pp. 6–7.

11. Leopold, "Some Fundamentals," p. 95.

12. For a discussion of this point, see J. Baird Callicott, "Conceptual Foundations," pp. 87–90.

13. David Hume, *A Treatise on Human Nature*, Bk. 3, pt. 1, sec. 1.

14. The classic twentieth-century discussion of the naturalistic fallacy can be found in G. E. Moore, *Principia Ethica*. Perhaps the best critical commentary on Moore is William Frankena, "The Naturalistic Fallacy," *Mind* 48 (1939): 464–477. A helpful collection of analytic essays on this topic is W. D. Hudson, *The Is/Ought Question* (New York: St. Martin's Press, 1970).

15. Leopold, *Sand County Almanac*, p. 261.

16. This defense is developed in greater detail by J. Baird Callicott, "Hume's Is/Ought Dichotomy and the Relation of Ecology to Leopold's Land Ethic," reprinted in *In Defense of the Land Ethic* (Albany, NY: SUNY Press, 1989), pp. 117–127. Callicott's interpretation and defense of the land ethic is always worth reading, even if it is not always clear where Leopold's work leaves off and Callicott's begins.

17. Marti Kheel, "The Liberation of Nature: A Circular Affair," *Environmental Ethics* 7 (Summer 1985): 135–149; and Eric Katz, "Organicism, Community, and the 'Substitution Problem,'" *Environmental Ethics* 7 (Fall 1985): 241–256.

18. Tom Regan, *The Case for Animal Rights* (1983), pp. 361–362.

19. Don E. Marietta, Jr., "Environmental Holism and Individuals," *Environmental Ethics* 10 (Fall 1988): 251–258.

20. Jon Moline, "Aldo Leopold and the Moral Community," *Environmental Ethics* 8 (Summer 1986): 99–120.

21. Ibid., p. 105.

22. Ibid., p. 106. This criticism is best known when directed against act and rule utilitarianism. See, for example, David Lyons, *Forms and Limits of Utilitarianism* (Oxford, England: Clarendon Press, 1965), p. 118.

23. Leopold, *Sand County Almanac*, pp. 240–241.

24. Arthur Tansley, "The Use and Abuse of Vegetational Concepts,"
pp. 284–307. See also an earlier article, "The Classification of Vegetation
and the Concept of Development," *Journal of Ecology* 8 (1920): pp. 118–149.
For a general history of ecology, see Donald Worster, *Nature's Economy*.

Discussion Questions

1. Should farmers and ranchers be allowed to kill wild predators such as
coyotes and wolves in order to protect their herds? How should the government balance these conflicting interests?
2. Compare what Singer and Regan (see Chapter 6) might say about hunting deer in an overpopulated area with what Leopold might say. Which
side do you support? Why?
3. Do you support the view that humans are equal moral citizens of the
biotic community? Is there a middle ground between humans as masters
of nature and humans as equal biotic citizens?
4. Leopold suggests that the "dead earth" is an organism that does possess
a certain kind of life. What exactly is the distinction between a living organism and a nonliving object? Is the earth "alive"?
5. Can land really be characterized as "healthy" or "unhealthy" in anything other than a metaphorical way? What exactly would a "healthy" ecosystem be?
6. Return to a question asked in Chapter 1 of this book: "Are all things
that are natural also good?" Has your thinking on this question changed
since that first chapter?
7. At this point, you should be beginning to think about your own "environmental ethics." Where do your environmental values lie? What is the
greatest challenge to your own views?

For Further Reading

Aldo Leopold's own writings are eminently readable. Beside the well-
known *Sand County Almanac*, *The River of the Mother of God and Other Essays*, ed. Susan Flader and J. Baird Callicott (Madison: University of
Wisconsin Press, 1991), is a collection of over 50 of Leopold's essays span-
ning over forty years of writing.

Susan Flader, *Thinking Like a Mountain* (Columbia: University of Mis-
souri Press, 1974), and Curt Meine, *Aldo Leopold: His Life and Work* (Madison: University of Wisconsin Press, 1988), are both solid biographical
studies of Leopold.

J. Baird Callicott, *In Defense of the Land Ethic* (Albany: SUNY Press, 1989),
develops a contemporary philosophical defense of the land ethic. Callicott
offers the best and most developed interpretive defense of Leopold.

10

Deep Ecology

Environmental Activism: Legal and Illegal

Faced with environmental and ecological destruction, we soon realize that science and philosophy can only take us so far. No matter what conclusions we reach from scientific and philosophical analysis, we still face the further political question of how best to influence and direct public policy. We might be convinced by scientific and philosophical reasoning that the most justified course of action involves, for example, preserving a wilderness area or protecting an endangered species. But the question remains: what is the best way, practically and ethically, to get these decisions made on the level of public policy? Such questions are particularly challenging when we recognize that a decision to protect ecological interests can often have high economic and political costs. Quite often environmental interests will be pitted against entrenched and influential corporate and governmental interests.

Mineral King Valley was a case in point. That case involved corporate and governmental interests, in the form of the agreement between Walt Disney Enterprises and the U.S. Forest Service, going against the environmental interests represented by the Sierra Club. In pursuit of its environmental goals, the Sierra Club relied on a traditional course of action; they filed a legal suit to block development of the valley. In the past two decades, litigation has been one of the primary political strategies for affecting environmental change.

Besides litigation, environmental activism also occurs within both the legislative and executive branches of government, as well as within the private sector. Lobbying for legislation, letter-writing campaigns, support for political candidates, Earth Day rallies and celebrations, protest marches, and economic boycotts have all, to various degrees, influenced contemporary environmental policy. These views share in common the assumption that change can effectively be brought about by working within existing political and economic systems.

But what happens when these legal means don't work? The political process is notoriously slow to react to social problems, and sometimes irreversible damage can occur before the legal system can intervene. Furthermore, in the eyes of some critics, the present political and economic system itself is responsible for many of the most pressing environmental problems. Economic and political influence of polluters and developers; lax enforcement of the law; biased or deficient media coverage; an economic system that rewards selfishness, competition, and consumption; and a system of private property rights that allows private owners almost total control over their property are just some of the factors that diminish the effectiveness of working within the system. In light of this, are *illegal* means ever justified in the pursuit of environmental and ecological goals?

We might distinguish between two extralegal strategies for environmental protection. The first we can identify as a variation on a long tradition of acts of civil disobedience. The second has been called "ecosabotage" or "ecoterrorism."[1]

The history of conscientious acts of civil disobedience can be traced from Socrates and Jesus through Thoreau, Gandhi, and Martin Luther King. For many in this tradition, civil disobedience involved choosing to disobey the law on moral grounds as a means of protesting or thwarting governmental policy. The leading defenders of civil disobedience typically were committed to nonviolence and to publicly accepting responsibility (and punishment) for the act.

In this vein, we recognize that many actions of environmental activists can be classified as acts of civil disobedience. The environmental group Greenpeace is perhaps best known for its activities that fit the civil disobedience model. Some Greenpeace members have been known to sail their ships into restricted nuclear testing zones, to climb smokestacks to hang banners denouncing pollution, harass and ram whaling and fishing vessels, and so on. Typically, these acts involve criminal trespass and other minor offenses but pose little or no danger to humans or property. Defenders of these acts will argue that they can be justified in the same ways that the civil disobedience of civil rights activists in twentieth-century America has been justified.

Essentially, one could argue that we live in a culture and at a time in which people are slow to recognize the serious wrongs being committed. The normal political and legal processes are unlikely to change things because much of the public is unaware of, or has failed to appreciate, the extent of the harms. Public acts of civil disobedience, especially if they are covered in the media and result in well-publicized arrests and trials, can be a very effective means for focusing public attention and stimulating public action. If done to minimize the detrimental effects that can accompany breaking the law, and this often means if done respectfully and nonviolently, the beneficial consequences can justify civil disobedience.

Might the dire environmental consequences of political inaction justify something more than civil disobedience? Might illegal acts directed against private citizens or private businesses be justified? Are acts of sabotage against property, what is often called "monkey wrenching," morally justified? Could violence against individuals, or what we might call "ecoterrorism," ever be justified?

"Monkey wrenching" has been popularized in a series of publications originating with Edward Abbey's novel *The Monkey Wrench Gang*. Monkey wrenching has been described and encouraged, if not advocated, in the publications of the radical environmental group Earth First! As defined by Bill Devall, monkey wrenching "is the purposeful dismantling or disabling of artifacts used in environmentally destructive practices at a specific site—dismantling fishing gear or logging equipment, for example." Devall goes on to define ecosabotage or "ecotage" as "disabling a technological or bureaucratic operation in defense of one's place."[2] Typical examples of monkey wrenching include tree spiking (driving large metal spikes into trees to discourage logging), pouring sand into the gas tanks of construction and logging vehicles, pulling up survey stakes, and cutting down power lines. Similarly destructive acts against property are performed by animal liberation groups who break into and sometimes destroy laboratories to save animals from experimentation.

Unlike classic instances of civil disobedience, monkey wrenching and ecosabotage are often performed under the cover of darkness with the intent of escaping detection. For example, a group called the Sea Shepherd Conservation Society sank two Icelandic whaling boats as they sat at harbor in 1986. These saboteurs secretly entered the boats at night and opened seacocks to flood and sink the ships. Unlike well-established cases of civil disobedience, these activities usually involve destruction of property and, if not themselves acts of violence, hold the potential of injuring or killing people. Loggers have been known to be injured when their saws hit spikes driven into a tree.

The Sea Shepherds refused to sink a third ship when they discovered a night watchman aboard. They had pledged not to injure human beings. This decision stands in contrast to the actions of the French government against Greenpeace protesters in 1985. Greenpeace intended to sail their vessel *Rainbow Warrior* into restricted waters where the French were planning to conduct nuclear weapons testing. The French government sent intelligence agents with false passports into New Zealand to sink the *Rainbow Warrior*. A crew member aboard the ship at the time was killed in the sinking.

This reminds us that throughout much of the Western tradition, governments have often justified violence and killing in pursuit of important social goals. The just war theory and the self-defense argument are two ways that violence have been ethically justified. Sometimes, as a last resort and if done as a way of protecting innocent life, violence has been accepted in our culture. Might violence against individuals ever be justified for the protection of nonhuman life? Could such rationales as the just war or self-defense arguments be extended to ecological issues?

10.1 INTRODUCTION

This chapter examines the *deep ecology* movement. Unlike the land ethic, deep ecology has not developed out of one primary source, nor does it refer to one systematic philosophy. The term "deep ecology" has been used in a variety of ways, ranging from a general description of all nonanthropocentric theories[3] to the highly technical "Ecosophy T" developed by Norwegian philosopher Arne Naess. In recent years, the phrase "deep ecology" has come to refer primarily to the approach to environmental issues developed in the writings of Naess, Bill Devall, and George Sessions.[4] This is how I use it in the present chapter.

The distinction between "deep" and "shallow" environmental perspectives was first introduced by Arne Naess in 1973.[5] Naess characterizes the shallow ecology movement as committed to the "fight against pollution and resource depletion." Its central objective is to protect "the health and affluence of the people in developed countries." Deep ecology, in contrast, takes a "relational, total-field" perspective, rejecting the "man-in-environment image" in favor of a more holistic and nonanthropocentric approach.

Perhaps a simpler characterization, which is still faithful to Naess's basic point, could be made in terms of symptoms and underlying causes. The shallow approach, by focusing on issues like pollution and resource depletion, looks only at the immediate effects of the environmental crisis. Just as a sneeze or a cough can disrupt one's daily routine, pollution and resource depletion disrupt the lifestyle of modern industrial societies. However, it would be a mistake for medicine to treat only sneezing and coughing while not investigating the causes that underlie these symptoms. So, too, it is a mistake for environmentalists to be concerned only with pollution and resource depletion without investigating their social and human causes.

Seen in this way, of course, "deep ecology" would refer to a wide variety of approaches. What distinguishes deep ecology as a philosophical approach is its belief that the present environmental crisis can be traced to deep philosophical causes. A "cure" for the present crisis can come, then, only with a radical change in our philosophical outlook. This change involves both personal and cultural transformations, and would "affect basic economic and ideological structures."[6] In short, we need to change ourselves as individuals and as a culture. But this change, according to Devall and Sessions, is not the creation of something new, but a "reawakening of something very old." It involves the cultivation of an "ecological consciousness," an "ecological, philosophical, and spiritual approach" to the present crisis that recognizes the "unity of humans, plants, animals, the Earth."[7]

As a philosophical movement, deep ecology presents a critique of what is called the dominant worldview, which is seen as responsible for environmental destruction. Deep ecologists then seek to work out an alternative philosophical worldview. For many people involved in radical environmentalism as a political movement—members of Earth First!, for example—deep ecology provides the philosophy that legitimates their form of activism.

But any call for a radical change in one's philosophical worldview immediately faces a major challenge. How does one even begin to explain the alternative if, by definition, it is radically different from the starting point? How does one step outside of one's own personal and cultural worldview or ideology to compare it with something radically different?

Deep ecologists employ a variety of strategies to meet these challenges, including reliance on poetry, Buddhism, spiritualism, and political activism, including acts of civil disobedience and ecosabotage. Perhaps the most helpful strategy involves seeking common agreement first on a "platform" of general principles. This platform serves as a core around which the diverse deep ecology movement can be unified. This is a useful starting point for our examination of deep ecology.

10.2 THE DEEP ECOLOGY PLATFORM

Let us stipulate that deep ecologists are committed to the view that solutions to the present grave environmental crisis require more than mere reform of personal and social practices. A radical transformation in worldview is required. Given this general characterization, deep ecologists proceed in two directions. On one hand, there is a commitment to work for the types of changes needed. Many people who can be identified as deep ecologists dedicate their work as scientists, artists, and political activists to bring about these changes. On the other hand, deep ecologists also seek to develop and articulate an alternative philosophy to replace the dominant worldview, which is responsible for the crisis. Naess calls the field that considers such questions and seeks alternative worldviews *ecophilosophy*, and any particular working out of an alternative worldview an *ecosophy*. Just as a variety of strategies for bringing about the necessary changes are possible, so, too, is it possible for a variety of ecosophies to be developed.

In light of this diversity of aims and formulations, Naess and Sessions developed the deep ecology platform as a statement of common principles. The principles provide reasons that can explain and justify the movement's activism. They also provide a less abstract focus for philosophical speculation. The platform is intended to be general enough to allow for a diversity of philosophical interpretations and specific enough to distinguish the deep from the shallow approach to practical matters.[8]

As developed by Naess and Sessions, the platform includes eight principles:[9]

1. The flourishing of human and nonhuman life on earth has intrinsic value. The value of nonhuman life-forms is independent of the usefulness these may have for narrow human purposes.

2. Richness and diversity of life-forms are values in themselves and contribute to the flourishing of human and nonhuman life on earth.

3. Humans have no right to reduce this richness and diversity except to satisfy vital needs.

4. Present human interference with the nonhuman world is excessive, and the situation is rapidly worsening.

5. The flourishing of human life and cultures is compatible with a substantial decrease of the human population. The flourishing of nonhuman life requires such a decrease.

6. Significant change of life conditions for the better requires change in policies. These affect basic economic, technological, and ideological structures.

7. The ideological change is mainly that of appreciating *life quality* (dwelling in situations of intrinsic value) rather than adhering to a high standard of living. There will be a profound awareness of the difference between big and great.

8. Those who subscribe to the foregoing points have an obligation directly or indirectly to participate in the attempt to implement the necessary changes.

We can see how these principles could serve to explain and support a wide range of specific positions on practical environmental controversies. In working against the continued destruction of rain forests, for example, one could appeal to the first three principles. Principles 5 and 7 would be important in developing an energy policy that would address such issues as resource conservation, population growth, consumer demand, and nuclear energy.

Importantly, the platform also indicates the ways in which the science of ecology influences deep ecology. In some sense, ecological science provides direct support for principles 4 and 5. Ecology is also relevant in explaining and defending principles 1 and 2. But ecology is also important for ecophilosophy in that it provides a model for a nonreductionist, holistic worldview.

We turn now to the relation between ecology and philosophy.

10.3 ECOLOGY AND ECOPHILOSOPHY

Like the land ethic, deep ecology relies on the science of ecology for a variety of purposes. Ecology provides a good deal of information about how natural ecosystems function. Ecology helps us diagnose environmental disorders and prescribe policies that can resolve these disorders. Thus, in general, ecology provides us with an understanding of natural ecosystems, and this understanding in turn is the basis from which evaluations and recommendations can be made.

More specifically, ecology also cautions against any quick-fix technological solution to environmental problems. Echoing a theme found in Leopold, Naess argues for a humble and constrained approach to environmental change. The conclusions reached in ecology and conservation biology "are often statements of ignorance": "Only rarely can scientists predict with any certainty the effect of a new chemical on even a single small ecosystem." Faced with this scientific ignorance, the burden of proof should rest with anyone who proposes a policy that intervenes in the natural environment:

> Why does the burden of proof rest with the encroachers? The ecosystems in which we intervene are generally in a particular state of balance which there are grounds to assume to be of more service to mankind than states of disturbance and their resultant unpredictable and far-reaching changes. In general, it is not possible to regain the original state after an intervention has wrought serious, undesired consequences.[10]

Accordingly, ecology contributes to ecophilosophy in the same sorts of ways that scientific understanding has often contributed to ethical analysis. We gain a better understanding of the world and, given this understanding, we are in a better position to offer ethical evaluations and prescriptions. Because ecological understanding offers new insights, an ethic that relies on ecology can be expected to offer new evaluations and prescriptions.

But Naess also warns against too great a reliance on ecology. While scientific ecology can contribute to the goals of deep ecologists, it should not be mistaken for the final authority on environmental disputes. There are dangers in what Naess calls "ecologism," the view that takes ecology as the ultimate science.

Essentially, two related dangers follow from raising ecology to a position as final authority. First, we should avoid the danger of turning ecology into an "all-encompassing worldview." This occurs when the science of ecology is treated as if it can provide resolutions to all environmental issues. "Ecologism" overgeneralizes and universalizes ecological concepts.[11] As a science, ecology can make significant contributions to our understanding of the natural world. But we must recognize that many problems are traced to epistemological and philosophical sources. Ecology is not a substitute for philosophical analysis.

Naess believes that ecology can provide us with a model for thinking about the deep philosophical questions that need to be addressed. These would include such questions as "What is an individual? What things have intrinsic value and moral standing? What is the most reasonable model for understanding nature?" Ecology might suggest insightful and new ways for approaching these questions, and these approaches might well prove helpful in developing alternative ecophilosophies. But we must remember that the model does not prove the validity of the philosophical position developed with its help.

A second danger arises when we rely too heavily on ecology for solutions to specific problems. Treating ecology as just another science that can offer scientific answers to specific problems is to be tempted by the standard shallow hope for a technological quick fix. Consistent with the deep ecology commitment, Naess believes that such environmental issues as wilderness destruction and species extinction point to fundamental questions about how we ought to live. These philosophical questions have political implications that the institutions and individuals who defend the status quo wish to avoid opening up for view.

The fear is that the recent development of an "ecological conscience" that shifts our attention away from models based in physics and mechanics and onto ecological models, will be used simply to substitute one shallow quick-fix approach for another. In this view, ecology would simply be a new means for treating the symptoms. Thus, it would subvert attempts to probe deeper into the underlying causes of the environmental crisis. Ecology might then become a diversion away from these more fundamental issues. The risk is that ecology will be used as a part of a political strategy to derail movements that question the fundamental assumptions of a culture. In Naess's words, we need to "fight against de-politicisation" to keep focused on the political nature of the deep ecology movement.[12]

10.4 METAPHYSICAL ECOLOGY

As suggested earlier, scientific ecology provides a model for thinking about the deep, fundamental issues that underlie the environmental crisis. Inspired by ecology, deep ecologists seek to develop alternative worldviews that echo ecological insights into such issues as diversity, holism, interdependencies, and relations. We have characterized deep ecology as tracing the roots of our environmental crisis to fundamental philosophical causes. Solutions can come only from a transformation of our fundamental worldview and practices. These fundamental questions include "What is human nature? What is the relation of humans to the rest of nature? What is the nature of reality?" These questions are traditionally identified as *metaphysical* questions. Deep ecology, therefore, is as concerned with questions of metaphysics and ontology (the study of what is) as it is with questions of ethics. This section addresses the nature of these fundamental questions of metaphysics.

Deep ecologists trace the cause of many of our present problems to the metaphysics presupposed by the dominant philosophy of modern industrial society. The transformation I have mentioned involves a shift away from this dominant model and onto an alternative worldview that takes its inspiration from ecology. Deep ecology is concerned with a *metaphysical ecology* rather than a scientific one.

The dominant metaphysics that underlies modern industrial society is fundamentally *individualistic* and *reductionistic*.[13] This view holds that only individuals are real and that one approaches a more fundamental level of reality by reducing objects to their more basic elements. These most basic elements, whatever they turn out to be, are related according to strict physical laws. But this dominant worldview also sees humans as fundamentally different from the rest of nature. As individual human beings, we have a "mind" or "free will" or "soul" that exempts us from the strict mechanical determinism characteristic of the rest of nature. Thus, the dominant worldview rejects the position identified in Chapter 8 as "metaphysical holism."

Rejection of these dominant beliefs is central to the metaphysics of deep ecology. Taking its cue from ecology, the metaphysics of deep ecology denies that individual humans are separate from nature, the so-called man-in-nature perspective. Instead, deep ecologists are committed to a version of metaphysical holism. We humans are fundamentally a part of our surroundings, not distinct from them. We humans are constituted by our relations to other elements in the environment. In an important sense, the environment—by which the deep ecologists mean both the biotic and abiotic constituents—determines what human beings are.

When Naess speaks of the "relational, total-field image," he is alluding to a recognition that we humans are formed by our relationships. Without the relationships that exist among humans and between humans and nature, human beings would literally become different sorts of beings. A philosophy that "reduces" humans to "individuals" who are somehow distinct from our social and natural environment is radically misguided.

This point has been expressed by Warwick Fox, an Australian philosopher and deep ecologist:

> It is the idea that we can make no firm ontological divide in the field of existence: that there is no bifurcation in reality between the human and the non-human realms . . . to the extent that we perceive boundaries, we fall short of deep ecological consciousness.[14]

Thus, in one sense, deep ecologists deny the reality of individuals—at least as they are typically understood in Western philosophy. There are no individuals apart from or distinct from relationships within a system, a "total field." Human "nature" is inseparable from nature. Viewing human beings as individuals is the way that the dominant worldview has understood humans, and has broken up reality, but it is a dangerous and misleading metaphysics.

No doubt such thinking can tempt many people to place deep ecologists on the fringe of environmental philosophy. This certainly is a radical shift from mainstream Western philosophy. But, as suggested earlier, any call for a radical shift in perspective faces difficulties in being understood. We can, perhaps, approach this outlook in a variety of ways in the hope that we can begin to understand the alternative.

In the spirit of deep ecology, we might begin by taking a hint from scientific ecology. If we think of ecosystems as energy circuits through which solar and chemical energy flow, we might begin to think of individual organisms as less permanent, and less real, than the chemical and biological processes themselves. Individual organisms come and go, but the process goes on as long as the environmental conditions permit. Individual organisms can be thought of as the location at which these chemical processes occur. In Naess's terms, scientific ecology "suggested, inspired, and fortified" the metaphysical conclusion that individual organisms are constituted by their relations to other entities.

Another way of approaching this conclusion is to consider what it means to say that an individual organism is alive. Minimally, an individual organism is alive only if certain chemical and biological processes are occurring. When these processes cease to occur, the organism ceases to live. Thus the processes are necessary for the existence of the organism. When the processes are present, life exists. Thus, the processes are sufficient for life. Because chemical and biological processes are both necessary and sufficient for the existence of life, we have some reasons for saying that the processes are at least as, if not more real, than individual living organisms.

A similar point is made by biophysicist Harold Morowitz:

> Viewed from the point of view of modern [ecology], each living thing is a dissipative structure, that is, it does not endure in and of itself but only as a result of the continual flow of energy in the system. . . . From this point of view, the reality of individuals is problematic because they do not exist per se but only as local perturbations in this universal energy flow. . . . An example might be instructive. Consider a vortex in a stream of flowing water. The vortex is a structure made of an ever-changing group of water molecules. It does not exist as an entity in the classic Western sense; it exists only because of the flow of water through the stream. If the flow ceases the vortex disappears. In the same sense the structures out of which the biological entities are made are transient, unstable entities with constantly changing molecules dependent on a constant flow of energy to maintain form and structure.[15]

Finally, we might better appreciate metaphysical ecology by considering the language of "individualism." Ordinarily, we seem confident that we know what we refer to when we speak of individuals. But although we often use "individual" as a noun (*an* individual, *the* individual), the word is perhaps more precisely used as an adjective (an individual person, an individual tree, and so on).

Imagine being asked to go out and count the individuals you see. You might assume that the assignment involved individual humans, or you would be well advised to ask, "Individual *what*?" This suggests that when we speak of individuals we have already adopted a worldview or metaphysics that has divided up our experiences in some one way rather than some other way. Our ordinary language seems to presuppose a metaphysics in which separate and isolated organisms are most real. But recognize that we might just as well refer to individual communities, individual ecosystems, individual species, and individual chemical cycles. Or, we might just as well refer to individual body parts, individual organs, individual cells, individual molecules, individual atoms, and so on. The individual human person can be seen either as a part of some larger individual (for example, species or ecosystem), or as a collection of other individuals (for example, organ systems, cells, and so on).

The implication of this is that the world doesn't come already broken down into such categories as "individuals" and "wholes." Rather, particular ways of understanding the world, and particular needs in so understanding it, determine what counts as an individual and what counts as a whole. Deep ecology argues that the dominant worldview assumes an artificial distinction between individuals and their surroundings. This particular metaphysics has proven itself dangerous by the ecological and environmental devastation that has followed from it. An alternative metaphysics, one inspired by scientific ecology, can offer an opportunity for reversing this devastation.

10.5 FROM METAPHYSICS TO ETHICS

Perhaps the most philosophically challenging aspect of deep ecology involves connecting the metaphysical views just sketched to the normative prescriptions derived from them. The early chapters of this book examined a variety of ways in which standard ethical theories were extended and applied to environmental problems. At the time, I mentioned recent critics who claim that traditional ethics has been stretched beyond the breaking point by environmental challenges. With deep ecology, we now see how radically different the alternatives can be.

Environmental challenges require not just new ethics, but a new metaphysics as well. In this section, we consider how deep ecologists move from metaphysical ecology back to ethical and political concerns. The goal of ecophilosophy is to provide a philosophical account of the metaphysics, epistemology, and ethics of this alternative view of reality. We have explored the metaphysics, and turn to the ethics in the following section. In this section, I briefly discuss the epistemological views defended by deep ecologists. Much of their thinking on these topics develops out of a critique of some common epistemic assumptions of the dominant worldview.

One of the most common and fundamental distinctions made within that Western philosophical tradition is between *objectivity* and *subjectivity*. Mainstream Western metaphysics, and particularly the field of ontology, investigates the nature of reality. The *real* world is taken to be that which exists independently of human beings and human understanding. This is the objective world, and it is the goal of science to comprehend this reality. In so far as it does this, scientific claims are "true" and "objective," because they correspond to reality.

But human beings ("subjects") interpret the world, make judgments about it, perceive it, value it, have feelings about it. These human factors are *subjective*, since they depend on the human subject. Because they depend on human subjects, they should not be mistaken as objective "truths" about the real world.

In general terms, this distinction has had significant implications for mainstream epistemology and ethics. Deep ecologists believe it has had a detrimental influence both on how we understand and how we value nature. Epistemologically, objective descriptions of nature could be measured, tested, verified, and so on. Subjective judgments about nature, however, were arbitrary, unpredictable, biased, and unverifiable. Objective descriptions could be rational and true; subjective judgments could not. In ethics, subjective judgments of value ("oughts") could not be derived from objective descriptions of fact ("is").

To elaborate this distinction, philosophers in the seventeenth century relied on a contrast between the *primary* and *secondary* qualities of physical objects. An object's primary qualities exist in the object and are taken to represent what the object truly and really is. Size, shape, mass, extension, and movement were understood as examples of an object's primary qualities. They existed "out there" in the object itself. In contrast, secondary qualities were said to exist as a result of the interaction between an object and an observer. An object's color, texture, taste, and smell were secondary qualities because they exist only in so far as there exists a perceiver who experiences them. Because secondary qualities depend on a perceiver, they are subjective and not really a part of the object itself.

Continuing this seventeenth-century perspective, the role of science is to fully describe an object's primary qualities. Because all these primary qualities could be fully described in mathematical terms, the "real" world turns out to be the world of mathematical physics and mechanics. "Real" trees, for example, do not "have color"—they "reflect light waves." If our eyes were constituted differently, trees would appear different. Trees are not "heavy"; they "have mass," which is subject to the force of gravity. If we were larger, stronger beings, trees would be less heavy than they now appear. Thus, descriptions of natural objects that refer to secondary qualities such as color, weight, and taste are scientifically irrelevant. They are not really true, rational, or objective.

Further, more complex descriptions of natural objects, called *tertiary* qualities, are even less objective and true than judgments about secondary qualities. For example, to describe a tree as "majestic," "beautiful," or "awe inspiring" is to say something that is merely personal opinion. Although color may exist as an interaction between object and subject (reflected light waves reacting with nerve cells), beauty is totally in the eye of the beholder.

Notice how these distinctions and the value conclusions that flow from them depend very much on a clear distinction between subject and object. When the human subject is viewed as essentially one with the natural world, as deep ecologists argue it should, the rationale for clinging to a strict distinction between objective and subjective, between real and perceived, between fact and value is weakened. We can still make these distinctions, they can be useful for us, but they lose their metaphysical priority. The "real" world ceases to exist "out there," separate and apart from us. We exist in the real world. Our perceptions, judgments, and evaluations are as real as the abstract judgments of science. Just as importantly, these judgments and evaluations can be as rational, true, and "objective" as the judgments of science.

Notice also how these distinctions can play a significant role in debating environmental controversies. Often environmentalists are dismissed as "sentimentalists" who allow their emotions to cloud their reason. A stand of oak really is only a collection of primarily carbon and water molecules that play a role in cycling carbon, oxygen, nitrogen, and so forth through the ecosystem. Rationally, we might just as well put the carbon to a more useful purpose, such as furniture or firewood, especially if we can find the technological means for replacing their function in the carbon, oxygen, or nitrogen cycles. To fight against development for the sake of a "majestic" stand of oak trees is mere emotional and sentimental feeling. When environmental positions are cast as emotional and sentimental, they can be dismissed as irrelevant. According to the dominant worldview, they are not "rational," "objective," or scientific.

Naess makes a similar point:

> Confrontations between developers and conservers reveal difficulties in experiencing what is *real*. What a conservationist *sees* and experiences *as reality*, the developer typically does not see—and vice versa. A conservationist sees and experiences a forest as a unity, a gestalt, and when speaking of the *heart of the forest*, he or she does not speak about the geometrical centre. A developer sees quantities of trees and argues that a road through the forest covers very few square kilometres compared to the whole area of trees, so why make so much fuss? And if the conservers insist, he will propose that the road does not touch the *centre* of the forest. The *heart* is saved, he may think. *The difference between the antagonists is one rather of ontology than of ethics.* . . . To the conservationist, the developer seems to suffer from a kind of radical blindness. But one's ethics in environmental questions are based largely on how one sees reality.[16]

According to many deep ecologists, as long as a strict distinction between individuals and nature is maintained, an equally strict distinction between objective and subjective judgments can also be maintained. This distinction provides a rationale for taking the judgments of science and technology as epistemologically justified, while dismissing the evaluative judgments of ethics and aesthetics. But when deep ecologists challenge the distinction between individual and nature, they also are challenging the strict distinction between objective and subjective. This leaves open the possibility that evaluative judgments about the value and beauty of a wilderness, for example, can be shown to be as rationally justified as the judgments of science.

Naess is careful to recognize that mere spontaneous feelings or emotional reactions and outbursts are not themselves rational arguments. The mere expression of a feeling does not advance rational dialogue and debate. However, we need to be equally clear in recognizing that evaluative judgments "motivated by strong feelings" do have "a clear cognitive function." The *feeling* of anger produced by the destruction of a forest, or the imperative to "Stop that destruction!" are neither true nor false in themselves. But the judgment that "This mountainside has been destroyed and ruined" is open to rational assessment and very well might be true. The challenge to ecophilosophers is to specify the conditions under which such environmental judgments can be demonstrated as true and rational.

Naess's approach to such challenges is phrased in terms of relational properties and gestalts. Properties such as "being destroyed" and "being ruined" can be understood only within a context, what Naess calls a "gestalt," or "totality." The conservationist and the developer experience different realities. Their concepts and perceptions occur within different contexts and are related to many different concepts and perceptions. Given these contexts, each of their judgments make sense, each is in that way "rational." At the same time, neither can claim a privileged status as better reflecting "reality."

But the point remains that conservationists and developers disagreed radically about what we should do. Their respective practical recommendations are embedded in their different gestalts. However, if each gestalt makes sense and if neither enjoys a privileged status, we are left without means for deciding which course of action, if either, is more reasonable. In general terms, how do we judge between the conservationist and the developer's worldviews?

In some sense, rational discourse breaks down at this point. Each worldview has its own standards of rationality, its own values, its own reality. But Naess believes that continued discussion is possible and eventually substantiation of one side or other can be attained. Naess suggests that this is possible if we avoid "absolutism," take care in clarifying our norms, and all the while remain open to honest and nonviolent communication with our opponents. "If a speaker's norm pronouncement 'It is right to deny x' is answered from the audience 'It is not right to deny x,' there is nothing to get in a fuss about. The situation begs to be debated. A debate requires clarification of value priorities."[17]

At this point other deep ecologists rely on stories, poetry, narrative, myths, and ritual. The religious concept of "bearing witness" in the way one lives one's life, along with the "forceful announcement" of one's values and living in accord with those values, are other methods for communicating the deep ecology worldview. The goal is to make the deep ecology worldview understandable to people who do not yet view reality in this way. Since, by definition, these people do not share the concepts, norms, values, and metaphysics of deep ecology, straightforward linguistic explanation typically is unsuccessful. The epistemology of deep ecology involves the search for ways to encourage people to make radical shifts in their worldviews.

10.6 SELF-REALIZATION AND BIOCENTRIC EQUALITY

The practical ethics of deep ecology is best seen in the "platform" discussed in section 10.2. These principles can be directly applied to concrete situations to explain and justify environmental activism. But at a more abstract and philosophical level, the ethics of deep ecology focuses on two "ultimate norms." These norms are ultimate in the sense that they are not derived from any further or more basic principles or values. They are the point at which ethical justification ends. We can perhaps best think of them as connecting deep ecology's abstract metaphysics with its more specific ethical platform.

The two ultimate norms of deep ecology are *self-realization* and *biocentric equality*. Self-realization is a process through which people come to understand themselves as existing in a thorough interconnectedness with the rest of nature. Biocentric equality is the recognition that all organisms and beings are equally members of an interrelated whole and therefore have equal intrinsic worth.

Although self-realization grows out of a tradition that is as old as philosophy itself, the particular version developed within deep ecology represents perhaps its most original insight.

The ancient Greek directive to "Know thyself" and Socrates' claim that "The unexamined life is not worth living" imply that the good life involves a process of self-examination and self-fulfillment. The teleological understanding of the good as the actualization of internal potentialities provides a similar insight. The suggestion from these traditions is that as one goes through a process of self-examination, one becomes able to separate trivial, superficial, and temporary interests from deeper, more central, and lasting interests. To understand the concept of self-realization, it is helpful to develop this contrast between superficial and deep interests.

We can start with a general distinction, used earlier in this book, between *needs, interests,* and *wants.* Needs can be understood as those elements that are necessary for survival. Food, clothing, shelter, and nontoxic air and water are obvious examples of needs. Interests are those factors that contribute to well-being. It is in a person's interests to have friendships, education, and good health. Wants are the immediate desires and goals toward which someone is inclined. I want a vacation, a glass of juice, a free lunch.

Notice that there can be obvious overlaps between these categories. Nutritious food and clean air are things I need, have an interest in getting and, in fact, want. But there can also be tensions and conflicts between these categories. Although it is in my interests to get a good education and therefore stay home and study, I want to go out to a party with my friends.

Wants seem to be a matter of individual psychology. They are those factors that provide a motive for acting. Wants come to be developed, chosen, learned, created by advertising, and so on. Interests are not a matter of immediate psychological states. They are connected to what is good for a person and, therefore, are not a matter of choice. (Even if being free to choose is in someone's interest, *that* it is in someone's interest is not itself something that is a matter of individual choice.) Interests can be understood and discovered, but not chosen.

Many diverse philosophical traditions rely on a general distinction such as this in developing an account of ethics. Wants are typically seen as a product of individual choice, culture, or society. They are superficial and temporary in the sense that they depend on a person's personal background, history, and culture. Various ethical traditions encourage us humans to separate these transitory wants from our basic interests as rational beings. The good life is a life spent in pursuit of our basic and true interests. Self-interest, properly understood, is the good for human beings.

Thus, in effect, these traditions see two "selves" in every person. One is the "self" constituted by the conscious beliefs, wants, intentions of the ego. The other self is the person's true nature that underlies this ego. "Know thyself" is the injunction to get beyond this surface self to discover and realize your true underlying nature. Thus traditions as diverse as Greek philosophy, Christianity, Buddhism, romanticism, and Marxism all see a process of self-realization as central to the good life.

Self-realization plays a similar role in deep ecology. But for the deep ecologists, the underlying "Self" (capitalized) is the self that is one with the natural world. "Self-realizing" is a process of self-examination in which one comes to understand oneself as a part of a greater whole. It is a process through which one comes to understand that "there is no firm ontological divide between humans and non-humans," between self and other. It is the process through which we come to know ourselves not as individuals separate and distinct from nature, but as a part of a greater "Self." This Self is the self described within metaphysical holism. If what we are as human beings, our nature, is constituted by our relations with other parts of the natural world, then Self-realization is a coming to understand and fully appreciate this oneness.

For many in the Western philosophical tradition, self-realization is a means for developing one's separate, individual, and personal nature. Deep ecologists retain a commitment to "self-realization," "self-interest," and "self-fulfillment," but they deny this individualistic understanding of the self. To distinguish their holistic and relational view of the self from the more individualistic model, deep ecologists typically use "Self" (capitalized) to refer to the holistic view and "self" (lowercased) for the individualistic view. Thus, Self-Realization is a process through which "self comes to understand itself as Self" and "self-interest" comes to be seen as "Self-Interest."

Devall and Sessions summarize these points in the following:

> In keeping with the spiritual traditions of many of the world's religions, the deep ecology norm of Self-Realization goes beyond the modern Western *self* which is defined as an isolated ego striving primarily for hedonistic gratification. . . . This socially programmed sense of the narrow self or social self dislocates us, and leaves us prey to whatever fad or fashion is prevalent in our society. . . . Spiritual growth, or unfolding, begins when we cease to understand or see ourselves as isolated and narrow competing egos and begin to identify with other humans from our family and friends to, eventually, our species. But the deep ecology sense of self requires a further maturity and growth, an identification which goes beyond humanity to include the nonhuman world.[18]

The second ultimate norm is that of biocentric equality. In Devall and Sessions's words, this intuition is that

> all things in the biosphere have an equal right to live and blossom and to reach their own individual forms of unfolding and self-realization within the larger Self-realization. This basic intuition is that all organisms and entities in the ecosphere, as parts of the interrelated whole, are equal in intrinsic worth.[19]

At one level, biocentric equality is the same insight described in Chapter 7 as biocentrism. Taylor's *Respect for Nature*, for example, also defends a biocentric ethics that is based on the notion of equal inherent worth. However, Taylor's biocentrism is well rooted within traditional Western philosophy. It develops out of an individualism that views organisms as centers of individual lives. The biocentric equality of deep ecology grows out of metaphysical holism with equally old Western roots. Members of the biotic community possess equal moral worth, not because as individuals they have intrinsic worth, but simply because they are members of that community.

Is there a significant difference? If there is any, it seems that deep ecologists are less willing to make tradeoffs between human and nonhuman interests. When human interests conflict with nonhuman interests, deep ecologists are less inclined to favor the human interests. We saw Taylor go to some lengths to work out a means for rationally resolving conflicts. For deep ecologists, this is likely to result in hierarchies that, inevitably, have human interests at the top.[20] Deep ecology seeks a more democratic, and less hierarchical, equality.

With that said, we must recognize that the deep ecology platform allows humans to "reduce" biocentric richness and diversity in order to "satisfy vital needs." It is difficult to see how something like Taylor's distinction between basic and nonbasic needs would be "hierarchical" when this statement is not. Perhaps part of the answer lies in how "vital needs" gets explained. For example, Naess suggests that unemployment in a country with a high standard of living would not violate a vital need. But Devall and Sessions suggest that vital needs include such things as "love, play, creative expression, intimate relationships with a particular landscape (or nature taken in its entirety) as well as intimate relationships with other humans, and the vital need for spiritual growth, for becoming a mature human being."[21] Thus the ethical and practical implications of biocentric equality within a deep ecological perspective differ from those generated by a more individualistic philosophy.

What are these practical implications? We can mention two. Deep ecologists are committed to promoting lifestyles that "tread lightly on the Earth." This means that humans ought to live in simple, relatively nontechnological, self-reliant, decentralized communities. Second, analogous to the concept of an ecosystem, communities ought to be organized regionally, existing as a "bioregion" rather than as more traditional political organizations. Our lifestyles ought to be simple in the sense that our consumer or material desires should be kept to a minimum. We need to recognize material wants as artificial products of human society. "We should live with minimum rather than maximum impact on the other species and on the Earth in general."[22] The ideal seems to be a situation in which local communities exist in a harmonious and self-regulating relationship with their surroundings. This ideal has been called an "ecotopia," a community that seeks harmony with rather than dominance over nature.

10.7 SUMMARY AND CONCLUSION

As mentioned at the start of this chapter, deep ecology does not refer to one specific and systematic philosophy. It refers to an assortment of philosophical and activist approaches to ecological issues that share some fundamental assumptions. It is perhaps best thought of as a movement that encompasses both philosophical and activist sides.

Given this diversity, it is difficult to offer any precise criticisms of deep ecology. A critique of, for example, the tactics of Earth First! could be rebuffed by deep ecologists as beside the point, because not all deep ecologists agree with these tactics. Likewise, a critique that accuses deep ecology of being too abstract and vague on such issues as self-realization, might be rejected by deep ecologists who are more inclined toward political activism.

Of course, this ambiguity itself can be grounds for criticism. In some ways, the claims of deep ecology are so sweeping and general as to become empty. A "movement" that can claim inspiration from such diverse sources as Taoism, Heraclitus, Spinoza, Whitehead, Gandhi, Buddhism, Native American cultures, Thomas Jefferson, Thoreau, and Woody Guthrie is certainly eclectic at best. At worst, it becomes unintelligible. This chapter has offered an overview of the most common philosophical themes and concepts involved in deep ecology.

More systematic critiques of deep ecology have been offered by thinkers associated with two other movements within environmental philosophy, *social ecology* and *ecofeminism*. These perspectives agree that in the search for the "deep" underlying causes of the present crisis, deep ecologists have focused their attention at too abstract a level. The more significant causes can be located at a much more localized level: the social, economic, and patriarchal structures of contemporary societies. The following chapter turns to these more recent environmental philosophies. I introduce them, in part, as critiques of deep ecology.

Notes

1. For an excellent discussion of this distinction, see Michael Martin, "Ecosabotage and Civil Disobedience," *Environmental Ethics* 12 (Winter 1990): 291–310.

2. Bill Devall, *Simple in Means, Rich in Ends: Practicing Deep Ecology* (Layton, UT: Gibbs Smith Publishing, 1988).

3. See, for example, the distinction between "deep" and "shallow" offered by Donald VanDeVeer and Christine Pierce, *People, Penguins, and Plastic Trees* (Belmont, CA: Wadsworth, 1986), pp. 69–70. Here "shallow ecology" is taken as the view that "nature has no value apart from the needs, interests, and good of human beings," and "deep ecology holds that nature has value in its own right independent of the interests of humans."

4. See Arne Naess, *Ecology, Community, and Lifestyle*, tr. and rev. by David Rothenberg (Cambridge, England: Cambridge University Press, 1989), and Bill Devall and George Sessions, *Deep Ecology: Living as if Nature Mattered* (Salt Lake City: Peregrine Smith Books, 1985).

5. Arne Naess, "The Shallow and the Deep, Long-Range Ecology Movement," *Inquiry* 16 (1973): 95–100.

6. Arne Naess, "A Defense of the Deep Ecology Movement," *Environmental Ethics* 6 (Fall 1984): 264.

7. Devall and Sessions, p. ix.

8. This description relies heavily on David Rothenberg's "Introduction" to Naess, *Ecology, Community, and Lifestyle*.

9. This platform is presented in Devall and Sessions, chap. 5, as the "basic principles" of deep ecology. They are also presented as "a platform" in Naess, *Ecology, Community, and Lifestyle*, chap. 1.

10. Naess, *Ecology, Community, and Lifestyle*, pp. 26–27.

11. Ibid., pp. 39–40.

12. Ibid., pp. 130–133.

13. For one sustained account of the "dominant modern worldview," see Devall and Sessions, chap. 3.

14. Warwick Fox, "Deep Ecology: A New Philosophy for Our Time?" *Ecologist* 14 (1974): 5–6, pp. 194–200. As quoted in Devall and Sessions (1974): p. 66.

15. Harold Morowitz, "Biology as a Cosmological Science," *Main Currents in Modern Thought* 28 (1972): 156. This section is quoted and discussed in J. Baird Callicott, "Metaphysical Implications of Ecology," *Environmental Ethics* 9 (1986): 300–315. Callicott's essay suggests that "a consolidated metaphysical consensus" might be emerging from ecological science that would supplant the mechanical model that emerged from seventeeth-century physics.

16. Naess, *Ecology, Community, and Lifestyle*, p. 66.

17. Ibid., pp. 70–71.

18. Devall and Sessions, pp. 66–67.

19. Ibid., p. 67.

20. Ibid., p. 68.

21. Naess, *Ecology, Community, and Lifestyle*, p. 30, and Devall and Sessions, p. 68.

22. Devall and Sessions, p. 68. See also, Naess, *Ecology, Community, and Lifestyle*, chap. 4, "Ecosophy, Technology, and Lifestyle."

Discussion Questions

1. Is civil disobedience in the defense of the environment justified? When and why? Is "tree spiking" a defensible means for preventing logging in old-growth forests?

2. What is an "individual?" What is an individual living thing? Does the meaning of this word change in different contexts? What implications for ethics follow from your answer?

3. Is the statement "This is a tall tree" any more objective than the statement "This is a majestic tree"? How would either statement be explained and defended?

4. Classical economists such as those discussed in Chapter 3 claim that humans are always motivated by self-interest. In light of the discussion of the "self" and the "Self" in this chapter, do you agree with that view of human motivation? Would the deep ecology view of Self-Realization require that "human nature be rewired" as claimed in Chapter 3?

5. Think about the connections between philosophical theory and political activism. Should theory guide activism, or should right actions determine acceptable theory? Should we first decide on our ethical principles and then decide what we ought to do? Or, having decided what we should do, do we then develop a philosophy that explains and justifies these acts?

For Further Reading

John Davis, ed., *Earth First! Reader* (Salt Lake City: Peregrine Smith Books, 1991), collects a wide variety of essays on and by radical environmentalists.

Dave Foreman, *Confessions of an Eco-Warrior* (New York: Harmony Books, 1991), by the best-known radical environmentalist.

David Ehrenfeld, *The Arrogance of Humanism* (New York: Oxford University Press, 1978), an ecologist's critique of anthropocentric thinking.

Gary Snyder, *The Real Work: Interviews and Talks: 1964–1979* (New York: New Directions, 1980), a collection of poems and talks by the "poet laureate" of deep ecology.

11

Social Ecology and Ecofeminism

Sustainable Agriculture and Appropriate Technologies

U.S. agricultural production, especially since the end of World War II, has enjoyed an unprecedented success. Few other U.S. industries have had such a long and productive history. The tremendous productive capacity of U.S. agriculture can be traced to a number of factors, but perhaps the development of highly mechanized and specialized farms, chemical fertilizers and pesticides, and specialized hybrid crops are the most important. In short, the U.S. farm seems like a classic economic and technological success story. Science and technology have increased efficiencies so that maximum output can be attained through decreasing inputs.

But modern agriculture, or perhaps what is more appropriately called "agribusiness," is not without problems. The highly efficient modern farm is increasingly dependent on borrowed money to pay for complex farm machinery, expensive fertilizers, pesticides, and hybrid seed. Population growth and the associated urban sprawl has also raised the cost of much farmland. In this heavily capitalized situation, many farmers, especially on smaller family farms, are extremely vulnerable. Despite their productive capacity, bankruptcy is a constant threat. During the 1980s, public attention was focused on the "farm crisis" brought about by foreclosures occurring at a rate unseen since the Dust Bowl of the 1930s.

These economic demands often encourage a type of farming that creates significant environmental problems. Soil erosion, loss of fertility, groundwater and soil pollution, pesticide contamination of both crops and workers are all by-products of many agribusiness farming techniques. The mechanized farm is also highly dependent on fossil fuels with their related environmental costs.

In response to these problems, there has arisen a growing movement concerned with developing alternative agricultural models. These models have been called by a number of different names: *organic, alternative, renewable, low-input, ecological,* or *regenerative agriculture.* The term gaining greatest acceptance seems to be *sustainable agriculture.*[1]

At first glance, sustainable agriculture appears simply to be a response to the specific problems associated with modern high-tech farming. Crop rotation and contour plowing, elimination of pesticides and chemical fertilizers, crop diversification, use of renewable resources and fuels, recycling and composting all seem to address specific agricultural problems. In general, sustainable agriculture advocates recommend adopting practices that ensure an agriculture that is sustainable and environmentally safe in the long term. The goal is to rely less on commercial resources produced elsewhere and more on those resources that can be produced on or near the farm.

Sustainable agriculture does not advocate abandoning technology and scientific farming. Indeed, it seeks a synthesis of scientific ecology, technology, and traditional conservation techniques. It does, however, require abandoning the priority that has been given to productivity and economic efficiency, or at least redefining our notions of what counts as "productivity." Thus it seeks to replace the image of a farm as a factory with the image of a farm as a natural ecosystem.

But sustainable agriculture involves more than simple "quick fixes" to specific farming problems. In the words of Wes Jackson (a well-known advocate of this approach), "As the sustainable agriculture effort unfolds, it is becoming increasingly clear that 'sustainable' is a complex political word."[2] How can a collection of farming techniques constitute a "political" movement?

First, it is obvious that agriculture has a tremendous social impact on the entire country. When tens of thousands of farms faced foreclosure and bankruptcy in the 1980s, the political repercussions were felt across the nation. Thousands of local communities, hundreds of counties, and a number of states suffered economically, politically, and socially during the 1980's farm crisis. In a straightforward sense, therefore, the farm crisis was also a political crisis.

Furthermore, any large-scale shift away from modern agribusiness faces formidable obstacles in terms of the social infrastructure already in place. All the institutions that supply agribusiness with capital, machinery, and supplies and that provide the means for transporting, processing, distributing, and retailing agricultural products will resist such changes in the status quo.

Shifts toward sustainable agriculture would also require changes in the ultimate consumer of agricultural products. Conveniences of price, availability, selection, and appearance could well be sacrificed in a society of low-tech, diversified, and organic agriculture. A conversion to sustainable agriculture would require substantial changes in our social, economic, and personal habits.

Finally, sustainable agriculture could have a profound impact on political values such as freedom and democracy. A sustainable farm is an independent farm, free from control and domination by external sources. Given this independence, decisions affecting a sustainable farm must be made at the local level by those people most directly affected by them. As Thomas Jefferson envisioned, small, self-sufficient farms can encourage a variety of civic virtues important for sustaining democracy.

Many people tend to think in dualistic, either–or terms. Critics of sustainable agriculture, for example, sometimes argue that if we abandon high-tech, highly mechanized and centralized agriculture, the only alternative is a subsistence, communal, back-to-nature model. Since that alternative is unrealistic, we have little choice but to accept the status quo. A similar challenge is raised against those who see technology as a major contributor to environmental destruction. Critics of nuclear power, automobiles, and other energy-intensive technologies are often cast as advocates of a pre-industrial asceticism. But this dualistic way of thinking ignores a third possibility, a more environmentally benign application of technology.

In its most simple meaning, the term *appropriate technology* refers to the practice of matching needs with a specific technology that is most suitable for these needs. "Suitable" as used here obviously is a value-laden word. A suitable technology is sufficient to accomplish human ends, but does so without waste and without unnecessary environmental, ecological, or social disruption. In this sense, it seeks a harmony between human ends and the natural processes used to attain those ends. Rather than seeking a technology that dominates and controls nature, appropriate technology seeks technologies that cooperate with nature. Of course, one by-product of this approach is that as the technology changes away from patterns of complexity and dominance, so too might the human ends and goals.

An example can illustrate this point. In order to provide heat and lighting for their homes, about 10 percent of the U.S. population presently relies on the extremely complex, expensive, centralized, and potentially dangerous technology of nuclear energy. Is society best served by using the technology of nuclear fission to heat and light its homes? Might there be more appropriate technologies for these tasks? Might there be technological alternatives to both nuclear power and returning to pre-electricity lifestyles? The appropriate technology strategy suggests local, environmentally benign energy sources to replace nuclear fission. Thus, renewable energy sources such as solar, wind, and hydropower, along with fuel-efficient and nonpolluting woodstoves, and energy-efficient appliances, provide technologies that are appropriate for the given human uses. The ideal of appropriate technology advocates is to attain the best of both worlds: energy to satisfy human needs and desires, without the environmental and other costs associated with highly centralized, complex, and bureaucratic technologies.

Of equal importance is the fact that appropriate technologies can also foster democratic virtues. Decentralized technologies support a process of localized decision making in a way that complex and bureaucratic technologies do not. Consider how decisions concerning nuclear power are made for example. As was discussed in Chapter 2, decisions concerning the location of nuclear power plants are made at the top of large public and corporate bureaucracies, far from the people most directly affected by them. The complexity, expense, and size of the technology ensures that decisions must be made by "experts" in government and industry. The average citizen, after all, understands little of what is involved in nuclear technology. Thus, citizens are taught to become passive and obedient, hardly virtues that democracies should promote.

On the other hand, with technologies appropriate to localized needs and abilities, decisions are much more likely made by the people directly affected by them. The energy-efficient household or the sustainable farm, for example, is free to make its own decisions: free technologically and economically, but also free in a political sense. Citizens are taught to become active participants in decisions concerning their life. Citizens become responsible for their lives in a way that democratic institutions require. Appropriate technologies and sustainable agriculture truly are political movements. Each seeks a world in which individuals are free from the control of people with whom they have no direct and personal relationship. Each also encourages individuals and local communities to take an active role in decisions that affect them.

11.1 INTRODUCTION

In this chapter, we examine one approach to ecological and environmental issues called "social ecology" and a variety of approaches that together can be identified as "ecofeminism." Although many differences exist between social ecology and ecofeminism, these approaches share important similarities that make it appropriate to examine them together within one chapter.

Social ecology is associated primarily with the work of one person, Murray Bookchin, and consists of a relatively unified theoretical perspective.[3] Ecofeminism, in contrast, reflects the diversity that exists among feminist thinkers, and might better be thought of as a general perspective on ecological issues rather than as a unified "theory" of ecophilosophy. In general, ecofeminism involves the use of any of the diverse feminist philosophies in the analysis of ecological issues. Since there are many different perspectives within feminist philosophy, we can expect to find diverse "ecofeminisms."[4] Nevertheless, there are important similarities both among perspectives within ecofeminism, and between ecofeminism and social ecology.

To help us understand these similarities, we can distinguish two facets of social ecology and ecofeminism. Each approach includes *analytical* aspects that offer analyses of the causes and issues underlying the contemporary ecological crisis. Each also has more *programatic* aspects that offer alternative visions of an ecologically sound future. Social ecology and ecofeminism have much in common in their general analysis of ecological problems. Each sees ecological destruction as related to social problems of control and dominance. They differ in the specific explanations offered for these social problems and on their programs for social change.

Social ecology and ecofeminism look to society to find the underlying causes of the environmental crisis. Unlike deep ecologists,
they do not identify the root causes of ecological destruction as a
dominant philosophy or world view. Each would hold that deep
ecology is concerned with factors that are too abstract and too general. Each would suggest that deep ecology tends to ignore the
very specific human and social causes of environmental destruction.
Each might also fault deep ecology for overemphasizing wilderness
concerns while ignoring the human costs of environmental harms.
Nor do they believe that the fundamental cause lies only in a failure
of traditional ethics, either in the scope or the application of those
theories.

Rather, social ecologists and ecofeminists argue that the root of
our ecological crisis lies in certain social factors. Specifically, social
ecologists and ecofeminists believe that human domination and
degradation of nature arises out of social patterns of domination
and hierarchy, patterns of social life in which some humans exercise
control or domination over others. Thus, both approaches shift
philosophical attention away from questions traditionally associated with metaphysics and ethics, and on to questions traditionally
associated with social and political philosophy.

A central insight of these views concerns the relations between
individual humans and the patterns of social organization in which
they live. We should always remind ourselves that societies are
human creations, organized and structured by human beings in
ways that serve human ends. Thus, when examining society we
should ask about the ends or purposes served by any particular
arrangement. But we also need to ask questions about what any
particular arrangement is doing *to* those humans who are living
within them. That is, we need to ask not only what does society do
for people, but what any particular society does *to* people. In the
views of social ecologists and ecofeminists, many social structures
serve to oppress some members of society for the benefit of others.
This oppressive social structure, in turn, works to re-enforce a way
of thinking and living that encourages domination in all forms, including the domination of the natural world.

This point is summarized by Bookchin in a short formulation:
"The very notion of the domination of nature by man [gender spe-
cific] stems from the very real domination of human by human."[5] In
a similar vein, Rosemary Radford Reuther, one of the first feminist
thinkers to address ecological issues, has written,

> Women must see that there can be no liberation for them and no
> solution to the ecological crisis within a society whose fundamental
> model of relationships continues to be one of domination. They must
> unite the demands of the women's movement with those of the ecologi-
> cal movement to envision a radical reshaping of the basic socioeconomic
> relations and the underlying values of this society.[6]

In this view, environmental and ecological destruction is best understood as a form of human domination, in this case the human domination of nature. To understand this crisis more fully, both social
ecologists and ecofeminists agree that we need to understand more
general patterns of human domination over other humans. In this
way, an adequate understanding of the ecological crisis must address fundamental questions of social and political philosophy. We
must identify and analyze patterns of domination and oppression
within societies and evaluate these patterns in terms of philosophical accounts of justice. An alternative ecological vision, in turn,
should be based on a model of social justice in which all human
beings are free from oppression and domination.

We can initially distinguish social ecology from ecofeminism by
looking to their analyses of the various types of social domination
and to their alternative conceptions of justice. Social ecologists liken
environmental destruction to what they see as general and widespread forms of domination and hierarchy. These include such social practices and structures as racism, sexism, class structures, as
well as private ownership, capitalism, bureaucracies, and even the
nation-state. These social practices and institutions establish social
hierarchies in which some humans exercise power and domination
over others. Social ecologists typically defend an anarchist conception of justice in which human freedom, understood as the absence
of external control and psychological manipulation, is the essential
element of justice.

Ecofeminists, however, identify the oppression of women as a
principal form of social domination.[7] Ecofeminists identify many
close connections between the oppression of women and the oppression of nature. As a result, they believe that the goals of the feminist
movement closely parallel the goals of the ecological movement.
However, ecofeminists offer various analyses of women's oppression and appeal to various accounts of social justice in critiquing
this oppression and in developing alternative nondominating models of society.[8]

In characterizing these parallel feminist and ecological concerns, philosopher Karen Warren emphasizes:

> the concern about connections—historical, empirical, conceptual, theoretical, symbolic, and experiential—between the domination of women and the domination of nature. According to ecofeminists, a failure to see these connections will result in the continued exploitation of both women and non-human nature and in the development of policy, theory, and practices which is grossly inadequate from a feminist point of view.[9]

In this chapter, I follow a similar pattern in describing the ecological philosophies of social ecology and ecofeminism. First, I trace the account offered of social domination and the connections with environmental domination. Next, I'll examine the evaluations of this social domination and discuss the philosophical basis of these evaluations. I then consider the alternative social visions presented in social ecology and various ecofeminisms and conclude with a review of some critical challenges to each of these approaches.

11.2 MURRAY BOOKCHIN'S SOCIAL ECOLOGY

Murray Bookchin is a social theorist who has been writing about the connections between social domination and the domination of nature for over four decades. His views have been characterized in a number of ways including "libertarian social ecology," "eco-anarchism," and most commonly "social ecology." In what follows, I limit the phrase "social ecology" to the social philosophy developed in Bookchin's writings.

Social ecology has its roots in a variety of philosophical traditions, including Marxist socialism, libertarian anarchism, and the "Western organismic tradition" associated with such philosophers as Aristotle and Hegel. Although a full description of these diverse traditions is well beyond the scope of this text, we need to consider them in passing to understand social ecology.

First we need to examine what Bookchin means by social domination and how this is connected to ecological problems. Specifically, Bookchin is concerned with *hierarchies*, which he explains as

> the cultural, traditional and psychological systems of obedience and command, not merely the economic and political systems to which the terms class and State most appropriately refer. Accordingly, hierarchy and domination could easily continue to exist in a "classless" or "Stateless" society. I refer to the domination of the young by the old, of women by men, of one ethnic group by another, of "masses" by bureaucrats who

profess to speak of "higher social interests," of countryside by town, and in a more subtle psychological sense, of body by mind, of spirit by a shallow instrumental rationality.[10]

Thus, hierarchies imply the existence of at least two groups, one of which holds power over the other. This power enables the "superior" group to command obedience from the "inferior" group. Hierarchies promote social systems of domination, in which the superior group is able to manipulate the inferior group to serve the purposes of the superiors while preventing the inferiors from pursuing their own true ends.

In this quotation, Bookchin distinguishes his views from both traditional Marxists and traditional anarchists. Unlike Marxists, Bookchin does not believe that the primary form of social hierarchy and domination rests with economic classes. Unlike anarchists, Bookchin also does not believe that the modern nation-state is the primary agent of social domination. In his view, it is quite possible to find structures of domination within societies that lack economic classes and the bureaucratic nation-state.

This quotation also suggests that physical domination and power is not the only kind of social control. Hierarchy "is also a state of consciousness" as well as a social condition. People can be oppressed by their own consciousness, their own understandings and beliefs, as much as by external forces. Thus Bookchin speaks of people who "internalize" social structures of hierarchy and learn to accept a life of "toil, guilt, and sacrifice" while their "superiors" enjoy a life of pleasure and satisfaction.[11] As suggested earlier, human freedom involves more than just the absence of external controls. In his classic book *The Ecology of Freedom*, Bookchin offers a history of the diverse forms of hierarchy and domination that have existed in societies from the Paleolithic era to the modern world.

But the most pertinent aspect of Bookchin's views concern his assertion that the domination of nature "stems from" these patterns of social hierarchy and domination. How, exactly, should this claim be understood?

An initial thing to note is that Bookchin essentially has reversed a standard Marxist interpretation. In the view of many Marxists, it was the human ability to dominate nature, in the appropriation of private property, that allowed the creation of wealth and class structures that, in turn, led to class conflict and oppression. Bookchin suggests that social structures of domination preceded the domination of nature.

Bookchin also distinguishes his views from a Marxist view by denying any necessity or determinism to the connection between social domination and the domination of nature. He allows for the possibility that hierarchical societies might actually have rather benign relationships to nature, and that nonhierarchical societies might abuse their natural environment.[12] Rather, he seeks to uncover how patterns of social domination can foster "a broad cultural mentality" or "ideology" that supports the domination of nature.

We can summarize these aspects of social ecology as follows. Societies characterized by a high degree of hierarchy are also likely to abuse and damage their natural environment. Social hierarchies provide both the psychological and material conditions, the motivation and the means, for exploiting and dominating nature. In hierarchical societies, social institutions and practices (which would include, for example, forms of agriculture and technology) are designed in ways to facilitate control. You might think of the concept of economic efficiency as one such social ideal. In such a society, success will be understood in terms of dominance and control. The more people who work for you, the greater wealth, power, and status you have, the more successful you are. In such a society, human success will also be identified with the domination and control of nonhuman nature. To understand the analysis further, it will help to discuss briefly another facet of social ecology, what Bookchin refers to as the "organismic tradition."

The "organismic tradition" in social philosophy focuses on the relations between individuals and their society. It seeks a middle ground between those who believe that individuals are simply the products of their society and those who believe that society is nothing more than a collection of individuals. An organic society, or what is more often called a "community," exists in what philosophers call a dialectical relationship with individual human beings. That is, communities are created by human actions and human decisions, but humans are also created by their community. Social institutions, practices, values, and beliefs all influence the person I become. My identity is constituted to a large extent by my social roles, my social history, my social circumstances. But the organic tradition does not reify the society, making it some "thing" out there that shapes and controls humans. Society itself is a product of human action and human decisions. Thus, the dialectical relationship sees humans as creating their society while at the same time being created by it.

Given this understanding of social history, we can now understand Bookchin's primary social and ethical value. Humans cannot help but be shaped and created by their social history. But this can occur in two ways. Humans can go through life being created by and in turn creating their social world without fully recognizing this reality, or they can be fully conscious of and responsible for this history. The pre-eminent human value is fully conscious, "self-determining activity" because only through this type of action do humans most fully attain their natural potential as conscious, thinking beings. This value is Bookchin's anarchist conception of freedom.

How is fully conscious, self-determining activity possible? It is possible only when humans are free from all forms of external control and domination, which includes not only physical but social, legal, psychological, intellectual, and emotional forms of coercion. Thus, the only truly just society is one in which humans are free from all forms of control or domination. This, then, is the goal of Bookchin's "libertarian anarchism." Philosophical anarchism holds that no coercive authority is ever justified. Put another way, philosophical anarchism maintains that all claims of authority are simply disguised forms of power or coercion.

In this model, the just community is one that is created to serve common needs and goals. It is a community that eschews domination in any form, whether domination of humans or of nature. It would be a community in which democratic values such as full participation and freedom are the norms. Bookchin characterizes this just community as one that avoids institutions and customs that place one person or group of people in positions of authority over others. They would be communities in which decision-making authority was decentralized, in which individuals complement and cooperate with each other, but do not dominate each other. Indeed, the ideal "anarchistic community would approximate an ecosystem; it would be diversified, balanced, and harmonious."[13]

Given these philosophical goals, one can see how practices such as sustainable agriculture and appropriate technologies would play a central role in Bookchin's ideal social and ecological community. Sustainable agriculture is seen not as a collection of solutions to specific farming problems, but as part of a lifestyle in which both humans and their natural surroundings can live free from dependence on dominating institutions and practices. So, too, appropriate technologies will free individuals from control by external forces. Both sustainable agriculture and appropriate technologies decentralize and diversify decision-making authority. In this sense, they are truly democratic practices. Decisions are made directly by the people most affected by them. Both sustainable agriculture and appropriate technologies re-enforce a community lifestyle in which local communities become sustainable and self-sufficient. In this type of world, humans will experience true freedom, and only in this type of community will humans be able to live in harmony with their natural environment. It is not coincidental, according to Bookchin, that nature's freedom from human domination can come about only in a world in which humans are also free from human domination.

11.3 CRITICAL REFLECTIONS

Several challenges can be raised against Bookchin's social ecology. One concerns the alleged connection between social domination and the domination of nature.[14] A second focuses on the role that humans play in guiding the evolutionary development of nature.[15]

We have seen that Bookchin explicitly denies that there is a necessary connection between social hierarchies and social domination on the one hand and attempts to dominate nature on the other. The former does not *cause* the latter. But what is the relationship? Bookchin's answer is not always clear. Yet without a clear answer social ecology loses much of its persuasive force, especially when we consider its practical implications.

A strong causal connection between social domination and the domination of nature would suggest that we will be unable to meet environmental challenges unless we first abolish social hierarchies. In this interpretation, our policy demands are clear: we must address social questions prior to ecological ones. Yet if the connection is less clear, then so too should be our policy priorities. If we can address ecological problems first, and independently of addressing social hierarchies, then the very relevance of social ecology is open to question.

In fairness to Bookchin, his view is more subtle than this challenge allows. As he sees it, the connection is less than a necessary, causal connection, but more than a mere accident. Bookchin speaks of the historical connection between real social hierarchies and the *idea* of dominating nature.[16] This suggests that, as a matter of historical fact, hierarchical societies encourage humans to identify social progress with control of and domination over nonhuman nature. Eventually, the connections can be thought of as mutually re-enforcing. By implication, we need to address both, and to address one is also to address the other. Changing to a more benign relationship with the natural world will provoke changes in social arrangements (as the discussion of the "political" nature of sustainable agriculture might suggest). Changing our social relationships to less hierarchical, more decentralized associations will encourage a more felicitous relationship with nature (as the discussion of appropriate technologies might suggest).

A second challenge to Bookchin focuses on the role that he allows for humans in guiding natural evolution. Bookchin casts humans as "stewards" of evolution, as capable of consciously serving and directing natural evolution. To some critics, this suggests a willingness to privilege human interests over nonhuman interests, to allow humans to "seize the helm of evolution" and direct nature to human ends.[17] Such anthropocentricism is rejected by critics as being exactly the attitude that created much ecological destruction in the first place.

This criticism grows out of Bookchin's description of human rationality and human society as themselves products of natural evolution, a "nature rendered self-conscious." On the basis of this description, Bookchin rejects any view that calls for humans to remove themselves from the natural world or that "denies or degrades the uniqueness of human beings." He lists both biocentric ethics and deep ecology among the philosophical views that degrade the rational abilities of human beings. Social ecology is described as *"humanistic* in the high Renaissance meaning of the term," which requires "a shift in vision from the skies to the earth, from superstition to reason, from deities to people—who are no less the products of natural evolution than grizzly bears and whales."[18]

Bookchin distinguishes "second nature," which includes such features of human evolution as rationality, communication, culture, and society, from "first nature," which refers to the nonhuman natural world. Although he emphasizes that this distinction is one of degree rather than kind, nevertheless it also suggests that humans are not simply the "equal biotic citizens" described in biocentric ethics, the land ethic, and deep ecology. The implications of this trouble critics, especially when Bookchin goes on as follows:

> Natural evolution has not only provided humans with the *ability*, but also the *necessity* to be purposive interveners into "first nature," to consciously *change* "first nature" by means of a highly institutionalized form of community we call "society". . . . Taken together, all of these human traits—intellectual, communicative, and social—have not only emerged from natural evolution and are inherently human; they can also be placed at the *service* of natural evolution to consciously increase biotic diversity, diminish suffering, foster the evolution of new and ecologically valuable life-forms, reduce the impact of disastrous accidents or the harsh effects of mere change.[19]

Bookchin explicitly denies that he is suggesting that humans take command over nature and control it for anthropocentric ends. As it exists today, "second nature" is thoroughly shaped by social hierarchies and ideas of domination. Hence, it would be a mistake simply to pass control of the natural world over to this type of thinking and reasoning. In a spirit reminiscent of Leopold, furthermore, Bookchin emphasizes the complexity of "first nature" and strongly recommends a conservative and prudent approach to any activity that changes nature. Nonetheless, he does not shy away from the ramifications of his initial claim. Humanity, as a part of natural evolution and the only part capable of sophisticated, rational thought, has a responsibility to act as stewards of the natural evolutionary process.

During the late 1980s, an acrimonious debate between Bookchin and several deep ecologists developed on this issue. Deep ecologists accused Bookchin of anthropocentricism and attributed to him the view that "human beings are a *higher* form of life."[20] Bookchin, for his part, had accused deep ecologists of advocating an oppressive and misanthropic philosophy.[21] A short review of this debate can provide a helpful summary of Bookchin.

Bookchin's critique of deep ecology can be generalized to apply to any biocentric or ecocentric ethics that attribute "equal moral worth" to human and nonhuman life-forms. During these debates, Bookchin highlighted the extreme views of several deep ecologists and members of Earth First!. These views suggested that famine and AIDS, for example, were "nature's revenge" for over-population and ecological destruction. The implication was that starving children in places like Ethiopia and Somalia should be allowed to die in the name of some natural ecological law concerning carrying capacity and population dynamics. Bookchin forcefully rejected these views claimed that they followed straightforwardly from the philosophy of biocentricism:

> If the deep ecology principle of "biocentricism" teaches that human beings are no different from lemmings in terms of their "intrinsic worth" and the moral consideration we owe them, and if human beings are viewed as being subject to "natural laws" in just the same way as any other species, then these "extreme" statements are really the *logical* conclusion of deep ecology philosophy.[22]

One problem with the principle of biocentricism is that it tends to treat all humans as equally responsible for ecological destruction. The cause of the ecological crisis is attributed to "anthropocentricism," a human-centered ethics. As an alternative, a biocentric, or life-centered, ethics is developed. But Bookchin rejects the view that "humanity" is at fault, that "we" are destroying the natural world:

> But, I have to ask, who is this "us" from which the living world has to be protected? . . . Is it "humanity"? Is it the human "species" *per se*? Is it people, as such? Or is it our particular society, our particular civilization, with its hierarchical social relations . . . ? One of the problems with this asocial, "species-centered" way of thinking, of course, is that it blames the victim. Let's face it, when you say that a black kid in Harlem is as much to blame for the ecological crisis as the president of Exxon, you are letting one off the hook and slandering the other.[23]

We can see the central insight of Bookchin's philosophy in these challenges to deep ecology and biocentrism. To understand the roots of our ecological crisis, we need to look to how societies are organized. Society is a human creation and some forms of society can lead to an attitude that encourages humans to dominate and destroy the natural world. But since society is a human creation, it can also be changed by human beings. Bookchin reminds us that while human decisions and human values have played a major role in ecological destruction, they can be a major part of ecological solutions as well.

11.4 ECOFEMINISM: MAKING CONNECTIONS

Ecofeminism identifies a variety of approaches that also see a connection between social domination and the domination of nature. Since the term was first used by Françoise d'Eaubonne in 1974, "ecofeminism" has generated a significant amount of interesting writing and research.[24] As described by philosopher Karen Warren, ecofeminism or ecological feminism "is the position that there are important connections—historical, experiential, symbolic, theoretical—between the domination of women and the domination of nature, an understanding of which is crucial to both feminism and environmental ethics."[25]

Ecofeminism is a recent development among environmental philosophers and, as this quote suggests, much of the work is still concerned with simply exploring the connections between the feminist and ecological movements. Nevertheless, significant philosophical contributions have already been made from this approach.

Since there exists a wide diversity among feminists concerning the nature and analysis of women's oppression, there also exists a diversity of views concerning the connections between the domination of women and the domination of nature. In what follows I review some connections that have been made between the domination of women and the domination of nature, and provide an overview of their philosophical and environmental significance.

Following the structure introduced in section 11.1, it would be convenient to begin with a discussion of the specific account of domination offered by feminists. However, as mentioned earlier, feminists offer a wide variety of explanations of the domination of women. Nevertheless, we can begin with a discussion of the most general features of any system of domination, or of what Karen Warren has called the "logic of domination."[26] This logic of domination is a pattern of thinking in which two groups (for example, men and women) are distinguished in terms of some characteristics (for example, men are rational, women are emotional), a value hierarchy is attributed to these characteristics (for example, reason is superior to emotion), and then the subordination of the one group is justified by the fact that it lacks this superior characteristic (for example, men ought to be in positions of authority because they are more rational, and less emotional, than women). If this is the most general pattern of thinking that feminists reject, different feminisms can be distinguished by their analyses of this logic of domination.

One framework for organizing feminist thinking that has influenced many ecofeminists was developed by philosopher Alison Jaggar.[27] Jaggar distinguishes between liberal, Marxist, radical, and socialist forms of feminism. Each offers its own account of the oppression of women and its own alternative social philosophy. For example, *liberal feminists* deny that there is any relevant difference between men and women. Liberals (like the utilitarians and Kant) argue that all humans possess the same nature as free and rational beings and that any unequal treatment of women denies this moral equality and therefore is unjust. As a result of this analysis, liberal feminists devote much of their energy to locating discrimination and fighting for equal rights and equal opportunity. *Marxist feminists* argue that women are oppressed because they are relegated to domestic, and therefore dependent, forms of labor. These feminists argue, for example, that the Lockean theory of private property rights makes sense only within a context in which women's labor is ignored. A necessary precondition for a "man" to "mix his labor" with some unowned land is that women are performing full-time domestic labor that allows the man the free time necessary to accumulate land. Domestic labor, of course, does not give women property rights of ownership over the home. They further argue only by becoming full participants in independent and productive forms of labor will women become liberated from economic and political exploitation. *Socialist feminists* reject the strict class analysis offered by Marxists and claim that a complex web of social relationships underlies the oppression of women. These relationships include both economic factors and the traditional patterns of gender roles and identities.

Radical feminists believe that biological and sexual differences between men and women have been made the basis of women's oppression. This type of feminism is "radical" in the sense that it denies that women's oppression can be reduced to some other more basic form of oppression. Women have been culturally defined in terms of their biology. This biological difference has been used to justify a wide-ranging gender system ensuring that women remain dominated by men, primarily by being cast exclusively in roles of mothers, wives, and sex objects. Because of their roles in child-bearing, child-raising, and human sexuality, women have been characterized as more controlled by their bodies, more passive, and more emotional than men. Given the logic of domination, it is a short step from these gender distinctions to the conclusion that men, by being more reasonable and active than women, ought to be in positions of authority over women.

Recognizing this pattern of thinking, some radical feminists conclude that women can escape oppression only when traditional gender roles are abolished. Some early radical feminists argued that women should strive for a "unisex" or androgynous culture, while others advocated separatism between women and men. Still other radical feminists turned this logic of domination on its head. Rather than denying biological, sexual, and gendered differences between men and women, these feminists seek instead to encourage and celebrate the female. Accepting the view that women do experience, understand, and value differently from men, some radical feminists seek to develop feminist politics, culture, and ethics as an alternative to the traditional masculine and patriarchal politics, culture, and ethics.

A significant amount of work on ecological issues has come from this branch of radical feminism. What has been called "cultural ecofeminism"[28] accepts the view of this type of radical feminism that there do exist authentic and particular "women's ways" of experiencing, understanding, or valuing the world. Cultural ecofeminism holds that women's perspectives historically have been and remain closely identified with nature and that women, like nature, have been systematically oppressed in the process. But rather than denying the link between women and nature (as liberal ecofeminists for example might do), cultural ecofeminists aim "to remedy ecological and other problems through the creation of an alternative 'women's

culture' . . . based on revaluing, celebrating and defending what pa-
triarchy has devalued, including the feminine, non-human nature,
the body and the emotions."[29]

The connections between alternative women's cultures and ecological concerns have been explored in a number of ways. I will
briefly consider two: an ecological ethics based on care and relationships, and a women's spirituality movement.

One contrast between masculine and feminine that has been a
part of past oppression of women views men as rational and objective while viewing women as emotional and overly concerned with
the personal. Consistent with this contrast, the dominant models in
ethics construed the moral realm in terms of abstract, rational, and
universal principles. The traditional theories of natural law, utilitarianism, and deontology are prime examples of ethics done in
this way. The domestic roles of women as mothers and wives
meant that those values important to women—caring, relationships,
love, responsibility, trust—remained outside of mainstream ethical
theorizing.

In recent decades, some feminists have brought many of the values traditionally associated with women's roles, what we shall summarize as an "ethics of care," into the forefront of ethical theorizing.
Drawing on the work of Carol Gilligan, Nel Noddings, Sara Ruddick, and others,[30] these feminists seek to articulate and defend a
perspective that de-emphasizes abstract rules and principles in favor of a contextualized ethics focusing on caring and relationships.
Traditional ethical concepts, such as moral laws, rights, duties, obligations, and justice, presuppose a world in which interests conflict,
in which the demands of justice restrict and limit human freedom,
in which morality battles egoism. An ethics of care begins with a
moral universe in which cooperation replaces conflict, relationships
replace confrontation, and caring for the other replaces rights and
duties. It is a moral universe in which mothering and friendship,
rather than abstract principles such as individual autonomy and
freedom from interference, serve as moral ideals.

Feminists offer different explanations for why an ethics of care is
particularly a women's perspective. In general, such feminists as
Noddings and Ruddick understand an ethics of care as more compatible with the life experiences of women, specifically as those
experiences follow from both reproductive biology and experiences
in mothering. Abstract ethical principles and rules seem irrelevant
in a life of child-bearing and child-rearing. The vocabulary of rights
and duties, autonomy and justice, rules and laws, is highly artificial
and inappropriate within the context of a mother–child relationship.

Some cultural ecofeminists build on these observations concerning an ethics of care. These thinkers acknowledge the fact that historically women have been portrayed as closer to nature than have men. But, rather than criticizing this portrayal as the basis for much of the violence done against women, as feminist Susan Griffin has done,[31] some ecofeminists build on this identification as a basis for a benevolent relationship between humans and nature. From this perspective, the ethics of care covers human–nature relationships as appropriately as it covers mother–child relationships. And women, as those who are taught to experience this caring more directly and more immediately than men, are the most appropriate voices for nature's interests.

To briefly develop this description of an ethics of care, reflect on some issues of virtue and character discussed earlier in this book. The care perspective moves beyond an ethics conceived of as abstract, universal rules that can be applied to specific problems and from which decisions can be deduced. The moral person is not conceived as a free and independent individual who must answer the question: "What should I do?" The care perspective focuses on specific relationships in all their detail, seeking to uncover the full nature of these relationships and affiliations. In such particularity, abstract and general principles are appropriately replaced by an ethics of character or an ethics of virtue. The good person—for example, the loving mother—is what an ethics of care seeks to describe. Moral actions would be those performed by the good person rather than those conforming to abstract general principles.

How might this be relevant to environmental issues? Again, reflect back on some earlier issues. Many philosophers have raised challenges concerning our duties to future generations in large part because future people do not conform to certain abstract and general conditions for moral standing. An ethics of care can shift our focus away from such abstract questions and start from the lived experience that many people do, in fact, care about what happens to future people. So, too, an ethics of care does not get bogged down with abstract questions concerning the moral standing of animals that characterizes so much of the animal liberation discussion. Instead, the questions "Do we care about animals? Do we have relationships to them? What is the basis for our attachments to animals?" become more central questions for ethics.[32] So, too, for the whole discussion of moral standing and moral considerability. We can and do exist in relationships with our natural surroundings, and an abstract ethical theory that ignores those facts will be inadequate. Finally, a view very consistent with an ethics of care is Leopold's injunction that we must first come to "love, respect, and admire the land" before we apply the more abstract principles of the land ethic.

The women's spirituality movement is a second area in which cultural ecofeminists have explored a bond between women and nature.[33] Within much mainstream Western religion, God was seen as outside of, or transcending, nature. Nature was mere matter: passive, inert, shapeless, dead; God created, formed, and breathed life into the dust. In much of this tradition, women again are associated with nature, because they are so dependent on their bodies and are so passive. Women are often seen therefore as lacking the special spirituality that would qualify them as priests, rabbis, bishops, popes, and so on. Thus, within much of this mainstream we again can witness the dual denigration of women and nature.

Many cultural ecofeminists seek a spiritualism or theology that reverses these trends.[34] We should instead observe and honor the identification of women, nature, and the divine. Often looking to ancient religions in which God was identified both as the earth itself and as a woman, some cultural ecofeminists honor a spirituality that views the Goddess as immanent in nature and views the natural world as revealing the divine. Thus, the earth itself is worshiped as divine, and caring for or loving the earth is a spiritual as well as an ecological responsibility. Celebrating Mother Nature or the Greek goddess Gaia, for example, becomes the way for women's spirituality to rejoice in the sacredness of women and nature.

11.5 ECOFEMINISM: RECENT DEVELOPMENTS

Despite these developments, many feminists are reluctant to accept the strategy of these feminists who embrace the view that there do exist distinctive and separate "women's ways" of understanding, experiencing, and valuing the world. They fear that by accepting the dualism implicit in viewing women as "closer to nature" than men, these feminists only reinforce the way of thinking that underlies hierarchies and the logic of domination. Philosopher Val Plumwood calls this "the feminism of uncritical reversal" and sees it as "perpetuating women's oppression in a new and subtle form."[35] Ynestra King suggests that an "unwitting complicity" in a patriarchal mind-set underlies the culture–nature split assumed by this view.[36]

In place of cultural ecofeminism with its roots in radical feminism, Plumwood and Warren seek a "third wave" of feminism that "is an integrative and transformative feminism, or that moves us beyond the current debate over the four leading versions of feminism and makes a responsible ecological perspective central to feminist theory and practice."[37] Although this approach is still very much in the early stages of its development, in the remainder of this section I sketch some of the directions in which this "transformative feminism" might be developing.

The view I am considering is represented in the writings of Karen Warren and Val Plumwood. To introduce this "third wave" of feminism, it is helpful to follow Val Plumwood's review of the first two waves. Feminism's "first wave," typified by liberal feminism, seeks to end discrimination and attain equality for women. The problem with this view is that in a culture in which masculine traits and characteristics dominate, equality for women will amount to little more than requiring women to adopt these dominant male traits. In effect, women can be equal to men only if they become masculine, and to the degree that strong cultural forces will work against this, women will always fall just a little short of full equality. (This point parallels the critical discussion in Chapter 6 concerning animal liberation. Only animals fortunate enough to resemble humans are granted moral standing.) The ecological implications of this first wave can be devastating: women can liberate themselves from an oppressive identification with nature only if they, like men, become oppressors of nature.

The second wave of feminism is represented by the "uncritical reversal" of some feminists. From this perspective, a distinctive female point of view is promoted and celebrated. However, as suggested earlier, this perspective risks being co-opted by the dominant male culture by accepting the very dualisms that have been used, via the logic of domination, to justify women's oppression.

The "third wave" seeks an alternative to both liberal and radical versions of feminism. This alternative sees the domination of nature and the domination of women as inextricably connected. They are connected in more ways than simply being two types of a more general pattern of domination. Women have been identified as closer to nature, and nature has been identified as feminine. These identifications have mutually reinforced the oppression of each. Thus, environmental philosophy and feminism need to develop in unison, each recognizing parallel interests.

Plumwood and Warren suggest that at a most general level, both feminism and the ecological movement need to address a cluster of dualisms and dualistic ways of thinking that underlie the logic of domination. This is not to suggest, of course, that distinctions are not to be made nor differences recognized. But we should challenge those distinctions that are made in order to reinforce superior—inferior,

oppressor–oppressed frameworks. This type of ecofeminism challenges both feminists and environmentalists alike to uncover the
patterns of domination common to the oppression of women and
nature, but also to begin exploring alternative and nondualistic
ways of thinking about both human and nonhuman nature. This
type of ecofeminism is also quite similar to Bookchin's more general
analysis of hierarchies and domination.

Some of these dualistic ways of thinking that are especially relevant to ecofeminism involve the split between masculine–feminine,
human–nature, reason–emotion, mind–body, and objective–subjective. Each of these dualisms typically gets used within our culture in
contexts that support domination: masculine over feminine, human
over nature, reason over emotion, mind over body, objectivity over
subjectivity. The goal, therefore, is to weed out these dualisms and
develop alternative patterns of thinking.

One of the most interesting directions in which this type of analysis has proceeded concerns science, technology, and a scientific understanding of nature. As I have pointed out, a number of feminist
scholars have chronicled the many ways that culture has identified
women with nature. But much interesting research has also been
done on how Western science has been influenced by that identification.[38] Science has typically been identified with the dominant part
of these dualisms: masculine, human, rational, mental, and objective. Feminist scientist Evelyn Fox Keller has detailed the ways in
which a particular way of understanding nature, women, and even
marriage, has also helped shape the early development of Western
science.[39]

Keller quotes the early scientist Francis Bacon to show how many
of the models and metaphors of early science betrayed an aggressive
attitude toward both women and nature. According to Bacon, science seeks to "establish a chaste and lawful marriage between Mind
and Nature." He says, "I am come in very truth leading to you
Nature with all her children to bind her to your service and make her
your slave." Science and technology do not "merely exert a gentle
guidance over nature's course; they have the power to conquer and
subdue her, to shake her to her foundations."[40] Bacon's images are
clear: Nature is a woman, and she is to become married to man, who
will subdue her and turn her into a slave. Not only does Bacon
associate nature with women and marriage, but he also associates it
with a particularly dominating and abusive type of marriage.

Sensitivity to these kinds of images should alert us to similar
attitudes within modern science. Typically, scientific theories are
judged by their ability to explain and predict natural phenomena.

But all too often the ability to predict natural phenomena is simply the first step in developing a technology to control natural phenomena, to "conquer and subdue her" and "make her your slave." This is a science and technology that sees value only in instrumental terms. How can we humans use nature for our own interests? Seldom does this science and technology consider noninstrumental values in nature, typically rejecting these values as a matter of "emotion," or "feelings" and therefore "subjective" and scientifically irrelevant.

Recent feminist scholarship alerts us to many of these very subtle, but very oppressive, patterns of thinking and patterns of acting. This scholarship also offers suggestions for alternatives. Keller has also written a biography of the geneticist Barbara McClintock titled *A Feeling for the Organism: The Life and Work of Barbara McClintock*. In this work, Keller describes an approach to science that exhibits this "feeling for the organism," an approach that is often called and then dismissed as "a woman's way of thinking." Keller does not suggest that mainstream science be abandoned in favor of this more particularized approach to knowing, but that science done only from the control-and-dominate perspective will likely miss much of what is important. You can review many of the cases discussed in this book to look for situations in which little "feeling" is exhibited toward nature by a science bent on domination and control. One might look particularly at the science and technology involved in building the Aswan Dam, harnessing nuclear energy, developing wilderness areas, experimenting on animals, and eliminating "varmints" and predators. For alternatives, you might consider the science and technology that would support sustainable agriculture and appropriate technologies.

A second direction for further environmental thinking that is encouraged by this type of ecofeminism develops from a much more modest conception of human action, ethics, and understanding. This third wave of ecofeminism encourages thinking that is *contextualist, pluralistic, inclusive,* and *holistic*.[41] It is contextualist in the sense that it seeks to avoid abstract and universal ethical pronouncements. This process of abstraction can prevent us from recognizing the rich diversity within both human and nonhuman nature. Too often, this process of abstracting to the universal has simply taken characteristics of the dominant group and turned them into ethical and philosophical ideals. We have already seen how this can reinforce oppression of women, animals, and the rest of the natural world.

This third wave of ecofeminism is pluralistic and inclusive in the sense that it respects diversity and difference. Perhaps the key aspect of a dominating ideology is the belief that there is only one right way of being, thinking, and acting. A philosophy that self-consciously avoids hierarchies and domination will celebrate diversity and resist attempts to establish one "correct" environmental theory.

Finally, this ecofeminism is holistic in that it encourages us to understand human beings as essentially a part of their human and natural communities. (Note how this common way of speaking already assumes a dualism, as if human communities were not "natural.") This ecofeminism rejects the view that humans are abstract individuals, fully constituted by their own private consciousness, their own thoughts, their own choices. On the contrary, humans are created by, and are an inextricable part of, their social and natural environments.

11.6 SUMMARY AND CONCLUSION

Like deep ecology and to a lesser extent Leopold's land ethic, both social ecology and ecofeminism advocate a radical shift in the ways in which the major and dominant sectors of the contemporary world think about and understand the relationships between humans and the rest of the natural world. But social ecology and ecofeminism are more specific about the root causes of environmental and ecological devastation. The domination of the natural world is part of more general patterns of domination and control. Until all patterns of domination are acknowledged and eliminated, we can expect little real progress to be made on the environmental front.

Both social ecology and ecofeminism face serious philosophical challenges. How exactly are we to understand the connections between human domination of other humans and the human domination of nonhuman nature? Has one caused the other? Are they mutually reinforcing? Should one have ethical priority? Are they simply parallel developments with little direct connection? What are the ethically and philosophically preferable strategies for resisting these forms of domination? What are the connections between the domination of women and other forms of social domination? Is ecofeminism a branch of social ecology?

Ecofeminism especially resists attempts to construct a unified and over-arching environmental philosophy, and we need to be aware of this when raising challenges to ecofeminist views. Many such challenges seek the type of universal and abstract answers that ecofeminists (and social ecologists) identify as part of the problem. Ecofeminism is also in the very early stages of growth and development, and it would be unfair to expect too much in the way of answers at this point. But social ecology and ecofeminism have already made significant contributions to environmental ethics and environmental philosophy. No longer can these issues be discussed independently of discussions of social domination and control. Furthermore, by calling attention to such issues these approaches also stimulate our understanding of the benefits of the type of alternative social arrangements typified by sustainable agriculture and appropriate technologies.

Notes

1. Sustainable agriculture is perhaps most often associated with the work and writing of Wes Jackson and the Land Institute in Salina, Kansas. See Jackson's *New Roots for Agriculture* (Omaha: University of Nebraska Press, 1980). Other helpful sources include Judith Soule and Jon Piper, *Farming in Nature's Image: An Ecological Approach to Agriculture* (Washington, DC: Island Press, 1992), and John Reganold, Robert Papendick, and James Parr, "Sustainable Agriculture," in *Scientific American* 266, no.6 (June 1990), pp. 112–120.

2. Wes Jackson, "Making Sustainable Agriculture Work," in Robert Clark, ed., *Our Sustainable Table* (San Francisco: North Point Press, 1990), p. 140.

3. For Bookchin's ecological views, see especially *The Ecology of Freedom* (Palo Alto: Cheshire Books, 1982) and *The Philosophy of Social Ecology* (Montreal: Black Rose Books, 1990).

4. A helpful resource for recent work on philosophical aspects of ecofeminism is the American Philosophical Association's *Newsletter on Feminism and Philosophy* 90, no. 3 (Fall 1991). This issue contains an overview of ecofeminist issues written by Karen Warren, and a solid philosophical bibliography compiled by Warren and Carol Adams.

5. Murray Bookchin, *The Ecology of Freedom*, p. 1.

6. Rosemary Radford Reuther, *New Woman/New Earth* (New York: Seabury, 1975), p. 204.

7. This is a general characterization. Descriptions of ecofeminism offered by Reuther, Val Plumwood, and Karen Warren suggest an understanding that sees the oppression of women as a major, but perhaps not the major form of oppression. Other feminists argue that women's oppression represents the principal form of social domination. Radical feminists, for example, explicitly deny that women's oppression can be reduced to any other more basic form of oppression.

8. See especially Alison Jaggar, *Feminist Politics and Human Nature* (Totowa: Rowman & Littlefield, 1988), for the best discussion of various feminist understandings of social justice.

9. Karen Warren, "Introduction" *Hypatia* 6, no. 1 (Spring 1991): 1.

10. Murray Bookchin, *The Ecology of Freedom*, p. 4.

11. Ibid., pp. 4–8.

12. Much of what follows is taken from Murray Bookchin, "Recovering Evolution: A Reply to Eckersley and Fox," *Environmental Ethics* 12 (Fall 1990), pp. 253–273.

13. Murray Bookchin, "Ecology and Revolutionary Thought" (1965), published in *Post-Scarcity Anarchism* (Berkeley, CA: Ramparts, 1971), p. 80.
14. See, for example, Robin Eckersley, *Environmentalism and Political Theory* (Albany: SUNY Press, 1992), pp. 148–154.
15. See Eckersley, *Environmentalism and Political Theory*, pp. 154–160, as well as her "Divining Evolution: The Ecological Ethics of Murray Bookchin," *Environmental Ethics* 11 (1989): 99–116.
16. See, for example, "Recovering Evolution," pp. 262–266.
17. Eckersley, "Divining Evolution," p. 99.
18. Murray Bookchin, "Social Ecology Versus Deep Ecology," *Socialist Review* 18, nos. 1–2 (1988): 27–28.
19. Ibid., p. 28.
20. Judi Bari, "Why I am Not a Misanthrope," *Earth First!*, February 2, 1991, p. 25. For other deep ecology critiques of Bookchin, see Christopher Manes, *Green Rage: Radical Environmentalism and the Unmaking of Civilization* (Boston: Little, Brown, 1990), and Warwick Fox, *Towards a Transpersonal Ecology* (Boston: Shambhala, 1990). An excellent overview of these debates can be found in Steve Chase, ed., *Defending the Earth: A Dialogue Between Murray Bookchin and Dave Foreman* (Boston: South End Press, 1991).
21. See Bookchin's *Social Ecology Versus Deep Ecology* (Burlington, VT: Green Program Project, 1988). Reprinted in *Socialist Review* 18, nos. 1–2 (1988): 11–29.
22. *Defending the Earth*, p. 125.
23. Ibid., pp. 30–31.
24. Françoise d'Eaubonne, *Le Feminisme ou la Mort* (Paris: Pierre Horay, 1974). Among the most recent philosophically helpful sources are *Hypatia* 6, no. 1 (Spring 1991), special issue on ecological feminism; American Philosophical Association *Newsletter on Feminism* 90, no. 3 (Fall 1991), and 91, no. 1 (Spring 1992). In addition to articles and interviews, the APA newsletters also contain helpful course syllabi and bibliographies.
25. Karen J. Warren, "The Power and Promise of Ecological Feminism," *Environmental Ethics* 12 (Summer 1990): 126.
26. See Karen J. Warren, "Feminism and Ecology: Making Connections," *Environmental Ethics* 9 (Spring 1987): 3–20; "The Power and Promise of Ecological Feminism," *Environmental Ethics* 12 (Summer 1990): 125–146. In the earlier article, Warren takes the logic of domination as characteristic of patriarchal frameworks, while in the more recent paper she has revised her views to include all "oppressive" frameworks. In this respect, there seems a closer parallel to Bookchin's general discussion of hierarchies.
27. This classic discussion of liberal, Marxist, radical, and socialist feminisms can be found in Alison Jaggar, *Feminist Politics and Human Nature* (Totowa, NJ: Rowman & Allanheld, 1983). For a discussion of these models as they relate to ecological issues, see Karen Warren, "Feminism and Ecology: Making Connections"; Carolyn Merchant, "Ecofeminism and Feminist Theory," in Irene Diamond and Gloria Feman Orenstein, eds., *Reweaving the World* (San Francisco: Sierra Club Books, 1990), pp. 100–105; and Val

Plumwood, "Feminism and Ecofeminism," *The Ecologist* 22, no. 1 (January–February 1992): 8–13.

28. This follows the usage of Val Plumwood, "Current Trends in Ecofeminism," in *The Ecologist* 22, no. 1 (January–February 1992): 10.

29. Ibid., p. 10.

30. Carol Gilligan, *In a Different Voice: Psychological Theory and Women's Development* (Cambridge: Harvard University Press, 1982); Nel Noddings, *Caring: A Feminine Approach to Ethics and Moral Education* (Berkeley: University of California Press, 1984); Sara Ruddick, *Maternal Thinking* (New York: Ballantine Books, 1989).

31. Two of the earliest and best sources that explore the "women and nature" connections and the oppression and violence against women that followed are Susan Griffin, *Women and Nature: The Roaring Inside Her* (New York: Harper & Row, 1978); and Carolyn Merchant, *The Death of Nature: Women, Ecology, and the Scientific Revolution* (New York: Harper & Row, 1980).

32. A very helpful bibliography on "Women and Animals" is included in a thorough bibliography on "Feminism and the Environment," edited by Carol Adams and Karen Warren, that can be found in the American Philosophical Association *Newsletter on Feminism and Philosophy* 90, no. 3 (Fall 1991): 148–157.

33. Irene Diamond and Gloria Feman Orenstein, eds., *Reweaving the World*, contains several articles on women's spirituality and includes another helpful bibliography. See also, Carol Christ, *Laughter of Aphrodite: Reflections on a Journey to the Goddess* (San Francisco: Harper & Row, 1987); Rosemary Radford Reuther, *New Woman/New Earth* (New York: Seabury Press, 1975); and Starhawk, *The Spiral Dance: A Rebirth of the Ancient Religion of the Great Goddess* (San Francisco: Harper & Row, 1986).

34. Two classic sources for exploring the more general issue of women's spiritualism are Rosemary Radford Reuther, *New Woman/New Earth*, cited earlier, and Mary Daly, *GYN/Ecology: The Metaethics of Radical Feminism* (Boston: Beacon Press, 1978). Neither Reuther nor Daly subscribes to the particular overview of spiritualism described here, however.

35. Val Plumwood, "Feminism and Ecofeminism," p. 12.

36. Ynestra King, "Feminism and the Revolt against Nature," *Heresies #13: Feminism and Ecology* 4, no. 1 (1981): 15.

37. This quote is from Karen Warren, "Feminism and Ecology," pp. 17–18. The phrase "third wave of feminism" is from Val Plumwood, "Feminism and Ecofeminism," pp. 12–13.

38. See especially Carolyn Merchant, *Death of Nature*, and Evelyn Fox Keller, *Reflections on Gender and Science* (New Haven: Yale University Press, 1985).

39. See especially Chapter 3, "Spirit and Reason at the Birth of Modern Science," in Keller, *Reflections*.

40. As quoted in Evelyn Fox Keller, *Reflections*, p. 36.

41. This is adopted from Karen Warren, "The Power and Promise," pp. 141–145.

Discussion Questions

1. Discuss the types of character traits, or virtures, that would be encouraged by living on a sustainable farm that relies on appropriate technologies. Compare these to those virtues that might be developed by working within a corporate bureaucracy. What type of character is created by these varied social structures?

2. How might a social ecologist analyze the Mineral King Valley (pp. 42–43) and the Hetch Hetchy (pp. 45–46) disputes? How might a social ecologist or ecofeminist analyze the decisions described in Case One (pp. 2–3)?

3. Review some of the common dualisms (for example, mind–body, reason–emotion) mentioned in this chapter. Discuss and evaluate the value hierarchies that are implicit within them.

4. Bookchin claims that human beings cannot help but be, nor should they seek to avoid being, "purposive interveners" in nature. That would seem to conflict directly with the views of many, including some deep ecologists and preservationists, who believe that humans ought to "let nature take its course." Discuss how these different views might evaluate the Yellowstone Fires (pp.164–165), predator policy (pp. 186–187), and population policy.

5. In his recent book *Earth in the Balance* (New York: Houghton Mifflin, 1992), Senator Al Gore describes the infamous nineteenth-century potato famine in Ireland as resulting from monoculture farming techniques. That ·is, the Irish overrelied on a single imported species of potato so that a single infestation destroyed their entire food supply. This brings to mind the claim of some deep ecologists that famines often are "nature's revenge" on humans abusing nature. In his book, Gore also notes that other crops, including wheat and sheep, were being exported to England at the same time that Irish people were starving. How might a social ecologist analyze the social causes of the Great Hunger in Ireland?

6. In Chapter 1, I quoted scientist Amory Lovins, who said, "the answers you get depend on the questions you ask." What different questions might be asked by someone taking a feminist approach to science and technology regarding such issues as the Aswan Dam, nuclear energy, predator policy, and population growth?

For Further Reading

The sources mentioned in Note 1 provide an excellent starting point for further reading on sustainable agriculture. See E. F. Schumacher, *Good Work* (New York: Harper & Row, 1979) and his classic *Small Is Beautiful* (New York: Harper & Row, 1973) for helpful discussions of appropriate technologies.

The American Philosophical Association's *Newsletter on Feminism and Philosophy* 90, no. 3 (Fall 1991) provides a substantial bibliography compiled by Karen Warren and Carol Adams on feminist and ecofeminist writings.

Janet Biehl, *Rethinking Ecofeminist Politics* (Boston: South End Press, 1991) offers a critique of ecofeminism from the perspective of a social ecology feminist. While helpful in understanding some differences between social ecology and some forms of ecofeminism, Biehl's criticisms are not always fair to the variety of feminist positions.

The debate between Murray Bookchin and both deep ecology and Earth First! is reviewed and evaluated by Murray Bookchin and Dave Foreman, in Steve Chase, ed., *Defending the Earth* (Boston: South End Press, 1991).

INDEX